Toward a New Film Aesthetic

Toward a New Film Aesthetic

Bruce Isaacs

continuum

NEW YORK • LONDON

122526501

2008

The Continuum International Publishing Group Inc
80 Maiden Lane, New York, NY 10038

The Continuum International Publishing Group Ltd
The Tower Building, 11 York Road, London SE1 7NX

www.continuumbooks.com

This book includes elements of the author's previously published essay "Non-Linear Narrative." In *New Punk Cinema*, ed. Nicholas Rombes, 126–138. Edinburgh: Edinburgh University Press, 2004.

Printed in the United States of America

Library of Congress Cataloging-in-Publication Data

Isaacs, Bruce.
  Toward a new film aesthetic / Bruce Isaacs.
    p. cm.
  Includes bibliographical references and index.
  ISBN 13: 978-0-8264-2870-7 (hardcover : alk. paper)
  ISBN 10: 0-8264-2870-3 (hardcover : alk. paper)
  ISBN 13: 978-0-8264-2871-4 (pbk. : alk. paper)
  ISBN 10: 0-8264-2871-1 (pbk. : alk. paper)
  1. Motion pictures Aesthetics. I. Title.
  PN1995.I77 2007
  791.4301—dc22

                                        2007013620

Contents

1

A Notion of Film Aesthetics

Engaging the Aesthetic Impulse

Contemporary cultural formations have been theorized through postmodern ideas of fragmentation, distillation, and a "politics of difference" that has questioned fixed notions of identity and subjectivity. How do we begin to understand and account for the popularity, the desires, and pleasures of contemporary cinema outside of these notions?[1]

It is important to acknowledge that a shift has occurred—at least within an important swath of contemporary visual culture—toward an aesthetic that foregrounds the dimension of appearance, form, and sensation. And we must take this shift seriously at the aesthetic level. . . . A rush into interpretation before the aesthetic has been more clearly apprehended may follow an all too easy dismissal of such a spectacle aesthetic on grounds that it is facile, already transparent or really about something else.[2]

The notion of an "aesthetics of sensation," which seems to have fallen out of favor with literary and cultural theorists, is necessary to make sense of the myriad ways in which a contemporary popular culture interacts with cinema. According to Barbara Kennedy, one of the shortcomings of film theory is a failure to engage with what might be called an "aesthetic impulse." And while such an impulse celebrates affectivity, or what Andrew Darley calls "questions of a sensual and perceptual character,"[3] it does not compromise the analysis of film as ideological or cultural artifact. I do not wish to disengage from the seemingly inexhaustible body of critical theory that privileges the structural or psychoanalytic approach to cinema, or the broadly Marxist project that charts in painstaking detail the formation of selves and others in a discursive system of studios, cultures, subcultures, and artistic commodities. Yet this body of work cannot account for what I perceive to be the contemporary obsession with film as an affective medium, nor the cinematic text as an aesthetically engaged product operating within a Western, or as some theorists have argued, global marketplace.[4] The nearest critical theory comes to this phenomenon is the relatively recent interest in fandom,[5] and even this field seems unfortunately to privilege the "cult" text or "alternative" voice, and is thus destined to repeat the exclusion of a text based on its popularity or, rather, the absence of a requisite degree of alterity. This exclusion is unfortunate; it is precisely *because* film franchises such as *The Matrix* and *Star Wars* draw the crowds at the box office that an engagement with this art is so necessary.

Film writing (scholarly and otherwise) has always been suspicious of the blockbuster, distinguishing between an art cinema that functions as an autonomous creative work and the pop culture entertainment spectacle that services a capitalist market ethos and the wish-fulfillment fantasies of a majority of the filmgoing populace. In this way, the film theorist is able to differentiate between, for example, Antonioni's *Blow-Up* and *L'Avventura* (*The Adventure*) on the one hand, and Spielberg's *Jaws* and *Raiders of the Lost Ark* on the other. Antonioni requires a spectator actively engaged in making meaning of the narrative, and indeed, of the visual contours of the shot. (*L'Avventura's* striking use of deep focus in almost every shot is an example of the unconventional visuality of the art-film aesthetic.) Both *L'Avventura* and *Blow-Up* present metaphysical conundrums that challenge the conventional separation of truth and deception, or of orthodox narrative continuity and a jarring discontinuity. Spielberg's output in the late 1970s and early to mid-1980s is a self-acknowledged sequence of "high concepts" structured into cinematic spectacles: a twenty-five-words-or-less pitch of the kind satirized in Robert Altman's *The Player.*[6] The high-concept entertainment spectacle is a business enterprise; the art film is an artistic endeavor founded upon a singularly creative impulse.

In spite of the token disclaimer that the distinction between high and low culture has been effaced in the postmodern milieu (apparently opening popular cinema to a veritable smorgasbord of analytic processes), film theory has in the main recuperated the distinction. While undertaking analyses of contemporary popular cinema (*The Matrix, Star Wars, Back to the Future, Jaws, The Lord of the Rings, The Silence of the Lambs,*

Forrest Gump, and *Scream* have each received a significant amount of attention from film and cultural theorists), theory directs its examination of popular cinema as far from a conventional aesthetic approach to art as it possibly can. *The Silence of the Lambs* is less an aesthetic work than a system of ideological significations charting late-capitalist, feminist, or queer subjectivity.[7] *The Matrix* services an examination of race and/or gender issues in contemporary America.[8] *Jaws* enacts a liminal space in which deviant female sexuality is imagined as an unrelenting predator.[9] The *Star Wars* franchise instantiates a return to the Manichean opposition of good and evil and allegorizes a neo-imperialistic ideological bent in late-capitalist Western societies.[10]

This kind of analysis, which made possible film theory's remarkable advancements into the academy between the 1970s and the late 1990s, is not confined to the blockbuster or popular film. Work on *film noir* undertakes a similar task, often arriving at striking and provocative conclusions. Examinations of the horror and slasher genres that burgeoned with the low-budget independents of the 1970s (*The Texas Chainsaw Massacre* [1974], *Halloween, The Howling*) service a similar analytical bent. Laura Mulvey's landmark turn to film theory with "Visual Pleasure and Narrative Cinema" is, as she states at the opening of the piece, intended to appropriate "psychoanalytic theory . . . as a political weapon, demonstrating the way the unconscious of patriarchal society has structured film form."[11] Equally, the aesthetic of the film (Mulvey's analysis implies that visual narrative is founded in its entirety on the patriarchal prejudices of society) is appropriated and reconfigured as structural or instrumental analysis of subjectivity and social conditioning. The image of Woman in Hitchcock's *Rear Window* and *Vertigo* is "as (passive) raw material for the (active) gaze of man [which] takes the argument a step further into the structure of representation, adding a further layer demanded by the ideology of the patriarchal order as it is worked out in its favorite cinematic form—illusionistic narrative form."[12] Illusion masks only patriarchal hegemonic practices and chained female subjectivities. (I do not wish to take issue with Mulvey's seminal analysis except to suggest that illusion in cinematic spectacle—and certainly in the work of Hitchcock—is a purveyor of far more than patriarchy, and that it is this kind of failure to engage with an alternative aesthetic practice in film that has marginalized film aesthetics altogether.)

What I perceive as a very real shortcoming in film theory is the lack of an analysis of film as aesthetically charged, or functioning affectively on the spectator. Manovich describes this "waning of affect" in relation to the demand for new modes of affectivity in computer culture and digital media:

> Affect has been neglected in cultural theory since the late 1950s when, influenced by the mathematic theory of communication, Roman Jakobson, Claude Levi-Strauss, Roland Barthes and others began treating cultural communication solely as a matter of encoding and decoding messages . . . By approaching any cultural object/situation/process as "text" that is "read" by audiences and/or critics, cultural criticism privileges the informational and cognitive dimensions of culture over affective, emotional, performative and experiential aspects. Other influential approaches of recent decades similarly neglect these dimensions.[13]

The orthodox treatment of the affective in film writing relies on the assumption of spectator passivity in the popular film, but the nature of the cinematic spectacle is rarely conceptualized in more conventional analyses that emphasize the study of film "cultures," or more fashionably, "film subjectivities." At the risk of sounding parochial: spectators are interested in the look and sound of film as a profoundly aesthetic engagement with the senses. Spectacle is rarely (and certainly not entirely) a matter of image absorption or spectator inculcation into an ideologized medium. Visual cinema (which I will distinguish from narrative cinema—of course, most cinema relies on narrative structure, but a visual cinema responds to the affective engagement with the visual impact of the image, shot, or sequence on screen) is a complex dynamic of camera movement, angles, positions, *mise en scène*, innovations in sound, and image technologies. In this film aesthetic, I contend that the spectator rises above the passivity conceptualized by Adorno, Jameson, and others.

Distinctions between passive and active viewing in contemporary, or more specifically, postmodern cinema, are incompatible with ways of seeing, or *spectating*, that contemporary culture employs. On one level, the activity of intellectually or emotively responding to *L'Avventura* is vastly removed from a response to a multimillion-dollar film franchise in which a complex engagement with the film text requires immersion in its performance as product in the market: soundtracks, computer games, action figures, clothing, and various other marketing strategies employed by most sections of the marketplace. Film theory must re-engage with the complexities of *how* a film is read, or viewed, and this analysis (if it is to be a qualitative analysis of popular culture) must begin with film aesthetics. In relation to what I will freely acknowledge is a consumerist popular culture, I reject Adorno's notion of a kind of industrialization that spawns only passivity, conformity, and the blandness of cinematic entertainment. In this formulation, mass culture (though distinctions between mass and other cultural bodies are vague) is a culture that "proclaims: you shall conform, without instruction as to what; conform to that which exists anyway, and to that which everyone thinks anyway as a reflex of its power and omnipresence." "The power of the culture industry's ideology is such that conformity has replaced consciousness."[14] Although I will explore this in some detail, I will say here that Adorno's piece was historically and culturally specific and could not have foreseen the rise of a *kind* of mass culture (I distinguish between Noël Carroll's notion of mass art as occurring with the printing press[15] and the phenomenon of *Titanic* as a billion-dollar-plus cultural and artistic industry) as a complex and diversely articulated movement.[16]

In his monologue at the 2005 Academy Awards, American comedian Chris Rock satirized the Academy of Motion Pictures by interviewing audiences at a South Central Los Angeles multiplex. Rock's claim was that relatively few Americans had seen the films nominated for Best Picture that year. While the Academy and Hollywood celebrated its filmic ascendance with Eastwood's social realist fable *Million Dollar Baby*, Scorsese's lavish biopic *The Aviator*, and the nostalgic piece of Americana *Sideways*, Rock's contention was that these films were honorific symbols of the Hollywood establishment. What signified the Hollywood product in 2005, among other things, was the Wayans brothers' "screwball" comedy *White Chicks*, in which two black men disguise themselves as white women to bring a white-collar criminal to justice. The reference to Billy Wilder's *Some Like It Hot* (albeit a reference that was vague amid a plethora of derivative scenes) was lost on this multiplex audience, but the Wayans did not need an allusion to Wilder to stamp their film with an establishment honor.

Rock's monologue was perceived as the Hollywood establishment "not taking itself too seriously." Yet while his investigation of mainstream American film interests takes a less-than-scholarly approach, the implicit distinction Rock makes between a "serious" cinema and a cinema of the multiplex is provocative. Consider the following selection of films:

Citizen Kane (1941), *The Third Man* (1949), *Sunset Boulevard* (1950), *L'Avventura* (1960), *Peeping Tom* (1960), *A Clockwork*

Orange (1971), *Don't Look Now* (1973), *Eraserhead* (1977), *Apocalypse Now* (1979), *Raging Bull* (1980), *The King of Comedy* (1983), *Paris, Texas* (1984), *Akira* (1988), *Sex, Lies and Videotape* (1989), *Clerks* (1994), *Chong Qing Sen Lin* (*Chungking Express*, 1994), *Strange Days* (1995), *Boogie Nights* (1997), *Todo Sobre Mi Madre* (*All About My Mother*, 1999), *Adaptation* (2002).

It must be significant that the majority of the filmgoing populace has not seen these films. I selected these in particular because many of them have been central to the formation of a corpus of film (and associated cultural, aesthetic, and philosophical) theory; others are exemplary of the contemporary scholarship of postmodernism, feminism and the gaze, psychoanalysis, structuralism, cultural theory and subcultures, and art-house/alternative cinema. Each one of these films merits serious analytical attention, but accepted analytical strategies have rendered a great deal of writing on film insular, self-reflective, obtuse, and, in its worst incarnation, elitist. Theoretical abstraction in film studies marginalizes the voice of the casual filmgoer, reviewer, and fan, who, in Graham McCann's analysis, watch "movies," while theorists view "films." In a caustic piece reflecting on recent trends in psychoanalytic theory, McCann writes:

> For all their demotic pretensions, film theorists continue to handle popular culture with ill-disguised distaste. The popular has to be transformed into the unpopular before it can be discussed without embarrassment . . . The transformation may occur through repackaging . . . accompanied by reassuring *Guardian* encomia and precious labels like "Connoisseur Video" and "The Elite Collection" . . . In this new form, the movie can be thought of as a film.[17]

He proceeds to discuss Žižek's use of Lacan in his writing on Hitchcock, implying that the abstraction of the film into theory fails to address its status as a popular culture artifact, "movie" more than "film." Robin Wood explores similar territory in his influential analysis of Hitchcock:

> The cinema—especially the Hollywood cinema—is a commercial medium. Hitchcock's films are—usually—popular: indeed, some of his best films (*Rear Window, Psycho*) are among his *most popular*. From this arises a widespread assumption that, however "clever," "technically brilliant," "amusing," "gripping," etc., they

may be, they can't be taken seriously as we take, say, the films of Bergman and Antonioni seriously. They *must* be, if not absolutely bad, at least fatally flawed from a serious standpoint.[18]

In response to François Truffaut's suggestion that *Psycho* is an experimental film, Hitchcock replies:

> Possibly. My main satisfaction is that the film had an effect on the audiences, and I consider that very important. I don't care about the subject matter; I don't care about the acting; but I do care about the pieces of film and the photography and the sound-track and all the technical ingredients that made the audience scream. I feel it's tremendously satisfying for us to be able to use the cinematic art to achieve something of a mass emotion. It wasn't a message that stirred the audiences, nor was it a great performance or their enjoyment of the novel. They were aroused by pure film.[19]

Both McCann and Wood allude to the need for a film aesthetic that takes account of the affective parameters of the cinematic text. Implicit in this is an acknowledgment that the affective response is fundamentally attached to the way film is viewed in mainstream society, or the way in which popular cinema engages with a wider audience. Of course, we cannot dismiss the material conditions in which the product enters the marketplace, subject to what Wood calls the "dominant ideology." But neither is popular cinema a blank slate upon which to work nefarious ideological conspiracies against the passive consumer. The oeuvres of Lucas and Spielberg have little in common with either Bergman's or Antonioni's. But in what sense should this result in the evaluation of Lucas or Spielberg as *lesser* filmmakers, or as the detritus of a once aesthetically engaged medium? If movies and MTV have taught us anything, it is that theorists must employ the age-old Leavisite-Arnoldian distinction of the classical aesthetic and culture with caution.

Film studies must concurrently engage with the material reality of the film industry and the qualitative features of what Adorno considered the industrialization of culture. Carroll suggests that mass or popular forms of culture and art are ultimately attached to notions of commonality and community: "A taste for easily accessible art will not evaporate soon, nor will the pleasure to be had from sharing artworks with large numbers of our fellow citizens. For people like to have commerce with the same artworks that their neighbours—far and wide—do. . . . It is an important element of possessing a common culture."[20] Adorno's industrialization of culture is also, in a literal sense, a process in which culture is made available to a wider audience.

It is indisputable that film is not only the dominant form of entertainment and art in contemporary Western cultures, but, for many of these cultures, the only one. This is a simplification only insofar as film is hardly singularly *mass* or *popular*. And yet the majority of filmgoers are surely oblivious to Antonioni or Tarkovsky. For a sense of cultural and aesthetic identity, I argue that cultures revert to a popular form of cinema, its ways of making meaning, and its affective impact on the self. This centrality of an art form to personal experience and subjectivity requires returning to an aesthetic inquiry, if only to forge a critical space for the *Matrix*-like franchises that dominate the box office and the individual and collective fantasies of a mass culture.

Realism: Foundations

A new cinematic aesthetic must necessarily describe and engage a body of films and critical theory that traces a diversion from cinematic realism. Realism, in this context, has a twofold definition. Traditional pictorial realism refers to the degree of verisimilitude of the reproduction of the real object. A photograph of a building façade is, in one sense, the perfect image reproduction of that façade. The advance in image-making technologies (traditional art forms [painting, sculpture, wood block print, etc.], photography, moving images, digital cinema, virtual imaging) allows a more perfect reproduction, an image more faithful to the object than that permitted by an earlier technology.

More generally, I use the term realism to refer to a broader "realist" aesthetic that has informed artistic traditions and analysis. This aesthetic refers to a degree of verisimilitude in the attitude of the text to the object it represents, but it also indicates a sense of the reproduction as *striving for* a realistic representation of the tangible object. Of course, it must be said here that the two definitions, or contexts, are interconnected. The verisimilitude of the reproduction functions as a template for the verisimilitude of a more general "truth"—for example, a truth manifested in the universal nature, or the Platonic ideal. Ultimately, discussions about nature or essentialisms in literary or cinematic characters stress the fidelity to the way that nature exists in a "real" world, or a world that antecedes the representation, the aesthetic object.

A new film aesthetic must simultaneously acknowledge the centrality of the realist aesthetic to contemporary film and film theory, and recognize the innovation toward spectacle cinema, virtual realism, genericity, and the transformation in the ontology of the spectator/theorist. Theorizing beyond the Real requires an appreciation of the ontology of the realist image. A theory of hyperrealism (in which Baudrillard's Real consists of a "generation by models of a real without origin or reality"[21]) or Neorealism (consider, for example, the influential Italian Neorealist cinema of the 1940s[22]) must acknowledge the residue of a classical realist aesthetics in its performance on the screen, or on the isolated subjectivity of the cinematic spectator. The realist aesthetic insinuates itself into critical theses on cinematic style as well as the dominant modes of qualitative cultural analyses.

I argue that critical theory esteems an essentialist notion of realism in which realism is a mimetic art, or a "reality myth," to paraphrase André Bazin. Cinema promises the possibility of the perfection of representative art: the revelation of truth and a profoundly humanist capacity for the illumination of nature and an essential reality. Kracauer offers a seminal formulation of this approach to cinema:

> All these creative efforts [of the filmmaker] are in keeping with the cinematic approach as long as they benefit, in some way or other, the medium's substantive concern with our visible world. As in photography, everything depends on the "right" balance between the realistic tendency and the formative tendency; and the two tendencies are well balanced if the latter does not try to overwhelm the former but eventually follows its lead.[23]

Andrew summarizes the pursuit of realism as a founding principle of cinema: "The history of cinema is usually measured as the progressive ad-equation of the rules of cinematic organization to the habitual ways by which we organize our life in our culture."[24] Cinema thus presents the capacity to reveal the Real in its fullest sense, in its image and process, which I would argue is the culmination of a humanist pursuit of the ideal in representative form. While this chapter will focus on Bazin's "ontology of the Real" (particularly as he formulates it in relation to Orson Welles), I hope to foreground the necessity for discussing the various cultures that receive cinematic texts and that continue to view, collect, reflect upon, and indelibly reconform them. In Chapter Two, I consider the major aesthetic models brought to bear on our accepted analyses of cinema, including Frederic Jameson's "waning of affect" and, to a lesser extent, the Marxist frame of critical and cultural analysis. In the following discussion, I touch briefly on these legacies, but more for their descriptive and applicative value in the criticism of cinematic style than in a meaningful discussion of their cultural (for my purposes, specifically popular cultural) impact.

This chapter will also comprise an extended introduction to the second part of this book, in which I attempt to conceptualize a contemporary filmic subjectivity (the performer of the "hypermyth," *Neo*) necessary for comprehending the ontological space carved out by contemporary cinematic practices. Christian Metz distinguishes between the "filmic" and the "cinematic,"[25] in which "filmic" connotes elements external to the film and "cinematic" elements internal to it: narrative structure, characterization, theme, as well as *mise en scène* and *mis en shot*. This is a distinction I will uphold. The filmic, in a Metzian sense, incorporates the processes of production and the act of consumption of the cinematic. Metz's distinction is useful because it allows a critical trajectory aimed equally at a stylistics of film and the instruments of its production and reception—i.e., producers and consumers—an approach that incorporates an analysis of the filmic and the cinematic. In my usage, consumers are partakers communally in the proffering of a product; filmmaking and film viewing are essentially consumptive practices.

Foregrounding the "reality" aspect of film is often perceived as a necessary component of criticism, particularly in popular media. The majority of film reviews (to distinguish these from the scholarly, and academically published, analysis of film) consider film's relation to a pre-existing and eminently discoverable reality for a sense of its aesthetic or cinematic worth. Thus, Mike Leigh or John Sayles are praised for their unique brand of social realism. Leigh's cinematic philosophy esteems realism over spectacle, the Real over the generic artifice. Discussing *Vera Drake*, Leigh asserts that his characters are "specific and idiosyncratic."[26] Of his artistic philosophy, Leigh suggests that "primarily, my films are a response to the way people are, the way things are as I experience them."[27] The implication here is that a notion of the indissoluble Real pours forth the artistic representation as near to verisimilitude as the medium will allow.

Moreover, the triumph of the Real finds form (or at least credibility) in the departure from the *non-Real*. *Secrets and Lies* employs naturalistic acting styles (that veer perilously close to melodrama, particularly in the early exchanges between Cynthia [Brenda Blethyn] and Hortense [Marianne Jean-Baptiste]) and camera angles to ground the image in the parameters of an external social reality. The naturalistic cinematography of *Matewan* or *Lonestar* compliments Sayles's political project, which engages with material working conditions and a contemporary class-consciousness.

Even more significantly, genre animation such as *The Incredibles* is valued for what it might say about the "real world," and by extension, real lived experiences and even a sense of the communal self. Lisa Schwarzbaum, writing in *Entertainment Weekly*, suggests that

> the family's escapades in the field are indeed stupendous, an homage to the exploits of classic comic-book masters of the universe. But the true heroism in this spectacular movie—as worthy of a best picture nomination as any made with fleshly stars—shines brightest in that suburban house, where Bob, with his midlife bulge and his thinning hair, pines nostalgically for the old days, and Helen marches anxiously forward, bending to her family's needs.[28]

The value of the digitally animated image is discovered by Schwarzbaum in character, theme, and narrative, rather than image, shot, sequence, or a broader notion of spectacle. *The Incredibles* is spectacular, but for the most unspectacular reasons. The genre film is subjected to critical scrutiny based on a conventional realist approach to cinema. Genre must ascribe its own "reality apparatus," to which the generic product must adhere or yet again stretch the sacrosanct bounds of filmed reality. Steve Neale uses the term "verisimilitude" to describe the way genre cinema conforms to particular types and cinematic styles. Neale suggests that a genre film must have a degree of verisimilitude to the generic form, whether western, musical, or gangster film.[29] We could equally extend this verisimilitude to the realist aesthetic, in which the Real is engaged less obviously with a "real world" than with its reproduced and ultimately generic aestheticization; Jim Collins refers to this mode as "genericity."

Genre cinema is less than "reality," but it functions for mainstream film reviewers in much the same way, evidenced by Schwarzbaum's approach to *The Incredibles*. The orthodox response to David Fincher's *Se7en* addresses the film as conforming to the precepts of the thriller or *film noir* before it can embark on a project of generic commentary to embody a "spirit of innovation."[30] Classical genre cinema of the 1930s and

1940s did a very similar thing, transposing an essentially classical real-ism for its contemporary audience. Consider, for example, the invisible editing of the Hollywood studio film of the 1930s and 1940s. Finding its business in the genre film (in which even the most naturalistic depic-tion [*The Grapes of Wrath, The Lost Weekend*] was a generic form and eminently reproducible), the studio aesthetic employed an editing pro-cess that diminished the degree of artifice in plot and characterization. The perfection of the *film noir* in *Double Indemnity* offers a depiction of a harsher reality of post-Depression America (servicing the traditional realist aesthetic) in spite of the stylized dialogue and acting.

The pervasiveness of the mode of classical realism infects even the casual filmgoer, such that she feels beholden to address the cinematic image in relation to an ideal measure of reality. The image on screen must be, *a priori*, a thing of itself, and what it was always intended to be: irreduc-ible, a perfect reproduction of the external reality from which it is drawn, yet simultaneously reproduced only once. In this sense, it is posited as an "authentic" reproduction, something to which Walter Benjamin moves in his essay "The Work of Art in the Age of Mechanical Reproduction."[31] The literal transposition of the Real into the reproduced image recalls Adorno in a similar context: "For no authentic work of art and no true philoso-phy, according to their very meaning, has ever exhausted itself in itself alone, in its being-in-itself."[32] In his essay, Adorno argues for a dialectic in which the artwork is autonomous yet simultaneously engaged with the external conditions into which it is placed for exhibition or consump-tion. The necessity for an "autonomously engaged" art can be applied to the autonomy of the image on a cinematic screen as an organizing factor in the viewing criteria of classical Hollywood cinema. The screen image was posited as distinct from reality (it was, in a very literal sense, a form of escapism from an external world), but it prompted the spectator to address the screen image as a faithful reproduction of the real world. The image was autonomous, yet engaged with the reality it sought to repro-duce. Cinema as an art form was thus founded on a realist aesthetic even as Hollywood prospered through its stories of heroes, villains, and dam-sels in distress. Ironically, Hollywood's enduring "classicism" in the studio era was always simultaneously an enduring form of realism.[33]

The contemplation of film as reality invites a consideration of the limits to which realism can be stretched as a meaningful aesthetic measure. In positioning the spectator in a relation to the Real, film is able to fore-ground this inherent limitation. Viewing a trailer of Michel Gondry's

Eternal Sunshine of the Spotless Mind, a two-minute montage, I was transfixed only by a single sequence, a three-second shot of Joel Barish (Jim Carrey), disheveled with unrequited love, the major theme playing over his shuddering (from the expurgation of grief) image. The chaotic complexities of the narrative dissolved into something vague and formless, yet the essentiality of the story remained. It cohered beautifully and elegantly (to my mind, uncorrupted) as a three-second sequence and would no doubt have done as well in a single image, in the way that the lines of streaming data on a computer screen can recall the experience of engaging with a film franchise, *The Matrix*. What struck me as significant in Joel Barish's image was the ease—and remarkable acuity—with which I substituted it for an entire film experience. I rented the film, watched it again, and lived the experience of the first viewing a year before, and the profundity of that second viewing, the three-second sequence.

What I am getting at here is the spectator's ability to substitute the signifier for the signified in the cinematic image, the reproduced segment for the original whole, and yet to maintain the veracity and incorruptibility of its authenticity. A contemporary film ontology is in this sense founded upon an artifice. In reducing the whole to a montage, the spectator substitutes the component part for the full composition. The substitution of the once irreducible whole into an infinitely variable composition of images, shots, montage sequences, etc., shares something with Nicholas Rombes's analysis of the component structure of the DVD:

> What if we think of the supplementary features on DVDs not as just simply bonus material, but as new forms of cinema? Experimental cinema? For instance, the *Blue Velvet* DVD includes a bizarre feature that's sort of a "deleted scenes," but not quite. Supposedly, the footage that didn't make it into David Lynch's *Blue Velvet* was lost, but production/publicity stills survived, and the deleted scenes are composed of these still images, set to music, and edited together to suggest movement.[34]

I would only add that the division of the cinematic whole into chapters and various alternatives to the "original" text (alternate endings are an obvious example) inscribes the DVD at an ontological remove from a classical cinema and its viewing practices. The fact that DVD enables chapter viewing, still shots without the stretching of videotape, reduction of the image to slow-motion *controlled* by the spectator—must fundamentally reorganize the relationship between the spectator (particularly the spectator/fan or spectator/theorist, distinctions I will further explore) and the unalterable "classic." It is now fascinating to read Robin Wood's analysis of *Rear Window* in the first edition of *Hitchcock's Films Revisited*. Wood confesses that his analysis is based on a "three year old memory and a few scribbled notes in the cinema."[35] Contrast this with Žižek's analysis of a single (panning) shot on *Vertigo*'s DVD:

> After seeing the entrance to Ernie's from the outside, there is a cut to Scottie sitting at the bar counter in the front of the restaurant and looking through a partition into the large room with tables and guests. A long panning shot (without a cut) then takes us back and to the left, giving an overview of the entire crowded room, the soundtrack reproducing the chatter and clatter of a busy restaurant. We should bear in mind that this, clearly, is *not* Scottie's point of view.[36]

The DVD is, if not revolutionary in its reproductive capacity, certainly an alteration in the way "cinema" (which is of course now vaguely anachronistic) is viewed, reviewed, analyzed, and, in the advent of the innovation of digital cinema, *made*.

The spectator's response to contemporary cinema (and to classical cinema made contemporary upon DVD release) is also anchored in a *cinematicality*, an awareness of the text as partaking of a filmic history, context, and aesthetic register. The image of the lovelorn Carrey is inserted into what Eco calls the encyclopedia of the "collective imagination."[37] The montage imbues the sequence extracted from the whole with a "cultural charge,"[38] an affective stimulus based on a complex cinematic and cultural awareness. Attending an opening-weekend screening of *Star Wars, Episode III: Revenge of the Sith*, I was astonished to hear a collective round of applause at the presentation of the gigantic STAR WARS title screen. The still image was imbued with the fullness of a filmic franchise, as Joel Barish's face had been imbued with the fullness of *Eternal Sunshine*. An exchange between image and spectator had taken place in the opening shot, rendering the image attentive to its own status as metonym, as signification of an entire mythic, cultural, and aesthetic reality. What is significant here is the transition of the cine-matic shot/image, the indivisible component (in lieu of the fullness of the text) into a continuum of subjective aesthetic values.

Engaging with the Real in a classical realist sense requires engaging with an idealization of the Real. Beneath my aesthetic engagement with *Eternal Sunshine* is the notion of an ideal text. An attempt at a dutiful post-structuralist rejection of the Real meets only images and sound bites that stand in for perfected texts, and wholly cohesive, contained film experiences. The Real need not be a tangible point of "reality" (as, say, the socioeconomic plight of youths in Brooklyn is in Spike Lee's *Do the Right Thing*). I recalled the basic narrative structure of *Eternal Sunshine*, but it was not narrative to which I turned for the film's aesthetic impact. In fact, it occurred to me, the less reality involved, the more Real the cinematic mind makes of the image. In this way authenticity can be a subjective experience, that is, if reality is substituted by an idealized vision that informs the subjective point of view, albeit only a three-second clip.

What I hope to illustrate is the tenuousness of the relationship of the cinematic image to the Real; in *Eternal Sunshine*'s case, this applies to the notion of an essential and holistic film experience. We simply do not experience films this way in contemporary Western filmgoing societies, if indeed we ever have. Films are no more texts on a screen for passive consumption than they are traditional interpretive phenomena in the service of a better cultural appreciation. I hope to reconstruct an aesthetic mode of looking at film, an aesthetic not divorced from an appreciation of art as ideology, or art as social reflection (or even cultural engineer), but certainly one that returns critical theory to its rightful place—equally commentary and complimentarity rather than a thing in and of itself.

Bazin and the Myth of Total Cinema

André Bazin's writings on cinema might appear an odd choice with which to level an attack on realism. For one, Bazin's work has already been critiqued and developed in several forums and in several inventive ways. One influential analysis of Bazin's realism myth can be found in Deleuze's *Cinema 2*, in which Deleuze considers depth of field in relation to Bazin's theory of the reality of the depth-of-field image. However, in my discussion, I am interested more in the legacy of realism in cinema than a detailed structural analysis of the shot and sequence, such as Deleuze undertakes.[39]

Bazin offers a vital point of origin of cinema as a predominantly realist medium. But rather than value his functional "ontology of the Real," I contend that his notion of reality is anchored in a historical privilege accorded to the representative or mimetic art form. Robert Ray suggests that "the American Cinema's apparently natural subjection of style to narrative in fact depended on a historical accident: the movies' origins lay in the late nineteenth century whose predominant popular arts were the novel or the theatre . . . it adopted the basic tactic and goal of the realistic novel."[40] Classical Hollywood cinema was thus connected to a realist aesthetic that achieved its zenith in the nineteenth-century realist novel and drama. Griffith's *Birth of a Nation* and *Intolerance* are essentially social-historical dramas that find an ancestor in American realism and naturalism of the late nineteenth century. I am not arguing here that all cinema was indebted to a realist aesthetic. Murnau's *Nosferatu* or Lang's *Metropolis* are striking for their unique departures from a classical realism and their deliberate incorporation of Expressionist and Surrealist art traditions. But the cinema that was taken up by the Hollywood studios was indelibly inscribed with the mark of the Real, whether this was Wilder's uncompromisingly realistic portrayal of alcoholism in *Lost Weekend* or the genre cinema of Hawks's *Scarface: The Shame of a Nation* and *The Big Sleep*.[41]

Classical cinema adopted the classical realist aesthetic in its attempt to perfect the reproduction of the image. The High Renaissance is deemed "high," among other things, for devising the complexity of perspective in painting and sculpture, and achieving a heightened realism in its depiction of the life form (Michelangelo's *David* is often mentioned in this context).[42] Film was very early considered an image medium (thus the formative and influential work of Sergei Eisenstein on the montage) rather than a field of free movement; it is this distinction that foregrounds Deleuze's influential books on film. Early cinema foregrounds the image and the cut rather than the sequence. This emphasis on the still representation (in photography, the perfect realization of the physical form) can be traced to classical realist aesthetics, distinguishable from modernist successors. Modern art movements of the late nineteenth and early twentieth centuries found their modernity in the departure from the representative image, whether a figure or a field of flowers. It is precisely for this reason that Adorno esteems Picasso's *Guernica* in its being "wholly incompatible with criteria of realism, gaining expression through inhuman construction." For Adorno, *Guernica* achieves a critical distance from realist aesthetics, which paradoxically allows it to engineer a frame of "social protest."[43]

In contrast, Bazin recuperates the ethos of classical realism as the aspiration of a new *kind* of image in the cinema: "Painting was forced, as it turned out, to offer us illusion and this illusion was reckoned sufficient unto art. Photography and the cinema on the other hand are discoveries that satisfy, once and for all, and in its very essence, our obsession with realism."[44] He is correct to begin with the assumption of realism as an obsession, a necessity to contort what is fundamentally artificial (in this case, the cinematic image) into the shape of what it is said to indelibly represent. The criteria of contemporary film-viewing conditions are based on the importance of the realist aesthetic. A mass audience views films in a darkened room, insulated from an external reality, as audiences once did in the presentation of silent cinema or at the advent of sound, to sustain disbelief that it is viewing a world fundamentally divorced from its own, a world based upon a technological and textual construct. But rather than address the ontology of realism as a representative standard (that is, the Real as aestheticized reality), Bazin addresses the technological evolution toward the perfect realization of the Real. In his work on the photograph, he explores the "ontology of the photographic image," which, he suggests, effects a profound ontological shift from the earlier, and inherently flawed, realism of the master painter. "No matter how skilful the painter, his work was always in fee to an inescapable subjectivity. The fact that a human hand intervened cast a shadow of doubt over the image."[45] However, in the ascendance of the photograph over the representative painting, "for the first time, between the originating object and its reproduction there intervenes only the instrumentality of a non-living agent" [the camera lens].[46] For Bazin, the photographic image is empowered with the greatest ontology yet to "lay bare the realities."[47]

In fact, the driving "myth" of cinema is toward the Real. Thus, even before the technological components of image-making had been realized, the mythic foundation of representative art was to reproduce the Real without the impingement of the subjectivity of the artist or the shortcomings of a primitive technology: the crudity of an artist's tools, the unreliability of the human faculties to reproduce perfectly what they perceived. Bazin summarizes this in the following passage: "Any account of the cinema that was drawn merely from the technical inventions that made it possible would be a poor one indeed. On the contrary, an approximate and complicated visualization of an idea invariably precedes the industrial discovery which alone can open the way for its practical use."[48] In realizing this myth, cinema achieves what it had been destined for: an art laying bare the world in "all its cruelty and ugliness."[49] This was an image that was pure in relation to its object, an art of the Real and a new artistic realism.

In his much discussed essay "The Evolution of the Language of Cinema," Bazin invests the cinematic image with the power he attributes to photographic realism. The aesthetic pursuit of realism thus achieves its culmination in the cinematic image. Crucially, Bazin was a cofounder of the influential French journal *Cahiers du cinéma*, which proved a fermenting ground for the philosophical aesthetics of the French New Wave auteurs, particularly Jean Luc Godard and François Truffaut; it proved a fermenting ground also for Bazin's realist aesthetics. According to Bazin, the inherent realism of the cinema is revealed in the stripping back of the complex (though "invisible") editing techniques of classical Hollywood cinema and the montage of Russian cinema explored in the films and writing of Sergei Eisenstein. In the 1940s and 1950s, Bazin looks to Welles, William Wyler, and early Renoir, and traces residues of the perfection of realism in the silent films of Murnau (*Nosferatu* [1922], *Sunrise* [1927]) and Eric Von Stroheim (*Greed* [1924]).

It is interesting to note that the films of Godard and Truffaut, especially those of the early sixties, expressed very little of Bazin's theories of the film image, particularly in his reification of realism. Both foreground cinematic style and the inherent artifice of the cinematic image. Godard's *A Bout de Souffle* (*Breathless*) is exemplary of what I will refer to as the metacinematic aesthetic. Michel (Jean-Paul Belmondo) plays a protagonist on the lam who embodies a Humphrey Bogart persona while addressing the camera; the narrative continuity of his adventure is hampered by Godard's incessant use of the jump cut. Truffaut's concluding shot in *Les Quatre Cents Coups* (*The 400 Blows*) (in which the protagonist's loss of innocence is conveyed in a camera rush on his striking features, followed by an unorthodox use of freeze-frame), merges the realist aesthetic with the cinematic flamboyance of the first of the New Wave auteurs. Truffaut's next film was the overtly "artificial" *Tirez sur le Pianiste* (*Shoot the Piano Player*). And indeed the French New Wave quickly came to embody the cool artifice of the cinematic medium, confronting and then succeeding the demands of a cinema that had exhausted, in Deleuzian terms, the possibilities of the action-image.

Depth of Field and Focus

In Bazin's work, cinema is essentially a narrative art form. He discusses Robert Flaherty's documentary *Nanook of the North* in the same critical vein in which he discusses Orson Welles's use of deep focus in *Citizen Kane*; in both films, the structure of the cinematic text is based on the telling of a story. The measure of the cinematic image is its capacity to convey the reality of life stories, characters, and ideals. For Bazin, the origins of an "intellectual cinema," postulated in the montage of Sergei Eisenstein, are less an exposition than a perversion of the Real. The intellectualism of the cinema, for Eisenstein, could be traced to the quality of the montage, "an essential method and device in any cinematographic exposition. And, in a condensed and purified form, it is the starting-point for 'intellectual cinema,' a cinema that seeks the maximum laconicism in the visual exposition of abstract concepts."[50] The intellectualism of cinema is thus initially a matter of form that organizes the nature of the content; the montage functioned as a comprehensive philosophical and aesthetic language.

Eisenstein's intellectual montage is particularly relevant to this discussion of Bazin, for while Bazin does not use the term "intellectual cinema," he more readily discusses the work of a Murnau or Dreyer than Hollywood's Cecil B. DeMille. Interestingly, Welles, Wyler, and Ford emerged in the U.S. from within a studio aesthetic and an industrialized film production. Hitchcock is perhaps the most interesting case insofar as his auteuristic impulse was attuned equally to the artistic and the commercial.[51] The notion of an intellectual cinema that developed separately from a commercial cinema is increasingly problematic after the 1930s, but it is a distinction that Bazin at least implicitly upholds.

Bazin locates the realization of the myth of total cinema after 1940, particularly in Welles's *Citizen Kane* (1941) and *The Magnificent Ambersons* (1942). It is his contention that Welles's use of "deep focus" and "depth of field" challenges the ontology of the montage as the cinematic purveyor of reality. Deep focus is a cinematographic device in which the focus of a single shot is broadened to encompass more than a central figure or a single point of reference. The dominant style of classical Hollywood cinema (1930s and 1940s) was a "shot-reverse shot" sequence in which the spectator is presented with a shot and a subsequent reverse shot contextualizing the arrangement. A shot would therefore have a focal point (commonly center screen), a high contrast with a background that remained out of focus, and a subsequent cut to a reverse shot to give the focal arrangement a point of reference. Robert Ray suggests that the shot-reverse shot was integral to the maintenance of the "invisibility of style" in classical Hollywood: "The shot-reverse shot figure, therefore, played a crucial role in a formal paradigm whose basic tactic was the concealment of the necessity of choice."[52] In contriving the invisibility-of-style editing process in its major, primarily genre films, the Hollywood studio system presented the cinematic image as unadorned, servicing only the structural requirements of the narrative. The shot-reverse shot drew the spectator into the action, collapsing the screen that ordinarily functioned as a point of demarcation between cinematic text and spectator. The screen was dissolved, arriving almost paradoxically at the perfection of the realist aesthetic through the immersion of the spectator in the story, characterization, thematic, and, by extension, the Hollywood studio system. The spectator, relinquished of the necessity to choose (or forge her subjective interpretation on the sequence of images), assumes that the reality on screen is identical to the one it represents.

In response to various strategies of montage, Bazin celebrates the cinematic image's potential to reproduce the Real, and thus to reject the inherent artificiality of "visible" editing, exemplified in the work of Eisenstein. If montage is a "collision of two factors which gives rise to an idea,"[53] Bazin considers the process of arrangement, or the ordering of single shots, an intrusion into the visual reality: "It is simply a question of respect for the spatial unity of an event at the moment when to split it up would change it from something real into something imaginary."[54] The montage is essentially a putting together of two or more otherwise unrelated shots into an ordered system, forming a narrative component. This ordered system does not permit the spectator to partake in the realization of the image on the screen because the order of the image sequence is determined wholly by the filmmaker.

The crucial distinction between Eisenstein and Bazin's philosophy of the cinematic image can be found in the notion of "spatial unity." Whereas Eisenstein attempts to trace a genealogy of the montage through Japanese symbols and hieroglyphs:

> For example: the representation of water and of an eye signifies "to weep,"
>   the representation of an ear next to a drawing of a door means "to listen,"
>   a dog and a mouth mean "to bark" . . .
>   But—this is montage!![55]

Bazin conceptualizes a transcendental Real, an *a priori* "spatial unity" that pre-exists the cinematic representation, the reproduced image. Bazin's "language of cinema" is essentially a language with which to reproduce the inherent "*continuum* of reality."[56] For Eisenstein, cinema is a system of production: "Cinema is: so many firms, so much working capital, such and such a "star", so many dramas. / Cinema is, first and foremost, montage."[57] For Bazin, it is a system of *reproduction*. Eisenstein *creates* something out of montage; Bazin perceives a revealing of the Real "in which the image is evaluated not according to what it adds to reality but what it reveals of it."[58]

This revelation occurs in the ontology of the deep-focus and depth-of-field shot (in which the "field" of the shot is longer than a façade or a standard setup). While deep focus holds more of the shot in focus simultaneously, depth of field is able to visually contrive the "centrality" of an out-of-focus object. The two cinematographic strategies are complementary. David Bordwell offers an excellent discussion of the use of depth of field in contemporary cinema in which he claims that what was once unique in Welles has been taken on board by the majority of mainstream filmmakers after the 1980s:

> Most postwar directors, modernist or mainstream, cannot be distinguished by their commitment to a distinctive aesthetic of depth. . . . Neither [can] most of the younger generation, including the various New Waves in Europe and the Third World. Virtually all of the *Cahiers'* canonised "modern" directors shot with deep focus in the 1940s and 1950s and shifted to telephoto lenses and zooms during the 1960s and 1970s. They quickly adapted the new techniques to their aims of more self-consciously realistic, reflexive and ambiguous storytelling.[59]

Contemporary filmmakers employ conventional focus for the majority of shots, though they frequently revert to deep focus for a single shot, and even occasionally an extended sequence. The scene in which Delilah (Anna Levine) offers William Munny (Clint Eastwood) a "free one" in *Unforgiven* is shot almost entirely in deep focus, achieving a naturalism in the relationship between the isolated figures, ostracized from their respective societies, and the desolate beauty of the American West. Antonioni's *L'Avventura* is shot almost exclusively in deep focus; the composition of the shots on the ocean and particularly on the island on which Anna (Lea Massari) disappears is striking.

While the majority of shots in contemporary cinema use shallow or medium focus, deep focus is still utilized, and often to striking and provocative effect. Bazin's notion of the deep focus as rendering the cinematic image "ambiguous," or at least subject to multiple interpretations, is illustrated, for example, in Scorsese's *Casino*. Ginger (Sharon Stone) speaks to Sam (Robert De Niro) on a pay phone while Lester Diamond (James Woods) "chastises" their daughter in the background. The spectator's gaze is divided between the separate shot segments (and thus separate dramas) that merge in a medium-focus shot. In a classical montage, the separate dramas would be rendered through a series of cuts that direct the spectator's gaze and, according to Bazin, code the meaning of the scene.

Citizen Kane: A Cinematographic Revolution?

Citizen Kane remains the most influential film produced in the Hollywood studio system, and perhaps the most influential film ever produced in the United States. After more than fifty years, it is still regarded by the influential *Sight and Sound* poll as the greatest film ever made.[60] Of course, measuring degrees of influence is largely subjective, and the reader ought to bear in mind Chris Rock's visit to a multiplex in South Central L.A. In any case, film theory attests to *Kane*'s centrality in its stylistic innovation rather than in the originality of the story. Reviewers, critics, and theorists return to *Kane*'s unique cinematography to find its distinction. Bazin discusses in particular the *function* of depth of field and focus, which allows the camera to maintain the spatial unity of the shot, or to reproduce it in its "true" form. Welles certainly did experiment with the conventions of editing in *Citizen Kane* and *The Magnificent Ambersons*, primarily in lengthening the takes and deepening the focus of the shot to include characters and objects on the periphery. The famous four-minute opening sequence of *Touch of Evil* was captured in a single take (and remains perhaps the most distinguished single take on film). However, I would argue that the ontology of the long take had altered significantly since 1941 or, for that matter, 1947, the year Hitchcock shot *Rope* in a "single" take.[61]

The use of the long take in *Kane* permits the action to unfold according to a natural spatial and temporal dimension. The extended take is favored over the cut, approximating the movement of the actor to real life and offering the spectator the depiction of movement as it would appear off-screen. Bordwell and Thompson offer a detailed reading of a sequence early in *Kane* in which the camera unobtrusively moves from a long exterior shot to an interior conversation involving characters positioned in various depths of shot.[62] The scene is imbued with a sense of intimacy, and yet there is a fluidity of movement from exterior to interior shot. The depth of focus emphasizes the inherent continuity of the shot—background to foreground becomes a space that remains in focus.

The immersion of the image in focus functions literally as a resistance to the cut. While the camera holds on Charles's aunt and uncle inside the house, Charles is never "out of focus" in the exterior, but merely off-screen. This is precisely the revolutionary component of deep focus that several critics have failed to appreciate. Deep focus and the long take equate to an inherent continuity of the image in which action and movement are in a sense always occurring. For Bazin, this offers the nearest approximation of an external reality in which, if a person turns her head from one direction to another, what thereby leaves her field of vision continues its own progression into the future while she remains oblivious. Space and time are in a state of perpetual movement in relation to the gaze of the spectator.

In contrast, the cut is for Bazin connected to an earlier fascination with the still-life image captured by an earlier form of reproductive technology:

> Orson Welles restored to cinematographic illusion a fundamental quality of reality—its continuity. Classical editing, deriving from Griffith, separated reality into successive shots which were just a series of either logical or subjective points of view of an event. . . . The construction thus introduces an obviously abstract element into reality. Because we are so used to such abstractions, we no longer sense them.[63]

One could contrast Welles's "continuous" shot with Kubrick's use of the cut as an organizing principle of space and time in the last chapter of *2001: A Space Odyssey*. For Welles, deep focus maintains continuity in the represented image. For Kubrick, the cut literally erases a figure from the shot. After Bowman (Keir Dullea) exits the wormhole, the first shot depicts him from outside the spaceship. The first cut fractures the causality of the conventional shot-reverse shot. Now the spectator sees Bowman positioned outside the spaceship, but the point-of-view shot positions the spectator *inside* the spaceship. The prior incarnation of Bowman (who materialized in the spaceship after exiting the wormhole) is now occupied subjectively by the spectator. The cut installs the spectator into Bowman's subjectivity, which has *simultaneously* been displaced to the exterior of the ship. This occurs three more times as a hard cut erases Bowman's presence from the scene. The cut is used throughout this extraordinary sequence to dissociate the new Bowman (the precursor to the Star Child) from a natural cause-effect

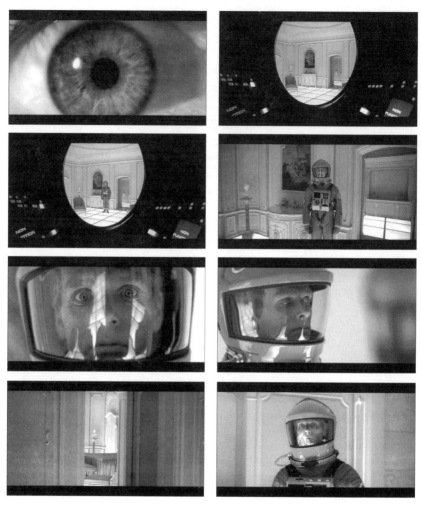

Kubrick's "quantum cinematography": subjectivity displaced through the cut.

determinism. In this case, the erasure is literally achieved through the cut, which alters the point of view of the sequence, transforming the (subjective) reality of the shot. This is Kubrick's remarkable visualization of a quantum space and time through cinematographic principles.

While Bazin in a sense acknowledges and even celebrates the aestheticization of reality, deep focus in *Kane* transcends this, exacting an affinity with the Real which maintains "an awareness of the reality itself"[64] apart from the abstraction into artifice.

A Note on the Mechanics of Style

For the discussion of *Citizen Kane* that follows, I am indebted to Roger Ebert's astonishingly detailed commentary on the film.[65] Ebert's "insider knowledge" in this respect is very useful and indicates yet again that film buffs and historians have access to source material beyond the reach or interests of the traditional film scholar. Only Bordwell to my mind has offered an analysis of film style that approaches the professionalism of the language of a filmmaker.[66] One need only contrast Scorsese's description of a shot in *Taxi Driver* or *Raging Bull*[67] with my own rudimentary terminology of shots and sequences in *Citizen Kane*. Ultimately, I would argue that film scholarship does not have an adequate knowledge of the filmmaking process. The advantage of such knowledge is twofold. The recuperation of any measure of auteurism (which I would argue is necessary in a study of contemporary cinema) requires a knowledge of the way the film is put together. Wood offers a reading of a sequence in *Marnie*, first as a literal exegesis of the action as it would appear in the script and then as a series of shots.[68] For Wood, the essential innovation of cinema (and particularly Hitchcockian cinema) is the uniqueness of the visual technique to the individual filmmaker, as well as a heightened affectivity of the visual image over the written word: "A novelist could give us some kind of equivalent for this, could make us react along the same general lines; but he couldn't make us react in this direct, immediate way, as image succeeds image—he couldn't control our actions so precisely in time."[69] An analysis of the cinematic stylistics of individual filmmakers is not misplaced in a study of film, nor easily negated by investigations of spectator subjectivities in psychoanalytic theory or analyses of hegemonies, cultures, or, by extension, selves.

Second, a knowledge of the filmmaking process is required to establish a measure of *intent* in the cinematic image, and this is equally necessary to an analysis of cinema. To take a very simple example, it is crucial in the narrative structure of *Psycho* that Hitchcock maintains the deception of the Norman/Mother duality until the final scene, in which Norman is literally unveiled. According to screenwriter Joseph Stefano, the most complex deception takes place in the scene in which Norman carries Mother (against her will) into the fruit cellar.[70] In the shooting script, Norman has a brief argument with Mother, which takes place inside the bedroom, off camera. The camera would be positioned at the top of the staircase. As Norman leaves the bedroom, coming into shot in the original setup of the camera, Hitchcock would cut the scene and show Norman and Mother from the doorway of the bedroom as they descend the stairs. Stefano's objection was that the spectator would sense something amiss and the deception would be compromised, perhaps even revealed. The cut from medium front shot on the staircase to a medium back shot from the bedroom doorway would be too conspicuous, and too obviously deceptive. Stefano suggested building a mechanism with which to capture an overhead shot, thus filming the exit of Norman and Mother from the bedroom, the passage through the landing, and the descent on the staircase in a single take. Hitchcock objected on the morning of the shooting due to the cost of the setup but changed his mind when it became clear that Stefano was right.

The point here is that the deception is maintained through the composition of the shot based on a visual strategy employed by the filmmakers (in this case, Stefano and Hitchcock). I would contend that the theorist who seeks to conceptualize the impact of a shot on the spectator must have a knowledge of the way the shot is composed. The composition is ultimately coordinated by a mechanistic process involving the camera and various contraptions that allow the camera to move. The innovation of digital cinematography is to transcend the physicality of the mechanized process, but I will have more to say about this in Chapter Three.

Conventional film theory has devoted little space to analyzing what David Sterritt has called the "physicality" of cinematic narrative, that is, the way in which the physical objects and bodies are arranged to give a sequence a systematic composition. Sterritt suggests that "even close analyses of Hitchcock's films tend to race past the *visceral* impact of *physical* events that pass across the screen."[71] It is not only the physicality of the cinematic shot but the mechanized processes involved in its composition that must surely be returned to any meaningful analysis of film. Without such an analysis, film theory is limited in its scope to spectator response, which accounts for its emphasis on subjectivity and the relationship of the subject to the cinematic screen.[72] While such analyses are central to an understanding of the way film functions on the spectator, I would argue also that a study of film as a uniquely visual text (incorporating the moving image) is just as crucial.

Auteurism and the Artifice of the Cinematic Image

I have thus far engaged with Bazin's theory of cinematic realism. Central as Bazin was to the *Cahiers* group, and central as auteur theory remains to film audiences (who invariably refer to a film as the singular possession of its director), I have also argued that Bazin's realism is a component of a broader realist aesthetics that pervades contemporary theories of cinema. Bazin was there first, so to speak, and his tenacious engagement with an ontology of the Real remains impressive in light of subsequent film theories and movements.

A critique of Bazin is necessarily formulated around two divergent arguments: the overemphasis on the auteur aspect of Welles after 1940 (particularly in the focus on *Kane* and *The Magnificent Ambersons*) and the challenge to the ontology of the image in post-structuralist semiotics—I draw on Barthes's work in this respect.

The notion of the auteur (or creative genius) was in its conception a retrospective theorizing and engagement with the presentation of content, that is, the auteur's unique way of formalizing the content of the story. In spite of an attack leveled by post-structuralist and materialist critics in the decades subsequent to the French New Wave, Andrew Sarris, the influential American film writer, reverts to the notion of the auteur as a meaningful criteria with which to measure the value of a film.[73] Sarris's "The Auteur Theory Revisited" is particularly interesting insofar as it offers a response to the attack leveled by Gore Vidal and others. I am somewhat sympathetic to theories of the auteur, in spite of Thomas Schatz's dismissive analysis of the theory as "adolescent romanticism."[74] While one ought to be suspicious of auteur theory in its mid-1950s incarnation, especially in relation to contemporary cinema produced within the Hollywood system, it seems facile to reject the possibility of a discernible "vision," albeit a vision constructed within a highly complex and fluid dynamic. Lynch's *Blue Velvet, Lost Highway*, and *Mulholland Drive* seem to me quintessential Lynch as much as *Taxi Driver, Raging Bull*, and *Goodfellas* are quintessential Scorsese. A large portion of the work of Lynch and Scorsese is focused on a similar thematic and stylistic project. One could argue, as Roger Ebert does pejoratively, that Lynch has been trying to make the same film his entire career and finally succeeds with *Mulholland Drive*.[75] Scorsese's "New York" films (*Mean Streets, Taxi Driver, Raging Bull, The King of Comedy, Goodfellas, Gangs of New York*) examine similar characters, stories, and themes while exploring a stylistics of cinema that can be traced throughout his work. The slow-motion entry of the protagonist as flaneur (who is more often than not also one of the film's narrators) occurs in *Mean Streets, Taxi Driver* (in which the enclosed urban space of the city substitutes for the social setting of a bar or restaurant), *Goodfellas, Casino*, and the brilliantly understated opening sequence of *The Departed*.

The retroactive declaration of Welles as an auteur in the tradition of Hitchcock or Ford seems premature in light of his career after *Kane* and *The Magnificent Ambersons*. Auteur theory credited certain directors with a uniformity or continuity of style, including a continuity of visual aspect in their films. There is a near uncanny uniformity in the way Hitchcock approaches his subject matter as a director. While he never looked through a viewing lens (leaving that to the cinematographer, whom he at times called a "cameraman"), the use of camera angles, movement, staging of the scene, etc., have a degree of congruence in each of his films. Rebello discusses the Hitchcockian obsession with subjective (or point-of-view) shots in *Psycho* that became almost synonymous with the director's work—in addition to *Psycho*, *Rear Window* and *Vertigo* are obvious cases in point.[76]

Bazin's conception of Welles as auteur focuses on a unique cinematographic strategy as an auteuristic impulse and thus as a purveyor of a perfect cinematic realism. What Bazin seems to argue for is the notion of the auteur as *philosopher* as well as creative genius; Welles's career is notable for what it says about "Film" rather than for his films themselves. Bazin has relatively little to say about the narrative or thematic continuity of Welles's films from *Citizen Kane* onward. While the freedom offered by depth-of-field cinematography was considered a remarkable and controversial aesthetic innovation in Hollywood cinema in the 1940s,[77] it surely does not constitute the *essence* of Welles's filmmaking. Most film audiences (including those niche audiences privileged enough to have seen *Citizen Kane*) remain oblivious to the concept of deep-focus cinematography.

Welles's turbulent years in the Hollywood studio system inevitably fashioned something auteuristic in his work and, perhaps even more significantly, in his persona as a Hollywood rebel. He is particularly interesting for his involvement with and ultimate exclusion from the studio system. *Citizen Kane* had been made through RKO Pictures, one of the major studios in 1940. He made only *The Magnificent Ambersons* two years later with RKO, but the studio considered the film such a disappointment that it altered its downbeat ending; the ending with which we are left, in relation to the majesty of the rest of the film, is laughable. Following *Ambersons*, Welles existed on the fringe of the studios. He made *The Stranger*, a less-than-noteworthy genre film which was marginally successful. *The Lady from Shanghai* appeared in 1948, though next to *Kane* and *Ambersons*, this is mediocre *film noir*, remarkable only for a tense, well-conceived first act and a wildly surreal concluding scene in a hall of mirrors.[78] He appeared briefly in *The Third Man* (1949), though his creative input on that film is questionable. *Touch of Evil* (1955), now regarded as a classic and the progenitor of the neo-*noir*, was received poorly by American critics and audiences: "While the New York critics were honoring Stanley Kramer's *The Defiant Ones*, the *Cahiers* critics were cheering Orson Welles's *Touch of Evil*. Obviously their eyes were quicker than our ears."[79] Thus, only *Kane* (which did not win a Best Picture or Best Director Oscar) and *Ambersons* support Bazin's thesis, and in relation to the peripheral nature of Welles's career after *Ambersons*, I would suggest that according him auteur status on the basis of two films is presumptuous. Bogdanovich describes this general response to Welles as a filmmaker toward the end of his career: "If Welles did have fears, he came by them honestly: since Orson's earliest theatre and radio successes, after *Citizen Kane*, his U.S. notices were mixed to negative. 'What else has he done since *Citizen Kane?*' was a popular refrain long before Welles died."[80]

Perhaps this criticism is not entirely fair to Bazin, who does not purport to describe his brand of realism as central to the Hollywood studio system. Along with Truffaut, he championed Welles as one of the great auteurs in the midst of an industry practicing a classical aesthetics: shot-reverse shot, theatrical sets, naturalistic focus, quick edits, etc. But the legacy of Welles as an intellectual filmmaker, to recall Eisenstein's term, is questionable in this regard, which must subsequently bring into question the significance of deep-focus and depth-of-field cinematography to subsequent filmic traditions. Welles's legacy will always revolve around the legacy of *Citizen Kane* to classic and contemporary Hollywood cinema, but one wonders how much that legacy has to do with cinematographic strategies or realist principles. An abiding legacy of *Kane* must also be located in the academy, most notably, among the theorists who turned to classical Hollywood in support of their theses. One such writer is Laura Mulvey, whose volume on *Citizen Kane* appropriates the film for an extended analysis of various theoretical legacies.[82] Mulvey concedes that her contribution to the legacy of *Kane*

> is an experiment in method. I am applying the film theory and criticism of my generation to a film that has been taken through the mill by each generation since it appeared fifty years ago. As the main influences on my thought have been psychoanalytic theory

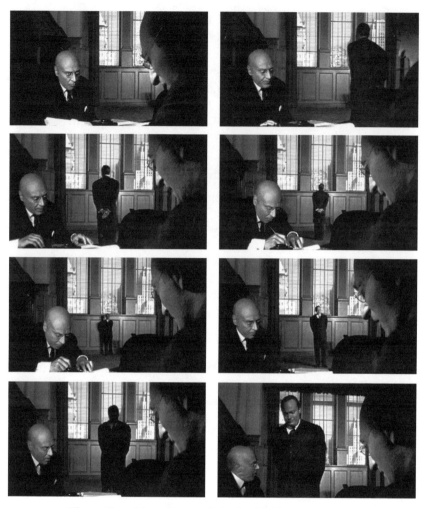

The artifice of deep focus and depth of field: Citizen Kane.

and feminism, both have strongly inflected my analysis of *Citizen Kane,* not just in terms of content—how the film depicts women and uses Freud—but as a film that challenges conventional relations between screen and spectator and constructs a language of cinema that meshes with the language of the psyche.[82]

In this sense, *Kane's* legacy will always manage to be reconstituted as the textual fabric of a new visual (or cinematic) consciousness.

A meaningful critique of Bazin's realism must also engage with his theory of the ontology of the cinematic image. We must begin with his notion of a possible cinematic realism realized in opposition to the montage. If the montage is a strategic connecting of unrelated images to form a narrative segment (the montage itself), deep focus allows the shot to maintain an inherent spatial unity by erasing the edit, the join, and by allowing a free flow of the temporal and spatial reproduction of the Real. Deep focus and depth of field allow the camera to photograph reality as it is. To address this, let us return to a scene in *Kane*. Charles Foster Kane sits in an office signing away his great fortune. Welles characteristically places this scene a third of the way through the narrative and returns to Kane's youth in the scene that immediately follows. The sequence in which Kane stands from the desk and walks to a rectangular window, pauses, and then returns to sign the document is striking for a number of reasons.[83] The single take is held in deep focus. The spectator perceives the contours of the desk, Mr. Thatcher, and Mr. Leland at the right of shot, as well as the rectangular windows in the background. Kane stands and moves toward the windows while the shot holds in deep focus. As Kane approaches the window, the spectator realizes that the depth of field of this shot is also a trick of perspective. The windows on the set are six feet above the ground. The critic Roger Ebert describes this as an "optical illusion,"[84] which of course it is. The spectator is deceived into thinking the windows are conventionally proportioned for an office building. Instead, the spatial dimensions of the shot are incongruent with an external reality while emphasizing the "reality" of the scene through long takes, deep focus, and depth of field. Thus, while the scene is exemplary of deep focus as a cinematographic device, it is also an example of Welles's ingenious use of deep focus to deliberately encode the Real with an inherent artificiality.

This illusion of realism is employed several times in *Kane*. The famous opening on Xanadu, Kane's pleasure palace, is a seamless blend of a constructed set and a matte drawing of Xanadu's façade; both set and drawing are held in the shot in deep focus. Rather than revealing the reality of the shot, deep focus positions a cinematic gaze that is subject to an inherent illusion: Xanadu, constructed in the spatial reality of the shot, does not exist. The trick of perspective is used a number of times in *Kane* to symbolize the rise and fall of a "great man." As Ebert suggests, it works as a "visual pun,"[85] but it works also as a cinematographic technique that signifies meaning in more than one way.

Welles employs a similar visual pun in the shot in which Kane walks toward a gigantic fireplace in Xanadu's great hall, exemplifying what Wood has called "the most artificial kind of cinema."[86] According to Ebert, *Kane* is "filled with special effects. When you look at the movie for the first time, you just see a political rally [Ebert is referring to a shot of Boss Jim Getty and Kane exiting a civic hall]. You don't think of it as a special effects shot, but it's as contrived as anything in *Star Wars* . . . it's made out of thin air."[87] Deep focus and depth of field are striking technical innovations in *Kane*, yet they are essentially cinematographic strategies employed to aestheticize a narrative in a visual medium. Welles employed depth of field precisely to foreground the contrivance of the cinematic shot (as Godard and Truffaut would do two decades later, inspiring a wave of innovative auteurs).

Cinema fractured as a mimetic form in the years after Welles, and *Kane* must surely be credited as a landmark film in this aesthetic revolution. Consider the famous opening of Billy Wilder's *Sunset Boulevard* in which a body lies floating in a pool. The shot was captured by placing a mirror on the pool floor and shooting from above the water. We thus see, floating from beneath the surface, the corpse of a traditional *noir* protagonist, who promptly begins to narrate the film. The setup is obviously not a conventional *mise en scène* or point-of-view shot.

The Hollywood auteurs (Wilder among them) explored the cinematic frontiers of the image. Hitchcock's oeuvre is a testament to film as a visual medium distinct from traditional textual practices, and to the shot as a site of innovation and variation on traditional realist aesthetics. How else can one account for the centrality of an ostensibly genre filmmaker to film theory after the 1950s? Broadly speaking, Hitchcock was never a "serious" filmmaker in the sense of a Spielberg, who started with the high-concept film in the 1970s (*Duel, Jaws, Close Encounters of the Third Kind*) but has attempted to transform himself into a director with artistic credibility with films such as *The Color Purple, Schindler's List, Saving Private Ryan*, and *Munich*. Hitchcock appealed equally to mainstream audiences and film theorists. I can only hypothesize that his centrality to film since the 1950s lies in his fascination with cinema as a unique form of spectacle divorced from prior art forms.

Mimesis was ultimately subsumed by the cinematic possibilities to contrive variations on the Real. In the work of Welles, Hitchcock, Godard, and others, the cinematic and the Real were absorbed into each other. The classic shower scene in *Psycho* is constructed out of forty separate shots in a sequence lasting less than a minute.[88] The cinematicality is foregrounded in the very deliberate arrangement of the sequence. In this scene, Hitchcock reveals only that the Real was extinguished when the cameras started to roll. It was already cinematic.

Bazin is relevant to any study of film aesthetics (and certainly any consideration of cinematic realism) simply because his concept of the film image is well defined and holds itself up to scrutiny. But why should depth of focus have anything at all to do with a more faithful reproduction of an external reality? He formulated his myth of cinema in response to what he saw as a transformation in signification practices, though he might have conceived of this transformation quite apart from the structuralist apparatus of Christian Metz and others.[89] But exactly what is transformed in Welles's *Citizen Kane* and *The Magnificent Ambersons*? *Kane's* cinematography does not allow a richer interpretation of the character. If anything, what I've argued is that the essential artifice of depth of field and focus mirrors the inconclusiveness of the narrative. Kane's story is subject to perpetual revision; a quasi-fictional account illuminates the ephemeral nature of identity and the discontinuities inherent in a narrative history. Formally, the film plays out as an expressionistic portrayal of a narrative conceit—the figure of Kane—visible intermittently through looming shadows, fractured accounts, and knowing subversions of narrative truth. Kane is equally a construct of news reports, personal anecdotes, and fragmented memories, and an overarching narrative trajectory that frames this collage. The narrative structure of *Kane* is perhaps most interesting in the context of the later European art films (*Hiroshima Mon Amour*, *L'Année Dernière à Marienbad* [*Last Year at Marienbad*]) that employed nonlinear narrative structures to foreground the notion of artifice in narrative composition.

Focus and Signification

The ontology of depth of focus and field realism fares poorly in light of post-structuralist theories of the image and the perpetual displacement of signification. Roland Barthes addresses the ontology of the photograph in a way that challenges Bazin's model. In his essay "The Photographic Message," he concurs initially with Bazin's ontology:

> The photograph professing to be a mechanical analogue of reality, its first-order message in some sort completely fills its substance and leaves no place for the development of a second-order message. Of all the structures of information, the photograph appears as the only one that is exclusively constituted and occu-

pied by a "denoted" message, a message which totally exhausts its mode of existence.[90]

Here the denoted comprises a first-order signification, the unmediated relation of the signifier to the signified, the photographic image to its representation, an external reality. As does Bazin, Barthes contrasts the fullness of photographic reality with the mediation of the Real in traditional representative arts: "In short, all these 'imitative' arts comprise two messages: a *denoted* message, which is the *analogon* itself, and a *connoted* message, which is the manner in which the society to a certain extent communicates what it thinks of it."[91] Yet Barthes very quickly reorganizes the ontology of the photographic image according to a characteristically Barthesian skepticism of the "unmediatedness" of the Real: "The photographic paradox can then be seen as the co-existence of two messages, the one without a code (the photographic analogue), the other with a code (the 'art' of the treatment, or the 'writing', or the rhetoric, of the photograph)."[92]

Barthes's system of denotation and connotation can be applied to Welles's use of deep focus. On the level of denotation, the depth of focus in the sequence in *Kane* in which the young Charles Foster Kane is removed from his home opens up the temporal and spatial dimensions of the shot: young Charles playing in the snow, the intrusion of his mother's head into the right of shot, the long track back through the window to rest on a high-angle shot of a table where Charles will be signed over to Mr. Thatcher (this scene has a remarkable congruence, stylistically and thematically, to the scene in which Charles signs away his beloved paper in Mr. Thatcher's office). The cinematic reality is denotationally faithful to the dimensions of the scene external to the shot. But the second-order meanings, the connoted "treatment" (to use Barthes's term), only proliferate with the use of deep focus. Deep focus results in an explosion of connotative meanings. This is precisely what Barthes has in mind with the paradox of the photographic message: "It is that here the connoted (or coded) message develops on the basis of a message *without a code*."[93] Deep focus lays bare the lack of a coding (or compositional arrangement): a scene literally without a code with which to view it.

The unconventionality (and invisibility) of the cinematography foregrounds the camera as a significatory mechanism. This invisibility is perfectly contrasted with the "invisibility of style" of classical Hollywood cinema. Hollywood achieved a classical realism through, paradoxically, a complex and highly structured editing style. In *Kane*, rather than "laying bare the realities," the gaze of the deep-focus camera, untethered from the edited cell and the montage, reorganizes the spatial and temporal sense of the shot. The depth of focus lays bare only the visibility of the contrivance in which the deep-focus shot is an *intrusion into* an assumed invisibility of style. The focal depth (in Bazin's notion of the continuity of the image, it is an infinite focal depth) provides the perfect canvas on which to explore the artifice of shot composition (as Welles did throughout his career, most deliberately in *Touch of Evil*). *Kane*'s visual sensibility is based on this duality: a freeing of the conventions of classical Hollywood editing to explore the boundaries of what Hitchcock called "pure cinema." The purity of the image achieves its resonance as a *photographed* (and thus reproduced) reality; deep focus allows the photograph to draw the entirety of the Real into its construction.

Consider the obverse to the deep-focus shot in a striking sequence in Wong Kar Wai's *Chungking Express*. After a short sequence in which a man and woman converse across a food counter for the first time (the spectator is informed that she will fall in love with him in six hours), the man leans forward and summons the woman to him with a gesture. The scene cuts to a close-up profile of the two faces, which now fill the shot.[94] The man's face, nearest the camera, is in macro zoom and perfectly in focus; the woman's face, according to the spatial unity of the scene, should be positioned slightly behind his and only marginally out of focus, if at all. However, her image is luridly out of focus. She has been positioned some distance behind the man to capture the extreme shallow focus of the shot.

If Welles's deep focus is striking for its unconventionality, Wong's shallow focus is equally provocative. Yet neither arrests a sense of an external reality. Both techniques foreground the artifice of the shot. In terms of Barthes's connotative reading, Wong complements the jarring shallow focus with the anachronistic music accompaniment, "California Dreaming" (The Mamas and the Papas), and a cool existentialism that recalls Godard's *Breathless*. *Chungking Express* (and Wong Kar Wai's impressive oeuvre) foregrounds its cinematic precocity. Shortly after this first meeting, a medium shot holds the man at left screen and the woman at right. The depth of field of the shot is visually striking and noticeably unconventional. Wong has the actors move in super-slow-motion and speeds up the film. Thus, the passersby move at twice the normal speed while the man and woman appear to inhabit a spatial and temporal frame in isolation.

Deep focus and depth of field are cinematographic performance spaces that express only an ontology of the constructed image. Cinema is and always has been about contorting a crude reality to the aesthetic elegance of the cinematic image. How can the spectator respond affectively to cinematic physicality (to use Sterritt's terminology) without an awareness of its status as constructed artifice? Welles and Wong explore a film aesthetics that contrasts with what had preceded it. Welles's deep focus stands out only in an era in which the Hollywood studio had encoded in its major pictures an invisibility of style. Welles, always a precocious talent, celebrated his pioneering of a technical innovation that has since become legendary to theorists and historians of film, if not mainstream film audiences. Rather than revealing a reality beneath the artifice of Hollywood, Welles exploded the connotative possibilities of the cinematic image, and Hitchcock, Godard, Scorsese, Tarantino, and Wong only followed suit.

A Brief Defense of Bazin

It would be remiss to overlook the genuinely revolutionary philosophy of the cinematic image attributable to Bazin's "The Evolution of the Language of Cinema." As well as suggesting that deep focus "brings the spectator into a relation with the image close to that which he enjoys with reality,"[95] he also alludes to a "more active mental attitude on the part of the spectator and a more positive contribution on his part to the action in progress."[96] Thus, in the deep-focus shot, the "reality" or "spatial unity" provides an avenue for the spectator to critically engage with the content of the image:

> While analytical montage only calls for him [the spectator] to follow his guide, to let his attention follow along smoothly with that of the director who will choose what he should see, here he will be called upon to exercise at least a minimum of personal choice. It is from his attention and his will that the meaning of the image in part derives.[97]

While I have critiqued the notion of an inherent congruence of the Real and a deep-focus reproduction, I agree with Bazin that the spectator's subjectivity enters the frame of meaning of the image. Indeed, my argument departs from Bazin only insofar as deep focus performs a veritable explosion of significatory mechanisms within the composition of the shot. Within the frame of the deep-focus shot, the image seems less attuned to what is externally Real than to what is internally presented (or photographed). But beyond this, I share Bazin's fascination with the complexity of the relationship between the cinematic image and spectator subjectivity. In critiquing Adorno's dialectic of the artwork and the culture industry commodity, as well as Jameson's "waning of affect" and passivity of the postmodern spectator, I return to Bazin and this critical juncture in the formulation of the cinematic subject.

The Transcendence of the Image

Reality, as it was visually experienced, became a staged, social production. Real, everyday experiences, soon came to be judged against their staged cinematic, video-counterpart.[98]

You're even better than the Real Thing.[99]

In spite of the critique of Bazin, his theories of cinema have a special place in the corpus of film studies. The majority of attacks of Bazin subvert his attempt to inscribe a realism myth into the cinematic apparatus. Comolli and Narboni introduce the "ideological" argument of the cinematic image: "Clearly, the cinema 'reproduces' reality: this is what a camera and film stock are for—so says the ideology. But the tools and techniques of filmmaking are a part of 'reality' themselves, and furthermore 'reality' is nothing but an expression of the prevailing ideology."[100] I have spent the greater part of my discussion in a conceptual engagement with Bazin's ontology of the Real and reproduced, the external reality and a cinematically reproduced image. This discussion has been specific to Bazin's model and may appear less than provocative in light of theories of cinema that have since prevailed. However, I have maintained that realism masks the essential artificiality of the cinematic image and that without a confrontation between cinema's inherent artifice and the spectator, an engagement with the aesthetics of contemporary film will be lacking. The greater part of recent film studies is a catalog of ways in which to *use* cinema. Consider, for example, Teshoma Gabriel's cinema of resistance, a politics and poetics of a cinema of the Third World.[101] The epistemological status of such a cinema is equated with a means to an end; the nature of that end is something I address in Chapter Two.

The legacy of cinematic realism is such that the spectator assumes a degree of passivity. Realism, essentialized as it has been in the work of Bazin and others, or the adoption of the studio's "invisibility of style" of the 1930s and 1940s, encourages the spectator to insert herself into the image or, paradoxically, remove herself from it. A knowing engagement with the dimensions of the spatial and temporal *disunity*—what I have referred to as the inherent artifice of the cinematic image—is forbidden. Consider, for example, Graeme Turner's conception of the point-of-view shot.[102] Turner's book is a detailed work on cinema as a "social practice," and to this end he attempts to establish the potency of the camera as a tool of signification. In discussing the sequence in *Citizen Kane* in which Kane stands over Susan Alexander (the sequence shot in Xanadu's great hall, discussed above), Turner writes: "In this sequence, the manipulation of camera angles is the major means by which the audience is informed about the changing relationship between the two characters."[103] That is, Kane looming over Susan Alexander conveys Kane's largeness and Susan Alexander's smallness. In this schematic, a high-angled shot connotes a relationship of superiority/inferiority (or dominance/submission), the low-angled shot the reverse. However, Turner fails to address the inadequacy of the shot as a (mimetic) significatory unit. The cinematic shot exists in a system of relations of various modes of signification: music, lighting, props, *mise en scène*, the physical presence of the actors, etc. Kane's point of view is challenged by subsequent shots of his diminishment in front of the gigantic fireplace or the wildly disproportionate interiors of the film. The point of view is less a physical space or the interior of a character's subjectivity than a *cinematic* reconfiguration of these physical (and psychical) dimensions. There is no point at which the shot—long, zoom, high angle, low angle, point of view—is a purely mimetic mechanism.

Turner goes on to address a sequence in Spielberg's *Jaws* in which the spectator apparently inheres in the shark's point of view:

> In *Jaws*, we are given numerous shots of the victims from the underwater point of view of the shark. The confusion caused by our discomfort with this alignment, and our privileged knowledge of the shark's proximity to the victim, exacerbates the tension and the impression of impotence felt by the audience and enhances our sense of the vulnerability of the victims.[104]

Jaws has two striking sequences in which the camera constructs a relationship between the shark and the spectator through the camera's point of view. The justly famous opening shows a young woman swim from shore, leaving her friend on the beach. After a long shot in which the woman is seen backstroking through the calm sea, the camera cuts to a close-up of the still water, ruptured from beneath by the woman.

The idyllic quality of the scene is maintained as the woman turns from camera toward the last sunlight and the shore, heightening the stillness and her isolation from the party. The scene then cuts to the first underwater shot. At this point, the spectator cannot inhere in the shark's point of view simply because the denotative message, to return to Barthes, has provided only the enchantment of the still water, a socially transgressive skinny-dip and the body of a naked woman treading water. The camera begins a slow movement toward the woman from beneath the water, and only then is the accompanying John Williams theme heard. The spectator is transported into a cinematic "space" through the rising theme and the slow zoom.

It is not only the intrusion of the shark into the idyllic setting that sustains the suspense. Prior to the zoom, the underwater shot positions the spectator in a realm of cinematic *otherness*, a voyeuristic distance. She does not vicariously share in the power and brutality of the shark, or the weakness and defilement of the young woman. The spectator enters the cinematic image and fractures the mimetic, and conventional, functionality of shot signification. The fracture occurs only at the commencement of the slow zoom and theme, anticipated with silence and a long pause. I agree with Turner about the "confusion caused by our discomfort."[105] I cannot agree, however, that Spielberg's camera is subject to the conventional parameters of mimesis. The point-of-view shot in this case (and several times in *Jaws*) is less than reliable as an indication, or initiation, of the spectator's subjectivity into the fictional subjectivity (of the shark) on screen.

Žižek offers a similar reading of a much discussed sequence in *Vertigo* in which Hitchcock corrupts the conventional shot-reverse shot as a signification of point of view. Scotty (James Stewart) enters Ernie's restaurant for the first time. The sequence in which the two "interact"[106] has been subject to several analyses that, Žižek charges, overlook the central panning shot in which the spectator is removed from Scotty's subjectivity. Žižek draws on a notion of the Lacanian *Real* that intrudes, or extrudes, from the alignment of spectator and conventional point of view. This Lacanian *otherness* (at least in terms of the spectator) shares something with the depth of the underwater shot in the opening sequence of *Jaws*, which is broken at the commencement of the slow zoom.[107] Raymond Durgnat suggests something similar for several so-called point-of-view shots in *Psycho*. It is Durgnat's contention that too much has been made of the point-of-view (or subjective) shot in Hitchcock's work to identify either the filmmaker or the spectator with his films' deviant psycholo-

gies: L. B. Jeffries (*Rear Window*), Scotty Ferguson (*Vertigo*), Norman
Bates (*Psycho*), Mark Rutland (*Marnie*). Durgnat has two objections to
this analysis:

> one, that in fictions like *Psycho*, camera and diegesis are logically
> incompatible, so that diegetic space and camera space read as a
> non-continuum, and, two, that most spectators overlook camera
> POV, much as they disregard cuts, which, if taken literally, would
> jump them about in space, like performing fleas. The reasons are
> well known in visual art theory and in scientific psychology.[108]

Steven Spielberg, a consummate stylist:
Jaws *and the construction of focus.*

While Durgnat does not take up the issue of the content of the camera space, as opposed to the diegetic space, it is significant that he recognizes a distinction between the two. This abstract though vital point
can be illustrated more simply in another sequence in *Jaws* in which the
spectator is positioned in the shark's point of view. My contention is simply that the spectator's subjectivity is at best imperfectly related to the
cinematic image. I reject the notion of a perfect congruence between
the spectator and Charles Foster Kane in the point-of-view shot. The
spectator embodies the temporal and spatial unity of Kane's presence in
the great hall, in which Turner perceives a "controlling [aspect] of the
audience's identification with the characters,"[109] but there is not the sense
of a literal transferal of the spectator's subjectivity into Kane. The spectator unconsciously appreciates and aestheticizes the inherent, cinematic
distance—the construction of the shot. In the sequence in *Jaws* in which
Brody (Roy Scheider) sits on the beach keeping a lookout during the
4th of July weekend, the gradual intrusion of the shark into an idyllic
setting is played out in much the same way as in the opening sequence.
The attack occurs suddenly and the viewer is inserted into Brody's point-
of-view. However, rather than a conventional point-of-view shot from
Brody's perspective, Spielberg uses what is referred to as the "push-pull."

The camera fast zooms on Brody's face while the focal length of the shot decreases dramatically. The effect is wholly unconventional and disorienting for the spectator because there is no recourse to the focal conventions of human vision. The shot is essentially a cinematic contrivance, a manipulation of the spatial and temporal reality (focal length and speed) into the artifice of the shot. The spectator, rather than being aligned with any of the primary characters—Brody, his wife, the boy who is attacked, or the shark—inhabits a contained, and contrived, cinematic space in which her subjectivity actively engages with the image. The quality of this engagement cannot be a literal and seamless transference of spectator/character subjectivity.

It is interesting to compare Spielberg's use of the push-pull in *Jaws* to Hitchcock's similar use of tracking and focus to achieve the famous "vertigo'" shot. Hitchcock employs the push-pull (or at least a variation of the device Spielberg uses) precisely to identify the spectator with Scotty; the disorientation of the shot perspective conveys what Scotty feels when he looks over an abyss. In Hitchcock's usage, the push-pull inserts the spectator (to some degree) into Stewart's character. In Spielberg's usage, a similar cinematographic trick inserts a space between spectator and character subjectivity. The use of the push-pull in *Jaws* disrupts the neat transference of the cinematic message. In fact, in light of the cinematic-*ness* (or the hypercinematic aesthetic) of the contemporary film, the relation between the image/shot/sequence and the reality it purports to represent is increasingly ephemeral, even as it attempts to correlate spectator and character subjectivity.

While it is necessary to appreciate the tangible relations between the Real and the cinematic reproduction (the subjective transference in the literal point-of-view shot, for example, which occurs frequently in Hitchcock, particularly *Rear Window*, *Vertigo*, and *Psycho*), it is equally necessary to appreciate the shortcomings of such a conceptual framework. Point-of-view shots are rarely an insular, wholly contained point of view. The notion of the "voyeuristic distance" of the cinematic image (which I've used above) compromises a perfect transference of the spectator/character subjectivity. However, this distance has little to do with Denzin's gendered gaze: "Always a gendered production, usually male, but not necessarily, the voyeur exposes the erotic, political sides of everyday life. In doing so, this figure shows how the gaze is inevitably gendered and structured by the laws of patriarchy."[110] In Denzin's analysis, the voyeur is an ideologized and, indeed, politicized position.

Without rejecting the ideological voyeur, central as it is to contemporary theories of gender and power in film, I would argue that the place from which the spectator views the cinematic image on a screen is dissociated from the space that appears on that screen, or the space that comprises the reality external to the movie theater. In regard to Denzin's notion of a cinematic distance as ideologized, I remain skeptical. In my opinion, *cinematic* voyeurism is ontologically connected to the cinema. Hitchcock's *Rear Window* is still the best example of the "romanticization" of the cinematic voyeur. Consider an early shot in which Grace Kelly is "presented" to the spectator. The camera offers a close-up of her features (she is simultaneously Lisa Freemont and Grace Kelly, a film icon, and the camera's adoration is directed toward both) as she advances toward the spectator. The spectator does not inhere in Jeff's (James Stewart's) point of view. Rather, the interaction is with a cinematic image *and* a film icon. The shot cuts to their "first kiss," a languorous slow-motion sequence, and a rarity for Hitchcock. While I concur with writers like Laura Mulvey[111] and Tania Modleski[112] that the cinematic voyeur and the average Peeping Tom have something in common, I would also argue that too much has been made of the sameness of these two (very different) ways of seeing.

Theories of the "society of the spectacle," a phrase I take from Guy Debord's famous work of that title,[113] vacillate between a grudging acceptance of the centrality of the image to contemporary culture and an extreme, almost religious embracing of the image as ontologically transcendent over the object. One need look no further than Jean Baudrillard's fashionable simulacrum of images, signs, and mediated ephemera for the location of this phenomenon: "Today abstraction is no longer that of the map, the double, the mirror, or the concept. Simulation is no longer that of a territory, a referential being, or a substance. It is the generation by models of a real without origin or reality: a hyperreal."[114] Baudrillard has since found his way into the conceptual framework of *The Matrix* franchise (Morpheus's "desert of the Real" echoes Baudrillard; indeed, in the shooting script of the first film, he explicitly references Baudrillard in explaining the relationship of the Matrix to the Real) and *Fight Club*, in which the disenfranchised narrator experiences postmodern America as "a copy of a copy of a copy."[115] Mass culture of the twenty-first century, it seems, has been taught to think in terms of the language of the simulacrum. Theorists like Baudrillard and writers like Don DeLillo (who seems to practice a "poetics" of the simulacra: consider DeLillo's notion of the Zapruder film of the JFK assassination as the simulacral expression of the Real [*Underworld*], a theme central to his earlier *Libra*) reflect on an apparent loss of the Real, a disgruntled sense of the fickleness of personal and social relations. Perhaps Bono, interviewed on the tele-visual set of U2's 1991 Zoo-TV tour, presents a way forward: "We saw all this information, all this bullshit . . . and wanted to surf it." Metaphors of surface and depth have proliferated since the announcement of the dominance of the Postmodern Condition by Lyotard,[116] yet depth unfortunately connotes the diverse, nuanced, subtle, complex, contextualized, historicized, reactionary Real, and surface the contemporarily transparent, superficial, sophomoric, simplistic, and ultimately valueless reproduction. Thus I reject such metaphors of cultural and aesthetic phenomena as inadequate to describe my own interaction with—and within—popular culture and its myriad signs, texts, and experiences. What does it mean to suggest that a cultural production—art, work, commodity—is *depthless*?

Conclusion

> It used to be that only movies were on film; now the whole world is. More than ever, visual technologies seem intent on striving for what Kracauer called "the status of total record." And not only does it seem at the start of the new century that everything is on film or video . . . but thanks first to video and then the Internet, scenes that were never shown before—from natural disasters and human atrocities to sexual intimacies and ecstasies—are now public spectacles that are instantly shown everywhere.[117]

Can the world be cinematic? And what would be implied in the dawning of a metacinematic aesthetic in which the external reality itself must submit to the ontology of the image/shot/sequence? Does the fact that the world (in whatever sense Black intends this) is captured on film alter the relationship of an external reality to its reproduced image? Of course it does. This chapter has attempted to theorize just such an alteration in the ontology of the Real. A classical realist aesthetics is incompatible with the cinematic medium; an engagement with a meaningful film aesthetics must confront a new ontology of the *cinematic* Real.

Notes

1. Barbara Kennedy, *Deleuze and Cinema*: *The Aesthetics of Sensation* (Edinburgh: Edinburgh University Press, 2000), 4.

2. Andrew Darley, *Visual Digital Culture*: *Surface Play and Spectacle in New Media Genres* (London: Routledge, 2000), 6.

3. Darley, 6.

4. For an analysis of the interconnectedness of various national cinemas, see Tom O'Reagan, "A National Cinema," in *The Film Cultures Reader*, ed. Graeme Turner (London: Routledge, 2002), 141.

5. For an analysis of fandom and its complex textual and cultural strategies, see Will Brooker, "Internet Fandom and the Continuing Narratives of *Star Wars*, *Blade Runner* and *Alien*," in *Alien Zone II*: *The Spaces of Science Fiction Cinema*, ed. Annette Kuhn (London: Verso, 1999), 50–72.

6. For an example of an influential exponent of this form of criticism, see David Thomson, *The Whole Equation* (New York: Alfred A. Knopf, 2005), 339–343.

7. See, for example, Annalee Newitz, "Serial Killers, True Crime, and Economic Performance Anxiety" in *Mythologies of Violence in Postmodern Media*, ed. Christopher Sharrett (Detroit, MI: Wayne State University Press, 1999), 66.

8. See C. Richard King and David J. Leonard, "Is Neo White? Reading Race, Watching the Trilogy," in *Jacking in to The Matrix Franchise*: *Cultural Reception and Interpretation*, ed. Matthew Kapell and William G. Doty (New York: Continuum, 2004), 32–47.

9. Robert Jewett and John Shelton Lawrence, *The American Monomyth* (New York: Anchor Press/Double Day, 1977), 148–164.

10. For the most lucid account of this widely held view, see Dan Rubey, "Not So Long Ago, Not So Far Away," *Jump Cut* 41 (1997). See also Koenraad Kuiper, "Star Wars: An Imperial Myth," *Journal of Popular Culture* 21, no. 4 (1988), 77–86.

11. Laura Mulvey, "Visual Pleasure and Narrative Cinema," in *The Sexual Subject*: *A Screen Reader in Sexuality*, ed. Screen (London: Routledge, 1992), 22.

12. Mulvey, "Visual Pleasure and Narrative Cinema," 32.

13. Lev Manovich, "Post-media Aesthetics," in *(dis)locations* (DVD ROM) (Karlsruhe: ZKM Centre for Art and Media, 2001), 5-6.

14. Theodor Adorno, "Culture Industry Reconsidered," in *The Culture Industry*: *Selected Essays on Mass Culture*, ed. J. M. Bernstein (London: Routledge, 1991), 90.

15. Noël Carroll, *A Philosophy of Mass Art* (Oxford: Clarendon Press, 1998), 172.

16. For a discussion of the influence of the Frankfurt School, and particularly Horkheimer and Adorno's "pessimism," see Joanne Hollows, "Mass Culture Theory and Political Economy," in *Approaches to Popular Film*, ed. Joanne Hollows and Mark Jancovich (Manchester: Manchester University Press, 1995), 18–20.

17. Graham McCann, "The Movie Killers," *Modern Review* 1, no. 9 (1993), 33.

18. Robin Wood, *Hitchcock's Films Revisited* (New York: Columbia University Press, 2002), 57. Original emphasis.

19. François Truffaut, *Hitchcock* (London: Granada, 1969), 349.

20. Carroll, *A Philosophy of Mass Art*, 13.

21. Jean Baudrillard, *Simulacra and Simulation*, trans. Sheila Faria Glaser (Detroit: University of Michigan Press, 1994), 1.

22. Roberto Rossellini's *Roma, Città Aperta* (*Rome, Open City*, 1945), *Paisà* (*Paisan*, 1946) and Vittorio de Sica's *Ladri di Biciclette* (*The Bicycle Thief*, 1948) are generally considered exemplary of this tradition. For a discussion of the legacy of Neorealism, see Jay McRoy, "Italian Neo-Realist Influences." In *New Punk Cinema*, ed. Nicholas Rombes (Edinburgh: University of Edinburgh Press, 2005), 40.

23. Siegfried Kracauer, *Theory of Film: The Redemption of Physical Reality* (London and New York: Oxford University Press, 1960), 39.

24. Dudley Andrew, *Concepts in Film Theory* (Oxford: Oxford University Press, 1984), 47.

25. Christian Metz, *Language and Cinema*, trans. Donna Jean Umiker-Sebeok (The Hague: Mouton, 1974), 55–61.

26. Quoted in Sean O'Hagan, "'I'm allowed to do what I want—that amazes me!'" interview in *The Observer*, Dec. 5, 2004.

27. Quoted in Michael Coveney, *The World According to Mike Leigh* (London: HarperCollins, 1996), 5. (Originally *International Herald Tribune*, Feb. 2, 1994.)

28. Lisa Schwarzbaum, "The Incredibles," *Entertainment Weekly*, Sep. 15, 2005.

29. Steve Neale, *Genre and Hollywood* (London: Routledge, 2000), 31.

30. Jim Hillier, "Introduction," in *American Independent Cinema: A Sight and Sound Reader*, ed. Jim Hillier (London: British Film Institute, 2001), 16.

31. Walter Benjamin, "The Work of Art in the Age of Mechanical Reproduction," in *The Norton Anthology of Theory and Criticism*, ed. Peter Simon (New York: W. W. Norton: 2001), 1166–1186.

32. Theodor Adorno, "Cultural Criticism and Society," in *Prisms*, trans. Samuel and Sherry Weber (London: Neville Spearman, 1967), 23.

33. See E. Ann Kaplan, "Classical Hollywood Film and Melodrama," in *American Cinema and Hollywood: Critical Approaches*, ed. John Hill and Pamela Church Gibson (Oxford: Oxford University Press, 2000), 46–48.

34. Nicholas Rombes, "A New Film Genre?" *Digital Poetics*, blog post Apr. 15, 2005, http://professordvd.typepad.com/my_weblog/2005/04/index.html (accessed Jul. 16, 2005).

35. Wood, *Hitchcock's Films Revisited*, 100.

36. Slavoj Žižek, "*Vertigo*: The Drama of a Deceived Platonist," *Hitchcock Annual* (2003-2004), 68–69.

37. Umberto Eco, "Innovation and Repetition." *Daedalus* 114, no. 4 (1985), 170.

38. Jim Collins, "Genericity in the Nineties: Eclectic Irony and the New Sincerity," in *Film Theory Goes to the Movies*, ed. Jim Collins, Hillary Radner, and Ava Preacher Collins (New York: Routledge, 1993), 256.

39. For example, see Gilles Deleuze, *Cinema 2: The Time-Image*, trans. Hugh Tomlinson and Barbara Habberjam (London: Athlone Press, 1989), 105–109.

40. Robert Ray, *A Certain Tendency of the Hollywood Cinema, 1930-1980* (Princeton: Princeton University Press, 1985), 34.

41. For an influential analysis of Hawks's contribution to studio cinema, and particularly for his brand of "noble realism," see Jacques Rivette, "The Genius of Howard Hawks," in *Cahiers du cinéma: The 1950s*, ed. Jim Hillier (Cambridge, MA: Harvard University Press, 1985), 130.

42. See André Bazin, "The Ontology of the Photographic Image," in *What Is Cinema, Volume 1*, trans. Hugh Gray (Berkeley and Los Angeles: University of California Press, 1967), 12–13. For an assessment of Bazin's theory, see David Bordwell, *On the History of Film Style* (Cambridge, MA: Harvard University Press, 1977), 70–71.

43. Theodor Adorno, *Aesthetic Theory*, trans. C Lenhardt, ed. Gretel Adorno and Rolf Tiedemann (London: Routledge & Kegan Paul, 1984), 337.

44. Bazin, "Ontology of the Photographic Image," 12.

45. Bazin, "Ontology of the Photographic Image," 12.

46. Bazin, "Ontology of the Photographic Image," 13.

47. Bazin, "Ontology of the Photographic Image," 15.

48. André Bazin, "The Myth of Total Cinema," in *What Is Cinema*, vol. 1, 18.

49. André Bazin, "The Evolution of the Language of Cinema," in *What Is Cinema*, vol. 1, 27.

50. Sergei Eisenstein, "Beyond the Shot (The Cinematographic Principle and the Ideogram)," in *Film Theory and Criticism*, ed. Leo Braudy and Marshall Cohen (Oxford: Oxford University Press, 2004), 14–15.

51. See Wood, *Hitchcock's Films Revisited*, 57–64.

52. Ray, 39.

53. Eisenstein, 19.

54. André Bazin, "The Virtues and Limitations of Montage," in *What Is Cinema*, vol. 1, 50.

55. Eisenstein, 14.

56. Bazin, "The Evolution of the Language of Cinema," 37. Original emphasis.

57. Eisenstein, 13.

58. Bazin, "The Evolution of the Language of Cinema," 28.

59. Bordwell, *On the History of Film Style*, 253.

60. "Sight and Sound Top Ten Poll," British Film Institute, http://bfi.org.uk/sightandsound/topten/ (accessed Jul. 16, 2005).

61. *Rope* is in fact shot over at least nine takes, with several rehearsals and attempts at each. A reel in 1947 could not shoot more than ten minutes of film. Hitchcock attempts to disguise the cuts, but a close viewing of the film reveals the process to be less than subtle and, in the context of the conventional narrative structure, unnecessary. See "Rope Unleashed," documentary, *Rope (The Hitchcock Collection)*, DVD (Universal, 2001).

62. David Bordwell and Kristin Thompson, *Film Art: An Introduction* (Reading: Addison-Wesley Publishing, 1980), 223–227.

63. André Bazin, "An Aesthetic of Reality: Cinematic Realism and the Italian School of Liberation," in *What Is Cinema*, volume 2, trans. Hugh Gray (Berkeley and Los Angeles: University of California Press, 1967), 28.

64. Bazin, "An Aesthetic of Reality," 27.

65. Roger Ebert, "Commentary," *Citizen Kane*, two-disc special ed. DVD (Warner Bros., 2001).

66. See, for example, Bordwell, *On the History of Film Style*. Of course, filmmakers have frequently waxed lyrical on the complexities of film technique. For the most influential work in this respect, see Truffaut.

67. Scorsese presents a fascinating account of the "cinematicality" of his films in *Scorsese on Scorsese*, ed. David Thompson and Ian Christie (London: Faber and Faber, 1989). See especially the section on *Goodfellas* (153–163).

68. Wood, *Hitchcock's Films Revisited*, 55–56.

69. Wood, *Hitchcock's Films Revisited*, 56.

70. See Stefano's account in Stephen Rebello, "The Inception," in *Alfred Hitchcock's Psycho: A Casebook*, ed. Robert Kolker (Oxford: Oxford University Press, 2004), 52–53.

71. David Sterritt, *The Films of Alfred Hitchcock* (Cambridge: Cambridge University Press, 1993), 17. Original emphasis.

72. See Christian Metz, "Some Points in the Semiotics of the Cinema," in *Film Theory and Criticism*, ed. Leo Braudy and Marshall Cohen (Oxford: Oxford University Press, 2004), 65–72.

73. Andrew Sarris, "The Auteur Theory Revisited," in *Film and Authorship*, ed. Virginia Wright Wexman (New Brunswick: Rutgers University Press, 2003), 26.

74. Thomas Schatz, "The Whole Equation of Pictures," in *Film and Authorship*, ed. Virginia Wright Wexman (New Brunswick, NJ: Rutgers University Press, 2003), 91.

75. Roger Ebert, "Mulholland Drive," *Chicago Sun-Times*, Oct. 12, 2001.

76. Rebello, 49.

77. Mikel J. Koven, "Citizen Kane," in *1001 Movies to See Before You Die*, ed. Steven J. Schneider (London: Quintet, 2003), 172.

78. Deleuze mentions *The Lady from Shanghai* several times in *Cinema 2*. However, his discussion relates specifically to Welles's narrative (and image) structure in which past, present, and future coalesce as frames of meaning (See Deleuze, *Cinema 2*, 112–115). Deleuze's books on film are perhaps more akin to filmic philosophy (equating to nothing less than a comprehensive theory of the moving image) than conventional film theory.

79. Sarris, 26.

80. Orson Welles and Peter Bogdanovich, *This Is Orson Welles* (New York: Da Capo Press, 1992), xxi.

81. Laura Mulvey, *Citizen Kane* (London: The British Film Institute, 1992).

82. Mulvey, *Citizen Kane*, 16.

83. *Citizen Kane*, two-disc special ed. DVD (Warner Bros., 2001), 27–28 minutes.

84. Ebert, "Commentary."

85. Ebert, "Commentary."

86. Robin Wood, "The Trouble with Marnie," *Marnie* (*The Hitchcock Collection*), DVD (Universal, 2001). While Wood refers to Hitchcock's "virtuosity" with the stylistics of the shot and sequence, this artificiality might equally apply to Welles's manipulation of field and focus in the manufacture of nonreality cinema.

87. Ebert, "Commentary."

88. See Truffaut, 348–352.

89. Metz, "Some Points in the Semiotics of Cinema." Here Metz draws on the semiotic structure of connotation and denotation conceptualized in the work of Ferdinand de Saussure. For a useful summary of the contribution of the structuralists to film semiotics, see Warren Buckland, "Film Semiotics," in *A Companion to Film Theory*, ed. Toby Miller and Robert Stam (Oxford: Blackwell Publishers, 1999), 84–104.

90. Roland Barthes, "The Photographic Message," in *Image Music Text*, trans. Stephen Heath (London: Fontana, 1977), 18.

91. Barthes, "The Photographic Message," 17.

92. Barthes, "The Photographic Message," 20.

93. Barthes, "The Photographic Message," 19. Original emphasis.

94. *Chungking Express*, DVD (Rolling Thunder Pictures, 1994), 42:30 minutes.

95. Bazin, "The Evolution of the Language of Cinema," 35.

96. Bazin, "The Evolution of the Language of Cinema," 35–36.

97. Bazin, "The Evolution of the Language of Cinema," 36.

98. Norman Denzin, *The Cinematic Society: The Voyeur's Gaze* (London: Sage, 1995), 32.

99. U2, "Even Better Than the Real Thing," *Achtung Baby*, compact disc (Island Records, 1991).

100. Jean-Luc Comolli, and Jean Narboni, "Cinema/Ideology/Criticism," in *Film Theory and Criticism*, eds. Leo Braudy and Marshall Cohen (Oxford: Oxford University Press, 2004), 814–815.

101. Teshoma Gabriel, "Toward a Critical Theory of Third World Cinema," in *Film and Theory: An Anthology*, eds. Robert Stam and Toby Miller (Oxford: Blackwell Publishers, 2000), 298–316.

102. Graeme Turner, *Film as Social Practice* (London and New York: Routledge, 1993), 52.

103. Turner, *Film as Social Practice*, 52.

104. Turner, *Film as Social Practice*, 53.

105. Turner, *Film as Social Practice*, 53.

106. This must surely rank as one of Hitchcock's greatest scenes. If the spectator considers that both Scotty and Madeline are "performing" their invisibility, the detail of the shot and scene, in which each is knowingly unaware of the other, astonishes. It is a motif that recurs throughout Hitchcock, but never more complexly structured than in this sequence.

107. See Žižek, "*Vertigo*: The Drama of a Deceived Platonist," 70. The eye of the camera functions for Žižek as the "organ without a body."

108. Raymond Durgnat, *A Long Hard Look at 'Psycho'* (London: British Film Institute, 2002), 4.

109. Turner, Film as Social Practice, 53.

110. Denzin, 58.

111. See Mulvey, "Visual Pleasure and Narrative Cinema."

112. Tania Modleski, *The Women Who Knew Too Much* (New York: Methuen, 1988), 73–85. However, it should be noted that Modleski's reading of *Rear Window* is a response to what she considers Mulvey's oversimplified account. Modleski finds room for greater female agency in Hitchcock than does Mulvey.

113. Guy Debord, *The Society of the Spectacle*, trans. Donald Nicholson-Smith (New York: Zone Books, 1994).

114. Baudrillard, *Simulacra and Simulation*, 1.

115. *Fight Club* (film). Dir. David Fincher (1999).

116. Jean-François Lyotard, *The Postmodern Condition*, trans. Geoff Bennington and Brian Massumi. (Minneapolis: Minnesota University Press, 1984). See especially the Introduction for a summary of Lyotard's argument.

117. Joel Black, *The Reality Effect: Film Culture and the Graphic Imperative* (New York and London: Routledge, 2002), 4.

2

Toward a Theory
of Popular Culture

Culture as Functionality

If we are asked to believe that all literature is "ideology," in the crude sense that its dominant intention (and then our only response) is the communication or imposition of "social" or "political" meanings and values, we can only, in the end, turn away. If we are asked to believe that all literature is "aesthetic," in the crude sense that its dominant intention (and then our only response) is the beauty of language or form, we may stay a little longer but will still in the end turn away.[1]

In titling this chapter "Toward a Theory of Popular Culture," I aim at something less grand than a unified theory of popular culture (or any culture, for that matter) in the way that physicists have aimed at a single theory of the physical world. If investigations into the nature of cultural institutions, narratives, and, broadly speaking, ideologies have told us anything, it is that culture is complex, always heterogeneous, and elusive. Culture cannot be explained holistically precisely because of its heterogeneity. It is a network of sources, texts, signs, symbols, and the paraphernalia of meaning, which is always, in a sense, beyond the grasp of the theorist. In this respect, I take Frederic Jameson's point: "The dilemma of the student of mass culture therefore lies in the structural absence, or the repetitive volatilization, of the 'primary texts.'"[2] I would only add that the problem lies equally with the texts (primary *and* secondary insofar as theory is implicated in these structures of meaning) and the individual subjectivities that receive them. In investigating culture through its texts, in this case primarily its cinematic texts, I begin with the assumption that it is transmitted through a variety of significatory mechanisms that incorporate values, ideologies, and politics, and that these systems of meaning are rarely conveyed unproblematically.

This second chapter functions as a correlative to the first. To conceptualize an alternative cinematic aesthetic, it is necessary to investigate the "content" of the form (the stylistics of the image), which I have done under the mantle of "cinematic realism." But it is equally important to consider historically the formation of the culture in which various texts are received. I have stated in Chapter One that I am interested in the style of cinema not merely for its controlled aestheticism, but also for its impact on the spectator, or what I have called *affectivity*. I share the view of Noël Carroll that mass or popular culture is a historical phenomenon.[3] I also agree with Jameson that there is at least the *perception*, subject to an effacement, of a distinction between high and low culture: "The second feature of this list of postmodernisms is the effacement of some key boundaries or separations, most notably the erosion of the older distinction between high and so-called mass or popular culture."[4] I use the term "perception" simply because the distinction has more veracity and currency as an imaginary standard or status symbol than an actual aesthetic tool. In relation to this effacement, which Jameson suggests is tantamount to an aesthetic revolution, an analysis of film must concurrently be an analysis of a culture that has made film its dominant textual form. Contemporary cinema demands a new kind of aesthetic system. Contemporary popular culture, it seems to me, requires a notion of culture that reflects what Anne Friedberg calls "'media fusion' or 'convergence' or the pluralist inclusiveness of 'multimedia'"[5] For Patricia Pisters, this is a new "mobile self [that] is individual but related, traversed by multiplicities, changing in time and informed by a camera consciousness."[6]

The collapse of a distinction between high and low culture, or popular and elite art forms (which comprise the artwork itself, but also its site of reception), is perhaps nowhere more apparent than in contemporary cinema. How can one distinguish between, for example, Pedro Almodóvar's *La Mala Educación* (*Bad Education*) and Christopher Nolan's *Batman Begins* in terms of high and low art? Both, I would argue, are commentaries on prior cinematic and textual traditions. *Bad Education*, rather than settling for the neo-*noir*, self-consciously reworks Wilder's *Double Indemnity*; the spectator might classify it as a "homosexualized" *film noir*. Nolan's adaptation draws on a pulp/mass culture tradition, yet is imbued with a cinematic realism that is unconventional in comic book adaptations; it seems a deliberate recuperation of the Real after Tim Burton's hyperstylization in *Batman* and *Batman Returns*.

Both films are a commentary on cinematic traditions, and equally on the distinction between high and low culture. Both perform a hybridity or genericity in which forms of the genre film "represent contradictory perspectives on 'media culture,' an ironic eclecticism" and "articulate a profound ambivalence that reflects the lack of any sort of unitary mass consciousness."[7] Collins locates a textual and cultural heterogeneity in the phenomenon of mass culture, which is a crucial advancement on Adorno's "consciousness as conformity" of the (mass) culture industry.[8]

Jameson appreciates the ephemeral and highly subjective (and thus ideological) nature of the distinction between high and low culture: "They [the "newer postmodernisms"] no longer 'quote' such 'texts' as a Joyce might have done, or a Mahler; they incorporate them to the point where the line between high art and commercial forms seems increasingly difficult to draw."[9] What is unclear is if "effacement" performs an eradication of the older distinction. If this is the contention, I would argue that it is premature. In spite of the deluge of intellectual work on cultures and subcultures, this academic mode (observing and indeed practicing the effacement of high and low art) operates primarily as a social science. Consider, for example, Graeme Turner's introduction to *The Film Cultures Reader*, a massive compendium of film writings that span the period from the advent of cinema to psychoanalytic perspectives on the horror genre, in which he writes: "These essays are not interested in establishing the artistic credentials of the texts in question. Rather, they are interested in establishing a more complex and nuanced understanding of the competing forces which frame the individual experience of popular culture in general, and popular film in particular."[10] Turner's comment is less an apology for the lack of consideration of popular art than an acknowledgment that recent film theory is simply not interested in considering popular film in aesthetic terms, as an earlier body of theory might have done of a Joyce or a Mahler. Equally, he does not claim that these films are less than art (or low art). This is perfectly understandable insofar as popular art offers a means of analysis of the culture that brings it to fruition—producers, consumers, institutions, social and cultural relations. For Turner, this is popular cinema's redeeming use-value. He merely affirms the acceptability of this position and closes off the avenue to an exploration of popular film as aesthetically motivated and received.

While I would argue that viewing a film is fundamentally an aesthetic experience, this process is predominantly theorized through a rubric of its *functionality*—that is, its *ideological* impact on the audience. Walsh suggests that "a lot of film theory and criticism has developed an eclectic mix of literary theory, Marxism, psychoanalysis, and other things. Generally the aim of such work is to show how films either cause or exemplify some wider social phenomena."[11] Implicit in such analyses is a notion of a popular audience, or at least an imaginary demographic upon which film makes its impression and inscribes its culture. But the notion of a popular audience is itself problematic. The theoretical model imposed on studies of audience is conventionally weighted one way or the other, on audience or text. Work that focuses on the formal characteristics of texts seems less interested in the reception of such texts by its audience; work that focuses on the demographics of audience, or the nature of spectator response seems less interested in the formal qualities of the cinematic text. In this way, Jancovich is able to critique one of the major exponents of genre theory, Rick Altman: "Despite his discussion of pragmatics and of the necessary indeterminacy of genre definitions, Altman shows little interest in the consumption of genres, compared with his interest in their production and mediation."[12] For Jancovich, genre theory has traditionally expended its analytic energies on understanding the formal parameters of genre: genre is a way of understanding form. However, he suggests that this mode of analysis is limited as a description of the aesthetic response of mainstream audiences: "The audience that he [Altman] constructs for himself in order to understand genre is, if not homogenous, at least quite placid."[13] Jancovich's piece is intended to "call attention to some important methodological issues" in formulating a theory of genre as it applies to horror;[14] I would argue that such a consideration is necessary when addressing contemporary film genres *per se*.

Considering that genre theory is founded on a collation and analysis of textual *types*, and apart from what I would consider the occasional analysis of the aestheticization of genre in Tarantino or Lynch, genre studies (and more broadly, film studies) functions as a way of *revealing* something of the historical, ideological, and political life of the spectator. While Paul Schrader has defined *film noir* as a specific mood or tone,[15] recent theory explores the sustained marginalization and subjugation of women in *noir*.[16] Similarly, while Amy Taubin offers a nuanced reading of masculinity in Tarantino's *Reservoir Dogs*, the film is for her *initially and predominantly* a site at which to consider masculinity (negatively) and abject femininity.[17]

My point here is that theory privileges a means-end, functional relationship between popular cinema and its audience. Films such as *The Silence of the Lambs* and De Palma's *Carrie* are useful vehicles for exploring the masculine gaze. Scorsese's *Goodfellas* or *Taxi Driver* or Spike Lee's *Do the Right Thing* become snapshots of a "kind of" urban America. The film, in theory, is always already a continuum of ideologized images.

Carroll draws a similar distinction between the scholarly obsession with "interpretation" (that is, a mode of analysis in which the text services a hypothesis external to it) and the popular mode of analysis, which he terms "evaluation," "an aspect of film-going to which recent film scholarship pays little attention."[18]

Of course, readings that inscribe an ideology into the film text are not in any way perverse. The opening shower sequence in *Carrie*, in which an otherwise ordinary locker room becomes the site of a hypersexualized encounter between the prepubescent girl and the dollying camera, offers the manifestation of a repressed masculine desire. De Palma's camera leaves little to the imagination. Similarly, Scorsese and Lee are useful chroniclers of a period and vision of New York City. Scorsese's masterpieces—*Mean Streets*, *Taxi Driver*, *Raging Bull*—are equally explorations of an urban myth and a reality that is vibrant, cinematic, and historicized. Scorsese's variations on the flaneur (Charlie Cappa [Harvey Keitel, *Mean Streets*], Travis Bickle [Robert De Niro, *Taxi Driver*], Jake La Motta [Robert De Niro, *Raging Bull*]) are voices of a kind of masculinity and a kind of urban subjectivity of post-Vietnam America. Spike Lee's *Do the Right Thing*, as Manthia Diawara suggests, "situate[s] spectators from the perspective of a Black 'once upon a time.'"[19] For Diawara, Spike Lee, John Singleton, and the New Black Cinema are addressed as a race cinema because their films are, ostensibly, about race relations "once upon a time" in America.

However, the exploration of a film's explicit or implicit politics or ideological engagements should not preclude its analysis as an aesthetic experience (which in any case it cannot, since film theory does not mediate the film experience for the majority of filmgoers, as it must inevitably for the theorist), nor the establishment of a body of work devoted to collating and analyzing a stylistics of film and its affectivity on the spectator. While this project of ideologizing the text is imbued with good intentions and sound methodology, it marginalizes the aesthetic response. Furthermore, its predisposition to read ideology in the image, shot, and sequence of the film renders its analytical "gaze" somewhat obtuse. Consider the reading of John Shelton Lawrence and Robert Jewett of the *Star Wars* franchise, in which they perceive an "American monomyth" tantamount to a brand of neofascism.[20] I do not wish to take issue with this intriguing reading except to suggest that cinematic ideology and an ideology of an external reality can simply not be *freely exchanged*. Of the conclusion to *Star Wars, Episode IV: A New Hope*, Lawrence and Jewett write:

> We were quite startled by the final awards ceremony for Luke, Han, and Chewbacca in *A New Hope*, an image reprised at the beginning

of *The Empire Strikes Back*. It seemed to "quote" the most famous of the Nazi propaganda films, *Triumph of the Will* (*Triumph des Willens*, 1935), which was made by Leni Riefenstahl as a celebration of the Nuremberg Nazi party rallies of 1934.[21]

The writers proceed to offer a detailed analysis of *A New Hope* as merely the most accessible and iconic performance in a long history of textual performances of the American monomyth. In Lawrence and Jewett's reading, this myth is equally connected to Leslie Fiedler's classic formulation of the obligation of the protagonist of the American novel to flee society[22] and Joseph Campbell's "hero with a thousand faces"[23] who must flee society as part of the maturation process. Lawrence and Jewett examine the *Star Wars* franchise as a set of discursive textual and cultural practices that ultimately revert to a form of fascism, suggesting that "[a]lthough American superheroes consistently strive to redeem corrupt republics, the definitions of their roles and the means of their triumphs reflect fascist values that ultimately undermine democratic processes and hollow out the religious faith of the enchanted."[24] They do not return to Riefenstahl's *Triumph des Willens* (*Triumph of the Will*) but rather assume that the ideological content of Riefenstahl's propagandist Nazi film is transposed unproblematically onto Lucas's studio-produced mass-culture entertainment. The intertextuality of Riefenstahl's film is thus a reflection of the text and subtext of *Star Wars*. Intertextuality, in Lawrence and Jewett's conception, has an outmoded ontological foundation insofar as the one text (Riefenstahl) literally informs the other. There is no consideration of intertextuality as an aesthetic conceit or broader textual strategy. The writers gloss over the fact that "Lucas'[s] Entertainment Company's encyclopedic 'Insider's Guide to *Star Wars*' frankly acknowledges it in its scene commentary: 'The final ceremony scene emulates, almost shot-for-shot, a similar segment in *Triumph des Willens* (1934).'"[25] The acknowledgment is frank precisely because *Triumph of the Will* is "quoted" self-consciously, deliberately, and *cinematically* (in much the same way that the conclusion to *Return of the Jedi* reenacts a sequence in Griffith's *Birth of a Nation*, an "objectively racist film"[26]). The shot-for-shot *fetishizing* (which is precisely what it is) of the earlier sequence is essentially an aesthetic practice. We can say the same thing of Gus Van Sant's shot-for-shot remake of *Psycho*, which is the perfect aestheticization (and fetishization) of Hitchcock's masterpiece. One suspects that Van Sant's fetishistic reproduction of the original is something of a commentary on Hitchcock's own obsession with this theme in his films, most notably *Rebecca* and *Vertigo*.

Lucas and cinematic quotation:
Leni Riefenstahl's *Triumph of the Will* and John Ford's *The Searchers*.

John Ford, The Searchers.

Leni Riefenstahl, Triumph of the Will.

Lucas's appropriation of a sequence in The Searchers.

Lucas's appropriation of a sequence in Triumph of the Will.

Lawrence and Jewett's willingness to install a detailed and discursive analysis of fascism in *Star Wars* on the apparent ideological reverberation of a film sequence does not take account of the hermetic cinematic image explored in Chapter One. The image in this case resonates as intertextual quote, but less in the sense of a literal transposition of ideological intent than as an aesthetically imbued textual practice. Lucas, Coppola, Scorsese, and others were of the generation that attended film school in Los Angeles and New York, were versed in American and international cinema, and willing to demonstrate the intertextual nature of film as an art form. Lucas quotes *Triumph of the Will* because there is an inherent artistic value in the cinematic utterance that is simultaneously quotation.[27] Furthermore, the fact that the quotation is of a Nazi propaganda film confers an element of subversiveness on what is otherwise conservative family entertainment for a mass audience. It is significant also that the reception of the *Star Wars* franchise has rarely crystallized into a consensus over fascism, neo-Imperialism, neo-Liberalism, or any other broad political or ideological rubric. Of a *Star Wars* poll conducted in 1986, Peter Kramer writes: "When asked whether 'the movie is in favor of the conservative idea of "peace through military strength,"' conservative respondents overwhelmingly said 'yes,' whereas the majority of moderate and liberal respondents said 'no'. This poll suggests that *Star Wars* allowed everyone to extract from it precisely the political meaning they were most comfortable with."[28]

Lawrence's piece on *Star Wars* is obviously not exemplary of an entire tradition of film and cultural analyses that seeks to transpose cinema and ideology seamlessly. But I would argue that film has generally been pressed too hastily into the service of an ideological project. Film (and all art, for that matter) coheres only in its reception and interpretation by its audience, and while ideology theory unveils the hegemonic practices of film production and consumption, its willingness to foreground the ideological reading over the aesthetic installs a new mode of appreciation divorced from the performance of the cinematic spectacle. It is for this reason that I find analyses of cinematic violence for the most part unconvincing and less than actively engaged with the cinematic image. These limitations are exemplified in Jane Caputi's reading of Oliver Stone's *Natural Born Killers*: "*Natural Born Killers* feels just like a prayer. It is not a critique, nor even a reflection of the 'demon'. It is a paean, an outburst of worshipful and exultant praise, a ceremony not of exorcism but of invocation [to violence]."[29] Caputi's reading of the film is founded on an interpretation of the motivations and actions of characters. She also draws on a comment made by Oliver Stone (who, of any filmmaker, should not substitute as an authoritative voice): "There was in me, I feel, a huge violence when I was born."[30] But little is made of the way violence is captured *on film* or the way it is manifested visually, which must surely inform any analysis of the impact of violence on a spectator or mass audience. Caputi's reading would benefit from a detailed shot and sequence analysis of parts of the film, an analysis that could offer a more nuanced reading of the way violence is transposed from character action to spectator participation. Ultimately, I reject the idea that the performance of *Natural Born Killers* on the spectator is an "invocation to violence," a notion I will consider in more detail in Chapter Four.

While I acknowledge the important—indeed, invaluable—contribution of cultural studies (and its predecessors, psychoanalytic theory and Marxism) to film theory, I contend that the emphasis on the text as ideological/political/personal footprint does not engage with the practicalities of film production or reception. It cannot record or qualitatively evaluate the aesthetic reverberations of a *Star Wars* logo or a blue filter on a camera lens in Michael Mann's *Heat*. It is even less successful in assessing the qualitative relations between an actor's performance and the film's aesthetic and cultural resonance. Consider Al Pacino, wielding two mini-guns in the last scene in De Palma's *Scarface*—"Say hello to my little friends." How does the film theorist evaluate the cultural and aesthetic discursivity of this filmic utterance? Perhaps it can be weighed in terms of an ethnicity, the immigrant taking what is held from him: *He loved the American Dream—With a vengeance.*[31] In *The Sopranos*, in the scene in which Christopher Moltisanti says, "This ain't negotiation time. This is *Scarface*, the final scene, fuckin' bazookas under each arm, 'Say hello to my little friends,'"[32] and the statement is a *re*-utterance, how does the theorist manage the shifting ontology of cinematic quotation? In what sense is the original utterance reorganized in relation to its subsequent quotation?

I do not wish to suggest that the aesthetic is purely an appreciation of beauty or form in an essentialist way but rather a complex and highly developed system of cinematic "reading," interpretation, and ultimately consumption. Carroll correctly suggests that "there is a great deal of audience activity involved in the response to mass art."[33] Aesthetically engaging with contemporary cinema requires something quite removed from a "heightened" though nonspecific appreciation of film; the nature of its distinction needs to be conceptualized in terms of the film itself and the context in which it is received. This context extends to its formulaic-*ness*, or generic foundations, its reflection on a discursive set of mythologies, and ultimately with its self-aware and self-acknowledged status as art. Traditional theories of art and aesthetics that privilege an essentialist notion of truth, beauty, and expression are incommensurate with the ontology of the cinematic image and quotation. Carroll suggests that "most art, maybe all art, is formulaic to some degree. All artists use some conventions, formulas, rules of thumb, traditional forms, donnees and so on."[34] The shift to an ontology of art as inherently formulaic is nowhere more apparent than in contemporary cinema. An aesthetics of popular cinema is founded in part on an aesthetics of the formulaic. In this sense, one can in fact embrace Adorno's "consciousness as conformity" (though of course Adorno intends it in quite a different way), if conformity is evaluated in the context of the textual *heteroglossia* that gives it meaning.

Culture as Commodity

The creature who emerges from postmodern thought is centreless, hedonistic, self inventing, ceaselessly adaptive. He thus fares splendidly in the disco or supermarket, though not quite so well in the school, courtroom or chapel. He sounds more like a Los Angeles media executive than an Indonesian fisherman.[35]

So jeans can bear meanings of both community and individualism, of unisexuality and masculinity or femininity. This semiotic richness of jeans means that they cannot have a single defined meaning, but that they are a resource bank of potential meanings.[36]

It is difficult, if not impossible, to theorize contemporary culture without observing what Lyotard, Jameson, and other writers address as the dominant aesthetic of postmodernity. As Eagleton indicates above, the postmodern condition is founded on a lack of center or origin, and the consequential discursive expression of the self and culture. Broadly speaking, the postmodern is an aesthetic founded upon *lack* while earlier aesthetic forms strive toward completion or fulfillment. Brian Singer's *The Usual Suspects* offers a remarkable transition of an earlier narratively focused cinematic aesthetic. It is an aesthetic innovation in which the film functions narratively on a narrative *lack*. Verbal's (Kevin Spacey) account of events on the Santa Monica pier is an inscription of a fictitious story onto the cinematic narrative. The demands on the spectator reorganize the relationship of spectator to film such that the spectator takes her place alongside Inspector Kooyong (Chaz Palminteri), fumbling over the narrative "truth" which is erased in the telling of the story. Similar narrative inversions, or what I will call "entropic narratives," inform some of Lynch's work (*Lost Highway* is perhaps the best example) and David Fincher's *Fight Club*.

The postmodern also refashions the earlier modern or classical subjectivity into a site of abjectivity, or the absence of an innate sense of self. The contemporary subject resides within this postmodernity divorced from an essentialist notion of truth, right, and existential purpose.[37] I do not share Eagleton's assessment of the merits of the postmodern subject, though the notion of adaptability or reinvention is useful. Discursivity in my usage connotes a sense of perpetual displacement of the subjective consciousness (or the space in which meaning is finally established). Fiske puts this nicely when he suggests that "making sense of anything involves making sense of the person who is the agent in the process."[38] It is important here to stress the nature of culture as processional, or in flux. This is not to say that culture eludes meaning but merely that part of that meaning is located in the sense of its perpetual movement or change. But the notion of a cultural process in Fiske's analysis is problematic because he does not indicate precisely what he means by "making sense." The cultural theorist is hampered by the project of having to make sense of the subject in a complex discursive cultural system. Must a film "theorist" be a "spectator" to make sense of the "person who is the agent" in contemporary cinema? What is the nature of that agency? The problem arises in the necessity of having to *make sense* because this implies in the subject a status of having an inherent sense, or static sensibility, and this must undermine the definition of culture as process. But Fiske's theoretical attunement to the cultural agent is a necessary starting point in any cultural analysis.

Fiske focuses on the ideology of the subject and cultural system in which the observer's (or agent's) consciousness is necessarily *already* ideological. I will begin here, using his paradigmatic analysis of popular culture as a point of departure.

Fiske discusses the semiotic potentiality of jeans in a contemporary university in which jeans are accorded the special power of making meaning out of cultural commodities and revealing the importance of the semiotic system within the economics of production and consumption. In this way, he formulates a mode of resistance to the "cultural logic of late capitalism," to use Jameson's famous phrase. "At the simplest level, this is an example of a user not simply consuming a commodity but reworking it, treating it not as a completed object to be accepted passively, but as a cultural resource to be used."[39] Fiske's efforts on behalf of a popular culture that engages semiotically with the market are to rescue popular culture from an "economic system which determines mass production and mass consumption . . . [in which] a commodity is ideology made material."[40] The commodity is not so much the perfect expression of the ideology that gives it life in the marketplace, but its ideology is *all that it is*. The ideology is not writ large on the product and its packaging as a unique and specific ideological statement; rather it is an all-informing, all-pervasive, ubiquitous system that incorporates the product and its consumer.

The problem I have with this notion of a cultural commodity is that, while a product might be ideology made material, it is surely only "the ideology" in the broadest sense. That is, the *act of consumption*, less an expression of cultural passivity, is an intervention in the process of the commodity from ideology to production to promotion to consumption. The franchise aesthetic in contemporary cinema reflects this process of the subject (usually a fan as opposed to the casual filmgoer) intervening in the system through the act of consumption in the marketplace. Purchase, possession, ownership, synthesis of product and self to form something new (for example, in the case of a fan donning the Matrix "mirrorshades" to alter her self)—are very real interventions in the process that connects ideology and commodity. In this sense, consumption is in its purest form an aesthetic intervention, and the commodity is much more than a materialized ideology.

Fiske reads popular culture as implicated within a semiotic and economic system, a culture that must ultimately accede to the market if all it does is consume and reinsert commodities into the system. He conceives the notion of cultural "excorporation," whereby "the subordinate make their own culture out of the resources and commodities provided by the dominant system,"[41] which may lead incrementally to "structural changes at the level of the system itself, in whatever domain . . . [which] occur only after the system has been eroded and weakened by the tactics of everyday life."[42] For Fiske, this act of *making culture*, refashioning the commodity so that it encapsulates and is encapsulated by a new field of meaning, is thus a significant step forward in the assessment of popular culture, which has commonly been one of passivity and aimless, "ceaselessly adaptive" conformity.

However, the model of the excorporation of the commodity has profound limitations. On the one hand, Fiske fails to acknowledge that culture must be "made" *within* the market, drawing on the market's semiotic system, as well as on the market's materials. I take on board his Marxist formulation of late capitalism and share his acknowledgment of its pervasiveness, yet reject the transparent relation between its ideology and its manifestation, the commodity. Disregarding this relation is tantamount to rejecting the ubiquity of the market, which I am perfectly willing to do. But such a rejection must constitute an obstacle to Fiske's excorporation as a tool of a "culture of resistance." After all, the individual must resist something, if only an ephemeral system of economic and cultural relations. In excorporation, Fiske offers what appears to be a vehicle to extricate the commodity from the dominant ideological agenda. But if the commodity is read *within* the marketplace, as it inevitably must be, the emancipatory possibilities of excorporation are diminished.

Consider a young Aboriginal boy seated in the back of a public bus, wearing a two-piece Eminem tracksuit. How would the cultural theorist, particularly one intent on charting the excorporation of the commodity, read such a confluence of cultural signs? On the one hand, the boy is aligned with (and aligns himself to) a minority disenfranchised culture, Aboriginal society in Sydney—he chooses to sit at the back of the bus, which is a well known gesture of resistance to orthodoxy. The Eminem tracksuit expresses his resistance to the hegemonic system, in this case a convergence of a conservative Liberal Australian government and the capitalist market. Conservatism is contrasted with the perceived poverty and oppression of black American culture represented in a "culture of rap." Rap has maintained its ethos of resistance to the dominant White society in spite of the dilution of rap resistance with hip-hop in the music of Destiny's Child or Snoop Doggy Dog. The coding of the commodification (Aboriginality/rap/Eminem) explicitly offers a message of resistance to a culture that is located as Other—White/conservative/wealthy/enfranchised.

Fiske establishes a dialectic of incorporation and excorporation in the process in which a dominant ideology is made material in the market. He suggests that

> popular culture is organized around various forms of the oppositional relationship between the people and the power-bloc. This opposition always has the potential to be progressive, and in practice it generally is. Insofar as the popular forces are attempting to evade or resist the disciplinary, controlling forces of the power-bloc, they are working to open up spaces within which progressiveness can work.[43]

There is a sense here that culture is either a site of resistance to hegemony or part of its mechanics—a solution to or perpetuation of the problem. But in my opinion, the image of the Aboriginal boy in an Eminem suit lays bare the profound limitations inherent in this mode of analysis. How would the theorist distinguish between incorporation and excorporation? The "Aboriginality" of the boy in the suit is itself incorporated into the hegemonic ideology insofar as the purchase of the Eminem tracksuit implicates the boy in the market (and thus maintains the status quo, rather than forming a site of resistance); the ownership of the suit challenges the abject poverty and oppression of the Aboriginal *and Aborigine*. Fiske addresses the "residual" ideology in the purchasing act:

> So how much of a resistance to this is wearing torn jeans? In the economic sphere there is a trace of resistance in that for jeans to become naturally ragged they need to be worn long past the time when they would normally be considered worn out and thus need replacing with another pair. Reducing one's purchase of commodities can be a tiny gesture against a high-consumption society. . . . One possible display of meanings here is of a display of poverty.[44]

The only way the tracksuit functions as excorporation (or display of poverty) is if it is stolen. And in any case, torn jeans are merely a commodification of poverty as romanticized image rather than an expression of resistance to a widely manifested social poverty. The act of theft might offer an expression of resistance to the conventions of production and consumption in the marketplace, but its ideology is made material as purchased object when worn, representative of the semiotic and economic relations of the marketplace. The suit functions as an expression of the market—brands, types, etc., and associated Eminem paraphernalia. The site of meaning is configured only as commodity.

As an expression of cultural resistance, Eminem is commodified in the production and consumption—exchange of goods for money—in the market. It is difficult to conceptualize just what the semiotic relation is between the young Aboriginal boy and Eminem, and by extension a suit bearing the Eminem brand name. If we consider a lyric like "I don't make black music, I don't make white music, / I make fight music,"[45] how would we locate Aboriginality in this context? How would we address the commodification of Eminem—as songwriter, rapper, brand name, movie star, icon, a plethora of pop-cultural images? I simply cannot perceive a way in which to insert the Aboriginal boy in his Eminem suit into a cultural model of passivity (Adorno) or resistance/excorporation (Fiske). I would perhaps side with Adorno only insofar as the suit as cultural commodity has nothing at all to do with resistance in a Utopian sense. Fiske's notion that torn jeans are a symbol of poverty is dubious. That such a symbol offers an incremental challenge to an "imagined" market (it is in fact an imaginary, or Utopian, vision insofar as the wearer of the jeans is not engaging with the ideology of the market except to reflect it back upon itself) is equally optimistic; poor is "cool," and "cool" is commodified through consumption. Ultimately, however, Adorno's model falls equally short of describing the empowerment of the Eminem suit and a genuinely discursive aesthetic of resistance, which I will address later in the chapter.

What is missing from this analysis is a meaningful way of addressing the subjectivity of the boy in the suit. If cultural discursivity is predicated on the proliferation of texts, myths, signs, symbols, and the various significatory mechanisms that are put together to formulate concrete meanings, the boy is implicated in this discursive process. Ultimately, the most complex and meaningful system of analysis of this "performance" of a commodity must be *aesthetic*. The consumption and expression of the commodity (and, if we are to follow Fiske, ideology made manifest) is founded on an aesthetic value accorded to the suit that occurs within the market system. The suit functions as a symbolic system of value, divorced from its ideological expression insofar as that ideology is incorporated in a discursive cultural process. Ideology no longer coheres in pure form at the site of representation in the commodity. Consumption alters the ideological fabric of the message, reconstituting the product at least in part as autonomous from the ideology of the prevailing system. The engagement with a product at the point of consumption is more than an ideological transposition.

There is something profoundly stimulating in the act of consumption because it is an intervention in an otherwise impersonal itinerary of the commodity. This is precisely the engagement with the consumption aesthetic that simultaneously reflects on and recuperates market ideology, and yet expresses the discursivity of the ideological symbol. The semiotic system in which the Eminem suit coheres is less the literal transposition of a hegemonic agenda than a discursive performance of meaning and, ultimately, subjective value.[46]

Perhaps this is better illustrated with a more concrete example. The image that opens each installment of *The Matrix* franchise is the classic Warner Bros. logo that heads the studio and signals the film's status as a major production and distribution enterprise. However, while the logo is ordinarily colored yellow, the Wachowski Brothers color it with the green tinge that colors the entire film. The reasoning behind this is explained by John Gaeta, Special Effects Supervisor on the three films:

> The opening of the movie was important in that we wanted to alter the logo of the studios because we felt that they were an evil empire bent on breaking the creative juices of the average director or writer. So we felt that desecrating the studio symbols was an important message for the audience that we reject the system.[47]

Unfortunately, as Gaeta speaks, Carrie-Anne Moss ("Trinity" in the film) can be heard laughing in the background. This renders Gaeta's intention in making the comment unclear. However, opting for the less-than-cynical approach, I will assume that Gaeta is entirely serious and that the Wachowski Brothers are indeed making a statement (or "excorporating the commodity") by altering the Warner Bros. logo. What is the impact of this on the studio system (which, though it might be crudely generalized, will be accorded the status of ubiquitous "system," as Fiske accords to the market)? What is the impact on the film itself? What is the impact on the spectator? And ultimately, what is the nature of the symbol as *performance* in the cultural sphere?

On one level, the symbol of resistance is an expression of the dominant (Warner Bros. and studio system) ideology. After all, the alteration to the logo has presumably been permitted by the studio executives. Yet it is, as Gaeta suggests, a perversion of the original and a challenge to its status in the system. When placed alongside Neo's exit from a phone booth to Rage Against the Machine's "Wake Up!,"[48] it appears that the film functions from first frame to last as an expression of resistance to a "system"—in the film, *The Matrix*, in the spectator's external reality, the market, and the Hollywood studio system. The fact that the logo appears "inside" the Matrix supports this reading. The logo is severed from its original ideological (and semiotic) intention; it is literally re-presented, and thus re-intentioned, in the film. And yet this alteration has been permitted by the system that has previously ideologized the message.

In this case, I would argue that the performance of the logo in the cultural sphere is discursive. It is a process that coheres and is ultimately signified only through networks of mediation. Resistance is aestheticized for the spectator, who simultaneously reconfigures the logo and yet affirms the residual ideology of the original. The reconfigured logo bears the aesthetic of individual heroic resistance to the system on behalf of the disenfranchised masses (in the film, humanity is a slave to Machine intelligence). But equally, it bears the aesthetic of *The Matrix*, a simulacral realm in which "residual self-image" transforms the desert of the Real into the hyperaestheticized imaginary of *The Matrix*. Immersion in the Real and the Matrix is thus founded upon an acknowledgment of the aesthetic value of the act of consumption (in this case, the logo is consumed in symbolic form at the ticket counter and onscreen). Fiske would no doubt suggest that the logo (or brand name) is merely the expression of the hegemony of the studio system, which it is: "Jeans are no longer, if they ever were, a generic denim garment. Like all commodities, they are given brand names that compete among each other for specific segments of the market."[49] But it is equally, and simultaneously, an expression of resistance to that system, an expression and strategy of resistance that will always be aestheticized (and thus severed from the initial ideological utterance) at the point of consumption—which is to say the point of inception of the hegemonic ideology.[50]

Perhaps this reading of Gaeta's comment moves perilously close to a rejection of the possibility of cultural resistance, particularly in the notion of the consumption aesthetic. This is certainly not my intention. Individual and collective expression is after all a kind of resistance that impacts on real individuals and real cultures:

> By repositioning and recontextualising commodities, by subverting their conventional uses and inventing new ones, the subcultural stylist gives the lie to what Althusser has called "false obviousness of everyday practice" (Althusser and Balibar, 1968), and opens up the world of objects to new and covertly oppositional readings.[51]

I merely argue here that this reality has rarely been theorized from its initial point of contact with the culture it addresses. Cultural meanings do not cohere neatly between producers and consumers of meaning. Commodities do not negate cultural meaning or aesthetic value to the consumer.

One can see such a conflation of means and end with simplistic analyses of the Hollywood studio system. The system is in a narrow sense a business that seeks to maximize profits; cultures and individuals are incorporated in market strategies; demographics carry more weight than individual opinions; the system is more carefully attuned to the mainstream than unconventional cinematic forms—and this is all in part a business interest. But Hollywood is also a site at which creative impulses are manifested in commodity form for mainstream consumption. The system is involved in engineering creativity, regardless of the form this creativity takes. *Apocalypse Now* and *Jaws* are both major studio films; *Apocalypse Now* is perceived as an artistic endeavor while *Jaws* is considered a mass-marketing phenomenon.

The cultural coding of the commodity is difficult, if not impossible, to stabilize. Commodity consumption is a cultural investment, and it is this aspect of contemporary popular culture that has been too easily overlooked or disregarded. The aesthetic value of consumption is literally devalued or rejected out of hand beneath a Utopian vision of social and cultural resistance that may begin incrementally but is projected as proceeding exponentially. I cannot see the value in this negation of a genuine aesthetic engagement of a commodity in the market. The painstaking investigation of an incremental excorporation of a consumerist culture does not engage with the reality of that culture, which seeks resistance for its commodity value within, and in relation to, the market system.

Theorizing a resistance that must inevitably augment the object of that resistance (I refer specifically to the nature of consumption, or a "consumption aesthetic"—I am not speaking of resistance *per se*) is fraught with complexity and abstract systems of meaning. Jameson acknowledges this: "The hypothesis is that works of mass culture cannot be ideological without one and the same time being implicitly or explicitly Utopian as well."[52] In this sense, he defends his project, which is essentially Utopian; resistance must be aimed at a particular, and highly specific, *end*. But he also acknowledges that "until the omnipresence of culture in this society is even dimly sensed, realistic conceptions of the nature and function of political praxis today can scarcely be framed."[53] In this stage of the omnipresence of late capitalism, theory has less than adequately analyzed the discursive nature of culture and its components in which resistance is concurrently radical and conservative. "No society, indeed, has ever been saturated with signs and messages like this one."[54] I would add that the discursivity of these signs and messages compromises the integrity of an ideologically organized system (hegemony) and at least raises the issue of a hegemonic practice (market production and consumption) that is divorced from the institutions that originally provided its meaning.

Culture as Industry

The problem of postmodernism—how its fundamental characteristics are to be described, whether it even exists in the first place, whether the very *concept* is of any use, or is, on the contrary, a mystification—this problem is at one and the same time an aesthetic and a political one.[55]

Guy Debord's powerful slogan is even now more apt for the "prehistory" bereft of all historicity, whose own putative past is little more than a set of dusty spectacles. In faithful conformity to poststructuralist linguistic theory, the past as "referent" finds itself gradually bracketed, and then effaced altogether, leaving us with nothing but texts.[56]

Frederic Jameson's writings on postmodernism are seminal works insofar as they attempt to formulate an aesthetics of the postmodern, drawing on various theoretical models, including Horkheimer and Adorno's *Dialectic of Enlightenment* and the culture industry. Rita Felski is correct to suggest that "Jameson does not do Cultural Studies. His work is closer in spirit to Marxist aesthetic theory, especially the Frankfurt school and its gloomy vision of popular culture as a form of capitalist domination."[57] While cultural theorists have examined the production and reception of popular culture, Jameson and Adorno, among others, are engaged in a project of evaluating culture in an aesthetic sense, in which the autonomy or *semi*-autonomy of art is connected to subjective consciousness. Each project is founded upon a comparison between an authentic art as socially generative and a false art spawning a false consciousness. For Jameson, the false consciousness[58] is less a matter of cultural signification than the relations between a dominant mode of capitalism ("late capitalism") and social life,[59] which transforms "reality into images" and "fragment[s] of time into a series of perpetual presents."[60] By his own admission, the conceptual paradigm in which he has mapped postmodernism is totalizing rather than founded on post-structuralism's staple methodology of heterogeneous signs, proliferating subjectivities, and an infinitude of meaning.[61] This totalizing approach permits (and requires) broad claims about history and art, and he has received criticism for a lack of specificity in both areas.[62] He proceeds to defend the totalizing approach on the grounds of a "level of abstraction." In this section, I apply Jameson's theories of postmodernism and its dominant aesthetic to my own conception of contemporary culture.

Lyotard's classic formulation of postmodernism as an "incredulity toward the grand narratives,"[63] including the Enlightenment rationalist project, Christianity, and Marxism, is central to analyses of the "cultural turn," to use the title of a collection of Jameson's writings on postmodernism. It is expressed in the theoretical trajectories of post-structuralism as well as the mandate of cultural studies to remain "open-ended."[64]

Jameson's writing on postmodernity constructs a set of grand narratives that describe the nature of the postmodern moment. In the following section, I attempt to formulate an "authenticity" of contemporary popular culture and film, focusing on Jameson, Baudrillard, Teshome Gabriel's "Toward a Critical Theory of Third World Films," and Walter Benjamin's "The Work of Art in the Age of Mechanical Reproduction."

Jameson's conception of history, insofar as it is coherent in postmodernity, reflects on the origins of a Marxist project that is equally totalizing and Utopian. This project is fundamentally attached to art as resistance and authentic expression, which "is dependant for its existence on authentic collective life, on the vitality of the 'organic' social group in whatever form."[65] It is Jameson's claim that "capitalism systematically dissolves the fabric of all cohesive social groups without exception, including its own ruling class."[66] This dissolution of the collective group and subject (the realization of the postmodern moment is commensurate with the "death of the subject") signals the emergence of a new self (though selves and others are also anachronistic terms in postmodernism):

> Yes, once upon a time, in the classic age of competitive capitalism, in the heyday of the nuclear family and the emergence of the bourgeoisie as the hegemonic social class, there was such a thing as individualism, as individual subjects. But today, in the age of corporate capitalism, of the so-called organization man . . . today, that older bourgeois individual subject no longer exists.[67]

In this way, late capitalism and its semiotic realization perform a *de-authentification* of its own standards and of historical systems of meaning and value, cultural and aesthetic.

> Both of these modes [high modernism and popular art] have attained an admirable level of technical virtuosity; but it is a daydream to expect that either of these semiotic structures could be retransformed, by fiat, miracle, or sheer talent, into what could be called, in its strong form, political art, or in a more general way, that living and authentic culture of which we have virtually lost the memory.[68]

Postmodernism is a self-creating and self-administering system in which authentic art is practiced only in "marginal pockets of the social life of the world system."[69] These pockets have forged a critical space within, and in opposition to, the market. In Jameson's formulation, art produced within the market is always already commodified and thus inauthentic. The collective production and consumption of commodities cannot be equated with an authentic expression that is in some vague sense a form of cultural resistance to the market, and which is emancipatory for the subjective consciousness. While Jameson rejects Adorno's notion of the culture industry, at least within the parameters of the culture Adorno conceptualizes, his dialectic of a culture of authentic resistance and the postmodern veers close to Adorno's model. While Adorno requires an autonomy of the artwork, Jameson's critique of this autonomy is less an argument about aesthetics *against* postmodern art than a devaluing of the culture that constitutes postmodern society. Adorno's parameters of the culture industry, while reconfigured in Jameson within an elaborate economic and cultural analysis, are ultimately maintained.[70]

For Jameson, resistance and authenticity are meaningless in a culture that is systematically ahistorical. Signs and symbols are merely expressions of the market, imbued with meaning only in commodity form, valued only as a mechanism of exchange: "There is some agreement that the older modernism functioned against its society in ways which are variously described as critical, negative, contestatory, subversive, oppositional, and the like. Can anything of the sort be affirmed about postmodernism and its social moment?"[71] In this gesture, Jameson negates the possibility of "art" in the postmodern creative space and renders the postmodern subject politically impotent, unaware, and unconcerned. In the reflective glass of the Bonaventure hotel, a "total space, a complete world, a kind of miniature city,"[72] postmodernism's inculcation of depth into so much surface area is perfectly realized. The city as historical space is here ahistorical, a textual trope or fluid motif, as in the postmodern city of *Blade Runner* or *The Matrix*,[73] doomed to exist in a perpetual present, reflecting only on its insularity from an external reality. Ahistoricism equates to a spatial dispersion into nothingness, and all that is maintained is the imaginary of a simulacrum. "For Jean Baudrillard, for example, the repetitive structure of what he calls the simulacrum . . . characterises the commodity production of capitalism and marks our object world with an unreality and a free-floating absence of 'the referent.'"[74] Equating commodity production in the postmodern era with the hyperreality of Baudrillard's simulacrum divorces postmodern expression from any possibility of authenticity.

The postmodern subject (I speak as a writer not on the fringe of the market, but immersed in it), who must forge into being some semblance of herself, and some space for individual expression and aesthetic value, must reject each of Jameson's claims. I have argued thus far that film (and art) is fundamentally aesthetic, and thus experiential. I concurred with Barbara Kennedy that what is required in the realm of popular culture to conceptualize its value is an *affective* theory,[75] in which "a new aesthetic theory, which accounts for how the affective is formulated through color, sound, movement, force, intensity,"[76] holds sway with the plethora of theories of ideology. What is disappointing in Jameson's writing is the willingness to reject all postmodern art (and thus all popular art, insofar as the phenomenon of popular art arises only with monopolistic capitalism, the second stage of Mandel's model[77]) as inauthentic within the parameters of a totalizing and Utopian project of personal, cultural, political, and social emancipation. In this model, art is again *functional*, exemplary of this or that phase of human history, demonstrative of a social and cultural practice (or, in the case of postmodernism, a lack thereof), ideologized into obsolescence,[78] aestheticized only as reflection, or collage, or the emptiness of an endless and pointless proliferation of postmodern expressions. Forbidden the authenticity of art, the postmodern subject is doomed to endless repetition, and in this way is implicated in the performance of the market and its dominant aesthetic. "The distorted and unreflexive attempts of newer cultural production to explore and to express this new space must then also, in their own fashion, be considered as so many approaches to the representation of (a new) reality (to use a more antiquated language)."[79]

Even beneath the guise of a possible creative agency of the postmodern subject, "distortion" and "unreflexivity" amount to working *within* the simulacra, or merely affirming the parameters of the prison-house. But surely the postmodern subject, *un*emancipated for the meantime, must reconceptualize postmodernity without recourse to a realm of inauthenticity. This is essentially where Jameson and I part in our approaches to an analysis of postmodernism or culture.

Teshome Gabriel offers a more pragmatic approach to emancipate the subject from the marketplace, focusing on recent cinema and the methodology of film theory. Gabriel draws on the existing methodology of structuralism and the emphasis in cultural theory on hegemony to engage with what he calls "the struggle for freedom from oppression [that] has been waged by the Third World masses, who in their maintenance of a deep cultural identity have made history come alive."[80] It is significant that both Gabriel and Jameson locate authenticity in the "recognition of 'consciousness of oneself'"[81] that is possible only in dialectical opposition to a unifying and totalizing system: for Jameson, the third and final phase of capitalism; for Gabriel the "Western Hollywood film industry."[82] Both look to contained pockets on the fringe of, or external to, the unifying system for cultural and aesthetic authenticity. Both initiate these cultural spaces as sites of resistance. Both idealize the oppositional agency in the authentic subjectivity, though for Jameson this idealization is justified as a "level of abstraction" and is in fact a defense against the systematic destruction of dialectical and critical distance in the postmodern sphere: "A system that constitutively produces differences remains a system, nor is the idea of such a system supposed to be in kind 'like' the object it tries to theorise."[83] Against criticisms of a lack of specificity in his analyses of postmodernism, he attempts to write from within the system while maintaining a subjective critical distance from the object of his writing. The system, if it is functional as a descriptor of economic and social differences, is necessary to conceptualize the "sheer heteronomy and the emergence of unrelated subsystems."[84] In this way, the Utopian aspect of the Marxist project is maintained and is in fact the radical aspect of the analysis.

Both Jameson and Gabriel are equally committed to an authentic aesthetics and an authentic cultural practice. In fact, the two spheres of society are intimately connected (perhaps in much the same way that Adorno perceives the "autonomy of art" as the criterion of an art of resistance—art inherently possesses a social meaning). For Gabriel, the Third World film "matures" from its first, originating phase of an "unqualified assimilation" into the system, to a "remembrance phase," and finally the "combative phase," in which is born a

> cinema of mass participation, one enacted by members of communities speaking indigenous language, one that espouses Julio Garcia Espinosa's polemic of "An Imperfect Cinema," that in a developing world, technical and artistic perfection in the production of a film cannot be aims in themselves.[85]

The imperfect cinema is contrasted with the apparent drive to perfection of the Hollywood film, exemplified in the genre films of the studio period. While I will expand on this later in the chapter, I will say here that the notion of an "imperfect cinema" that is unique to the Third World is simplistic. Consider, for example, imperfection as a cinematic aesthetic. The French New Wave, as well as the Hollywood "auteurs" of the seventies, experimented with quality of film, minimalism in sets and performances, stark realism. Godard's jump cut edit was a direct challenge to the seamless "perfection" of the traditional cinematic image.[86]

Gabriel and Jameson share a distinctly Marxist trajectory in their train of thought, particularly in the willingness to reject historical specificity in favor of an instrumental periodization. Both paradigms are founded on a structural and functional appraisal of art and the culture that receives it. Jameson's postmodernity is summed up by a crumbling of the "center," at which point earlier models of history and society are simply not applicable. He perceives this lack as pervasive, that is, as having infected every sphere of the postmodern present—personal, ideological, and political. A critique of these models must begin by reinstalling a mechanistic historicity in postmodern society, a connection between the subject and her history, culture, art, agency, and sense of belonging. This is achieved by, among other things, employing an empiricist approach to the realities of postmodern culture.

Discussing his own brand of postmodernity, Jean Baudrillard relies on a wholly nonspecific approach to a critique of contemporary society. Baudrillard writes:

> Above all, it is the referential principle of images which must be doubted, this strategy by means of which they always appear to refer to a real world, to real objects, and to reproduce something which is logically and chronologically anterior to themselves. None of this is true. As simulacra, images precede the real to the extent that they invert the causal and logical order of the real and its reproduction.[87]

It is essential to recognize here that Baudrillard theorizes not only a simulacrum of the Real, the imaginary and real space in which the reproduced consumes the Real, but its *precession*, its anteriority to the ontological truth of the real object. Baudrillard adds: "Benjamin, in his essay 'The Work of Art in the Age of Mechanical Reproduction,' already pointed out strongly this modern revolution in the order of production (of reality, of meaning) by the precession, the anticipation of its reproduction."[88] Benjamin does indeed conceptualize the ontology of art in the age of mechanical reproduction precisely in its *reproducibility*: "To an ever greater degree the work of art reproduced becomes the work of art designed for reproducibility."[89] But in what sense is this compatible with a *precession of a simulacrum* in which the Iconoclasts reveal only "that deep down God never existed, that only the simulacrum ever existed, even that God himself was never anything but his own simulacrum."[90] Baudrillard is pronouncing a final effacement of the Real in which the postmodern individual inhabits a simulacrum of images divorced from an anterior ontologically sound reality. Benjamin is pronouncing a cultural and economic system in which art is transformed from the authentic (possessing an "aura") to the reproduced, which enables a qualified measure of social resistance, and in which "the public is an examiner, but an absent-minded one."[91] Indeed, conceptualizing the mechanized society and its profound impact on popular art requires returning to Benjamin's analysis of mass culture and the institutions responsible for mass art, such as film studios and the star system. I cannot see that Benjamin envelops all in an already existing simulacrum. In Baudrillard's simulacrum, war is realized only in a perfectly mediated form, through an infinite regression of images and signs.[92] Thus we are to believe that the anteriority of the image (CNN or Fox News, or Coppola's *Apocalypse Now*) to the object *effaces* the object, or erases its ontological core from existence. Baudrillard is quite explicit on this point:

> The War in Vietnam "in itself" perhaps in fact never happened, it is a dream, a baroque dream of napalm and of the tropics, a psychotropic dream that had the goal neither of a victory nor of a policy at stake, but, rather, the sacrificial, excessive deployment of a power already filming itself as it unfolded, perhaps waiting for nothing but consecration by a superfilm, which completes the mass-spectacle effect of this war.[93]

If we contrast this reading of the Vietnam War as simulacral procession with Coppola's assessment of *Apocalypse Now*—"This film isn't about Vietnam; it is Vietnam"[94]—we have some sense of how far Baudrillard departs from Coppola's objective to achieve the realism of war as a surrealist composition.

Theories of reproductions and repetitions are, as Jameson acknowledges, part and parcel of the dominant discourse of postmodernism: "At this point, I will merely note one further such theme, which has seemed to me to be of the greatest significance in specifying the antithetical formal reactions of modernism and mass culture to their common social situation, and that is the notion of *repetition*."[95] He sees this as originating with Kierkegaard and finding fruition in Baudrillard. I would add that

Baudrillard's simulacrum only makes sense after the "crisis of significa-tion" posited by the major post-structuralists. In fact, the simulacrum shares something with Barthes or Derrida's deferment of meaning: "Text, on the contrary, practices the infinite deferment of the significant" that "accomplishes the plurality of meaning: an irreducible (and not merely acceptable) plural."[96] If anything, the Barthesian "plurality" is a simula-crum, though it was Baudrillard who gave the term currency in post-structuralist parlance.

In Jameson and Baudrillard, one perceives a common trajectory chart-ing the subjectivity of the postmodern subject in terms of her immer-sion in that which was always already reproduced, in what is essentially inauthentic and fake. Gabriel theorizes something quite similar in his conception of Western cinema: "The Western experience of film viewing—dominance of the big screen and the sitting situation—has naturalized a spectator conditioning so that any communication of a film plays on such values as exhibition and reception."[97] But what are "such values as exhibition and reception"? In what way are they con-ceptualized? Is "exhibition" equated with immersion in the spectacle, and thus of the ills of what Debord calls a "society of the spectacle"? And in what way is an alternative to the spectacle compatible with an alternative "film-making as a public service institution?"[98] Public-service cinema presumably engages with a collective culture and in the service of that culture; its political project must thus be founded on a social reality rather than a spectacle. But Gabriel's resistance cinema falters, in much the same way as Jameson's somber assessment of post-modern culture, in a lack of detail and specificity. In fact, it is precisely in this area that Gabriel reveals his reliance on the "passivity" of the Western Hollywood-inculcated spectator. Whereas the "performance effect" of the folk or oral art form "expects viewer participation, there-fore arouses activity and prepares for and allows participation," the "print or literate art form" (and, by association, the cinematic art form) "discourages viewer participation. Puts an end to activity. Inhibits par-ticipation."[99] This is merely one comparison Gabriel makes between an enlightened, resistant, *authentic* art and its Western counterpart founded on hegemonic practices over its own culture and, in an impe-rialist sense, over the cultures of a marginalized Third World.

I would argue that the richness of the Hollywood cinematic tradition attests to a diverse range of aesthetic practices. Hitchcock's *Vertigo* surely encourages the spectator's participation in the viewing of the spectacle, as well as in interpretation. David Lynch's *Lost Highway* demands repeated viewings to make sense of its nonlinear, self-destructive narrative. If participation is literally to interact with the text, I would argue that cinema (and the "print or literate art form") is an inherently participatory art. I revert here to Barthes's "playing the text," in which

> the generation of the perpetual signifier . . . in the field of the text (better, of which the text is the field) is realized not according to an organic process of maturation or a hermeneutic course of deepening investigation, but, rather, according to a serial movement of disconnections, overlappings, variations.[100]

Recent experiments in digital cinema, nonlinear and real-time narrative, and cinematic "quotation" surely have their origins in an innovative spirit that one can trace to Welles, Hitchcock, and, later, Resnais, Truffaut, and Godard. Mike Figgis's *Time Code* or Tom Tykwer's *Run Lola Run* require the audience's interpretation and *organization* of a dominant narrative (though ultimately both films maintain a field of resistance to the linear narrative).[101] Singer's *The Usual Suspects* and Nolan's *Memento* are neo-*noir*, but they are equally narrative experiments that require the participation of the spectator in formulating a coherent narrative structure. *The Usual Suspects* presents the most interesting narrative experiment in recent genre cinema, particularly in its lack of a sound narrative "ontology." Verbal's (Kevin Spacey) account of the events on the pier are simultaneously a construction of the film's narrative; thus the narrative trajectory is not instigated by an objective "storyteller" but guided by a component of that narrative. Italo Calvino's "reader as writer"[102] translates seamlessly to film.

Theories of simulacra and late capitalism are abstracted from the specificity of reality—of real, lived, social conditions—as well as from the *reality* of textual participation in contemporary culture. Aesthetic experience that is incompatible with a Marxist aesthetic model or a nascent Third World filmic revolution is devalued, declared empty, or, in the worst sense, *inauthentic* for its commodification of that which once was socially and culturally generative. Both Jameson and Gabriel contrive the aesthetic and cultural authenticity of an *anti-popular* art. That is, authenticity is realized only in opposition to—and ultimately in extrication from—the system. But neither Jameson nor Gabriel investigates popular art in any detail. Gabriel suggests that Third World films "see a concentration of long takes and repetition of images and scenes. In the Third World films, the slow, leisurely pacing approximates the viewer's sense of time and rhythm of life."[103] I have two objections to this claim. First, filmmakers have self-consciously used the long take since the 1940s, most famously in *Citizen Kane, Rope,* and *Touch of Evil.* It can then not be employed as a symbolic or "Third World" cinematic tool of resistance; it falters at the second phase of maturation, the "assimilation" phase. Second, the notion that "leisurely pacing approximates the viewer's sense of time and rhythm of life" requires that these times and rhythms are shared by all spectators, which is clearly not the case. Joseph Natoli offers an interesting discussion about the viewing sensibilities of two generations separated by a proficiency in the reception of analog (outmoded) and digital (the new cinematic aesthetic) images: "Human consciousness and perception are undergoing a revolutionary change: the young are not only processing everything faster but they are not analogizing; they have no need to fill in the connect between word and world as a book reading generation is shaped to."[104] I would argue also that leisurely pacing, prevalent in avant-garde cinema since the late fifties (consider John Cassavetes's *Shadows*), is less an attempt to depict images in "real time" than a very obvious contrast to the rigid editing and fast cuts of genre cinema (though even this is too generalized if we consider something like Welles's *Touch of Evil*). The long take and leisurely pacing has been a staple of David Lynch's work since *Eraserhead* (1977), but neither device functions as an approximation of real time or "real life."

Jameson's conclusions of the postmodern moment are often founded on textual readings that are generalized or superficially engaged with the text. Walsh suggests that Jameson reads texts as "symptomatic" of a social or cultural reality.[105] While Jameson has defended himself in this respect, I consider the notion of a text as "symptomatic" of a cultural condition dubious—for one, it fails to take account of the post-structuralist notion of the discursive and perpetually displaced textual signifier. Consider, for example, his notion of "pastiche" and its perfect expression in the "nostalgia mode."[106] One of the inaugural films of what Jameson refers to as a "new genre" (though he hastens to add, "if that's what it is") is Lucas's major success in 1973, *American Graffiti,* which

> set out to recapture all the atmosphere and stylistic peculiarities of the 1950s United States. . . . Polanski's great film *Chinatown* (1974) does something similar for the 1930s, as does Bertolucci's *The Conformist* (1969) for the Italian and European context of the same period.[107]

Jameson employs these films to signal the arrival of a new genre, the film of nostalgia, which will fit into his assessment of postmodern subjectivity which lives in a "perpetual present" and is thus perpetually reflecting on a lost (idealized) past. Yet anybody who has seen *American Graffiti*, *Chinatown*, and *Il Conformista* (*The Conformist*) must be suspicious of the "similarities" between these films. The profound *dissimilarities* in plot, character, narrative structure, production, and distribution *must* bring Jameson's model into question. I will concede that Lucas's film is a nostalgia piece in the mode of Rob Reiner's *Stand by Me* (which appeared in the mid-1980s). I will also concede that the "nostalgia mode," for lack of an adequately defined genre, finds its seminal film in *American Graffiti*. But in what sense is Polanski's *Chinatown* exemplary of the nostalgia mode apart from the obviousness of its period setting? It can hardly function as a pop-culture barometer alongside films such as *Jaws* and *Star Wars*, which would be released shortly after *Chinatown* and credited with establishing the "blockbuster" phenomenon.[108]

Jameson places *Star Wars* in the nostalgia mode, but even so I cannot perceive a similar nostalgia in Polanski and Lucas's sensibility. Of *Star Wars*, he writes: "Unlike *American Graffiti*, it does not reinvent a picture of the past in its lived totality; rather, by reinventing the feel and shape of characteristic art objects of an older period (the serials), it seeks to reawaken a sense of the past associated with these objects."[109] I disagree that *Star Wars* functions for a popular audience even remotely in the fashion Jameson describes. Merely on a level of textuality, the franchise is far broader and discursive than its aesthetic veneer of 1930s and 1940s serials. Certainly Lucas had conceived of a classic serial as a feature film, as he had with his story outline of *Raiders of the Lost Ark*. But I cannot perceive that this serial aesthetic is transferred as pastiche to a popular audience (the majority of which engage with the film through numerous viewings and a wide knowledge of cinematic traditions) in the categorical way described in Jameson's model.

Lucas has characterized *Star Wars* as "the fairy tale or the myth. It is a children's story in history and you go back to *The Odyssey* . . . the myths which existed in high adventure, and an exotic far-off land."[110] He recalls here a system of mythology Fiedler describes as central to the American novel, which is certainly in keeping with the mythic structure of serials such as *Flash Gordon*. *Chinatown*, if anything, declares its contemporaneity with its critique of American capitalism and the rise of conspicuous consumption in middle-class America. Gittes's (Jack Nicholson) classic lines, uttered to Noah Cross (John Huston,) exemplify this as a subtext in the film: "How much better can you eat? What can you buy that you can't already afford?" Jameson says very little about the film apart from: "as witness the stylistic recuperation of the American and Italian 1930s, in Polanski's *Chinatown* and Bertolucci's *Il Conformista* respectively."[111] Why "recuperation" and not "representation," which would at least grant the film a sense of historical realism? Recuperation is literally the mode of pastiche, "the allusive and elusive plagiarism of older plots,"[112] and thus denies a sense of aesthetic authenticity that is the privilege of art prior to its commodification in the market.

If *American Graffiti* "set out to recapture . . . the henceforth mesmer-izing lost reality of the Eisenhower era,"[113] I would argue that *Chinatown* was a decidedly *contemporary* film in 1974, in which an entanglement in a convoluted plot in traditional *film noir* transforms into a profoundly existential crisis for the anti-hero. Robert Towne's screenplay is ultimately an exploration of the deterioration of American "certainties." The over-tones of conspiracy reflect the American fascination with conspiracy that began in the mid-seventies and found its most accessible expression in *The X-Files* in the nineties.

If *Chinatown* is a nostalgia film in which "generational periods open up for aesthetic colonization,"[114] then surely *The Godfather, Parts I and II* are equally nostalgia (which is commodified reflection, or reflection detached from historicity), equally condemned to repeat the perfor-mance of the expressionless gesture, the "imitation of dead styles."[115] De Palma's *The Untouchables* must be counted among these, particularly in the echo of De Niro's Jake La Motta (*Raging Bull*) in his performance as Al Capone. Reiner's *When Harry Met Sally* must be a reenactment of the relationship comedies of Ernst Lubitsch or George Cukor's *The Philadelphia Story*; Sally's (Meg Ryan) faked orgasm is merely the vul-gar expression of earlier symbolic representations of sex (a train entering a tunnel in Hitchcock's *North by Northwest*, or a searching spotlight in *Casablanca*),[116] doomed to repeat prior performances. Jameson's reading of Lawrence Kasdan's *Body Heat* is particularly nuanced, yet always cir-cumscribed by a desire to find pastiche "in which the history of aesthetic styles displaces 'real' history."[117] Viewing *Body Heat* as pastiche celebrates it merely as the culmination of the postmodern aesthetic, exemplifying not only the requisite lack of *historicity*, but achieving a unique aptitude for reveling in the condition.

In these postmodern paradigms—Jameson, Baudrillard, and Gabriel—postmodernism *requires* a lack of specificity; without the symptoma-tizing (and, to my mind, superficial) reading of the text, the totalizing aspect of the model is brought into question. The nostalgia mode is one model in which the cultural theorist might approach *American Graffiti*, *Chinatown*, and *Il Conformista*, and an idiosyncratic one at that. The narrative strategies and characterizations of these films have very little in common. The claim that they demonstrate a common mode is specious in the absence of a far more rigorous and detailed textual analysis. The notion that camera angle in Western cinema is "mostly governed by eye-level perspective which approximates to our natural position in the world"[118] conflates a traditional cinematic style with a perceived lack of political intent. *Film noir* is often shot from low angles or from overhead. Overtly political films like Warren Beatty's *Bulworth* or John Sayles's *Matewan* use traditional film stylistics (eye-level shots, shot-reverse-shot editing) as well as the more flamboyant innovations used by David Fincher or Quentin Tarantino.

Jameson's aesthetics of the postmodern is intimately connected to Baudrillard's theory of the simulacrum, though Baudrillard does not explicitly mention the connection between the simulacral precession and the dawning of late capitalism; in fact he seems to suggest that the simulacrum is the only true ontological Real, and that it has always been this way. Both are totalizing visions from which nothing can escape. Presumably Jameson theorizes from within the postmodern stranglehold over linguistics and modes of expression, and is doomed to conceptualize only "new realities" that are in actuality new mimetic, and thus, unreal, forms.

The totality of these visions allows for the inclusion of all texts into the dominant aesthetic (apart from those that oppose it from the cultural fringe). The ontology of this postmodern, or dominant Western art, is precisely as dead, as recuperative or reperformative, as having manufactured a dominant mode of expression in postmodernity: "Nostalgia films restructure the whole issue of pastiche and project it onto a collective and social level, where the desperate attempt to appropriate a missing past is now refracted through the iron law of fashion change and the emergent ideology of the generation."[119] The postmodern subject is hopelessly immersed and, it seems, entranced. If I have argued for a reconsideration of cinema as *affective*, Jameson installs into the fabric of the postmodern (culture and subject) a pervasive "waning of affect," which signals "the end of the bourgeois ego or monad."[120] It signals also the end of "style," "the distinctive individual brushstroke."[121] I can only attempt to refute these claims with a consideration of the complexities of contemporary cinema and the culture that interacts with it.

Is popular cinema unable to engage with an authentic subjectivity and culture? In what sense is it unable to provide an aesthetic experience that is personal and distinctive? Is the spectator truly no longer attuned to the text or actively engaged in interpretation? Is cinema no longer involved in its historical milieu and in a perceived hegemonic structure that it can resist?

The triumph of capitalism in its third manifestation (and the consequent commodification of creativity) precludes the possibility of aesthetic and cultural authenticity. I do not wish to argue that Jameson's assessment of the "omnipresence" of the market (to use his term) is misguided or inadequately researched. However, if authenticity is incommensurate with popular art, it would benefit the cultural theorist to investigate the reality of postmodern aesthetics *from within* the marketplace and thereby address what I would consider a point of origin: the subjective experience of film viewing and the diversity of cinematic texts. Duvall is correct to suggest that "one of the great ironies of Jameson's *Postmodernism, or the Cultural Logic of Late Capitalism* is that even "as he announces the death of modernism [and a stillborn postmodernism], and hence of its critical distance and emancipatory hopes, he reinscribes those same modernist hopes in his own writing practice."[122] Ultimately, Jameson's model of a postmodern society is *reflective*. The Utopian schema of a system of thought arresting a cultural deterioration for the emancipation of that culture must reflect on a point of origin, an ideal (and idealized) imaginary in which the Utopia was once realized. For Jameson, it is the realist phase of capitalism, equating with the rise of the bourgeoisie and a predominantly realist aesthetic. I have argued thus far that it is precisely this realist aesthetic that must cease to function as a nostalgic point of reflection. It is not the irreducibility of the realist aesthetic that has been recuperated in pastiche, but pastiche itself that reveals the nostalgia of a Marxist hermeneutics that seeks only to recuperate old forms.

> Indeed, there is a kind of return of the repressed in *Diamond Dust Shoes*, a strange compensatory decorative exhilaration, explicitly designated by the title itself although perhaps more difficult to observe in the reproduction. This is the glitter of gold dust, the spangling of gilt sand, which seals the surface of the painting and yet continues to glint at us. Think, however, of Rimbaud's magical flowers "that look back at you," or the august-premonitory eye-flashes of Rilke's archaic Greek torso which warn the bourgeois subject to change his life.[123]

The comparison between Warhol's *Diamond Dust Shoes* and Van Gogh's "original," or Marilyn Monroe's commodification in pop-iconomania with the reality of her person (which is effaced at the point of commodification), reveals only the detachment of a profoundly modernist aesthetics of emancipation from contemporary popular culture. As Hutcheon has convincingly argued, the reproduction is historically empowered precisely through the recuperative gesture.[124] She is equally critical of Jameson's apparent obsession to recover an old aesthetics: "What interests me is that, when he [Jameson] finds something nostalgic—be it in the theorizing of the Frankfurt School or the novels of J. G. Ballard—nostalgia is meant to be taken negatively as "regressive." Yet his *own* rhetoric and position can themselves at times sound strangely nostalgic."[125] Contemporary culture (and its theorists) must stake a claim for its own innovative aesthetics (and at the very forefront of this aesthetic revolution is pastiche) without looking over its shoulder at what once was and could still be.

Authenticity and Spectacle

A canon—a shared understanding of what literature is worth preserving—takes shape through a troubled historical process.[126]

The fact, however, is that when one speaks today of the aesthetics of seriality, one alludes to something more radical, that is, to a notion of aesthetic value that wholly escapes the "modern" idea of art and literature.[127]

To celebrate the status of popular art in contemporary society—that is, an art of the masses and an art dialectically opposed to the masses, but which is still a commodity in the marketplace—is to acknowledge that authenticity is contextual, as Ohmann argues convincingly of the canon of literature. Authenticity can thus equally be anchored in the contemporary—in the ontology of the art and culture that must sustain the eye of the critic, theorist, and consumer. To look outside popular culture for its authenticity (taking Jameson's and Adorno's lead, to look for this authenticity in some earlier point in history) is merely to affirm tired distinctions inscribed into the history of art and theory that privilege certain cultures and groups, and certain epochs over others.

But what does it mean to apply these standards to what Debord calls a "society of the spectacle"? Presumably for Debord, this society is founded on a shared history, a shared spatial and temporal reality, a shared sense of its interconnectedness. We who are immersed in the spectacle are immersed together, companions in our collective passivity. But while Debord is explicit in his attack on this society, I maintain that the immersion in the spectacle is necessary for affectivity; it is paradoxically this awareness of and immersion in the spectacle that recuperates affect, the essential aesthetic response that Jameson contends has "waned" in postmodernity.

Spectacle is not merely the visual, that is, the singularly visual aspect of art (in this case, and in my analysis, the art of contemporary cinema), although this is a vital aspect of the growth of the spectacle aesthetic. It is more fundamentally a transformation of the traditional interpretive mode in which realism functioned as a standard of excellence.[128] For Manovich, new forms of representation are "precisely a code [used] to communicate all types of data and experience":

> new media transforms all culture and cultural theory into an "open source." This opening up of cultural techniques, conventions, forms, and concepts is ultimately the most promising cultural effect of computerization—an opportunity to see the world and the human being anew, in ways that were not available to "a man with a movie camera."[129]

I concur with Carroll when he says that "the realist approach to film theory, either as an ontological thesis, or in its more contemporary psychologized variations, is a dead end."[130] In this piece, Carroll attempts to conceptualize the reasons for the "intensity" of experience provided by the "movies"—what he describes as "popular mass media films, the products of what might be called Hollywood International."[131] It is this intensity, he claims, that cannot have its foundation in a traditional realist aesthetic.

Spectacle comments on this mode of realism and in so doing refashions it into the already textual, or the "spectacle" of that which was once authentic. It is my endeavor to understand this new "authenticity" anchored in the spectacle that I have argued is endemic to contemporary popular culture and its aesthetic mode. Eco discusses the "seriality" of the art of mass culture, though he acknowledges "that we still know very little about the role of repetition in the universe of art and in the universe of mass media."[132] This seriality, in which the spectator is accustomed to the *series*—that is, the inherently connected and reproduced, rather than the authenticity of an original—is no doubt another crucial aspect of the society of the spectacle. It is possible in this sense to talk about the tendentiously "lowbrow" cinema of a Michael Bay (*Armageddon, Bad Boys*) or a Roland Emmerich (*Independence Day, The Day After Tomorrow*) as exemplary of the spectacle aesthetic in which seriality, repetition, and the visual foreground its attachment to, and reproduction of, prior forms of cinema and art. Thus, while the miraculous first twenty minutes of *Saving Private Ryan* (that seemingly carried the film in critical and box-office circles) were lauded for their unprecedented realism, it is the acknowledgment of this "presentation" of the Real that inaugurates the set piece as spectacle. At best, Spielberg's storming the beaches of Normandy is an unprecedented *cinematic* realism.

The spectacle of cinematic realism, to my mind, has been rarely acknowledged, yet its departure from the real is very obvious. Consider, for example, the stylistics of *Ryan*'s opening set piece. The color has been drained from the image to resemble the black-and-white photography of the stock film footage of World War II. The spectator is positioned in explicitly *cinematic* spaces, underwater (recalling *Jaws*), extreme close-up, medium-overhead shot. The cacophony of the maelstrom, less than an indistinct barrage, maintains a cinematic clarity: the spectator is allowed an intimate audience with the dying, particularly those suffering brutal or cinematically visceral deaths. The sequence is painfully distended—a number of critics noted favorably the *length* of the set piece. These are cinematic tropes that conjure a reality on celluloid. Ridley Scott's *Black Hawk Down* or even Terrence Malick's *The Thin Red Line* offer similar cinematic images of war that poeticize the Real into the spectacle. Is Spielberg's stylistics of cinematic realism any different from Lynch's hyperrealism in *Blue Velvet*? Spielberg drains the color from his opening set piece, Lynch saturates the images with colors and light/dark contrasts. Both spectacles are a form of *hyperreality*. The spectacle is ontologically far removed from the realism of the 1940s European cinema that Bazin cherishes, which was motivated by the theatricality of its film predecessors. The first twenty-minute segment of *Saving Private Ryan*, installed as cinematic spectacle, divorced from the reality of carnage and brutality, is also perhaps the most beautiful war sequence on film.

Darley locates a new affectivity in an analysis of a diverse range of media practices and concludes that "we must resist the temptation to essentialize: the aesthetic dimension of late modern culture is not homogenous. On the contrary, it is highly sedimented with a multiplicity of image forms and corresponding kinds of spectator experience."[133] Rather than assume the starting point at an imaginary and wholly ahistorical paradigm of artistic authenticity, he locates the authenticity of a society of the spectacle precisely in its immersion within and manipulation of the mechanism of the spectacle: in his case, a new media poetics of "cinemas, special venues, amusement arcades, television, video players, game consoles and personal computers."[134] Perhaps this is merely to say that at some point the aesthetic of a society of the spectacle and its varied forums must begin to interest—and impress—the cultural theorist.

But there is something else at stake here. Popular audiences are increasingly willing to challenge the supremacy of the canon by theorizing and conceptualizing their own art forms. Contemporary writing on film is simply not aware of the gulf that separates it from the culture it purports to describe. Consider the following passage that, while not exemplary of film theory, is indicative of what happens when mainstream film criticism addresses the popular cinema aesthetic:

> Just look at our top Oscar contenders. *Gump* was well made and had a certain sweetness, if you like that sort of thing, but it's still a lot closer to *Beaches* than *The Bridge on the River Kwai*. *Pulp Fiction* was lively and clever, but at bottom it's just an MTV version of old Hollywood themes, with all the boring parts left out. *Quiz Show* and *Nobody's Fool* get points for trying, but they don't exactly rank with *The Third Man* or *Annie Hall* or *The Godfather*. They're closer to good efforts than good movies.[135]

In this statement, Richardson falls back on the imaginary of the authentic work of art and thereby effaces the possibility of authenticity from the contemporary *and* the popular. "*Pulp Fiction* was lively and clever, but at bottom. . . . " The quest for a bottom*ness*, the eternal wellspring of authenticity, occludes the authentic from the contemporary. Authenticity is anchored only in the past, manifested in reflection, and is in this sense reactionary. Discussing Susan Stewart's study of nostalgia as a social disease, Hutcheon writes: "Nostalgia makes the idealized (and therefore always absent) past into the site of immediacy, presence and authenticity . . . nostalgia is, in this way, 'prelapsarian' and indeed utopian."[136] This crucial aspect of Utopianism as nostalgia has been little acknowledged.

But for Richardson, exiling authenticity from the present is never enough. It must be relocated to the essence of a particular cultural entity/discourse that is historical, contextual, and aesthetically dominant—traditionally the polar opposite of what has been perceived to be popular or of the masses: a *high or elite culture*.

> After that, the bottom drops off dramatically: the dreary sameness of all the erotic thrillers and buddy-o-matic action epics, the dispiritingly endless stream of sequels and remakes and Disney comedies. So many movies feel cobbled-together these days—

action films like *True Lies* and *Patriot Games* are so distended by their set piece action sequences that the rest of the movie feels like filler, and comedies from *Wayne's World* to *The Addam's Family* are so perfunctory about their stories that they make the Bob Hope and Bing Crosby road movies seem downright sophisticated."[137]

At bottom here is Richardson's failure to appreciate the spectacle aesthetic, and even the willingness to investigate what it might be. This arises from the implicit rejection of the possibility of authenticity from the contemporary and popular *at the point of its inception* in a nostalgic and idyllic past. To argue that *True Lies* and *Patriot Games* have distended action sequences fails to appreciate the cinematic literacy of the contemporary spectator, for whom action set pieces are deliberately distended into performative spectacles.[138] In fact, I would argue that the aestheticization of the spectacle occurs only in the distended sequences in which movement and contrast are foregrounded, and narrative, thematic, and character continuity de-emphasized. For the lack of characterization that Richardson perceives in *True Lies*, the film compensates in a fabric of intertextual references. When Tasker (Arnold Schwarzenegger) removes his wet suit to reveal an uncreased tuxedo beneath, the spectator recalls an almost identical sequence in *Goldfinger*—Tasker is equally an original characterization, inhabiting a textual present, and a reflection on Sean Connery's James Bond. The extended (and distended) chase sequence in which Tasker pursues a terrorist on horseback is a marvelous set piece in which the pursuit begins gradually but gains momentum exponentially, accompanied by increasingly complex visual compositions and a rising music theme. The chase sequence in *The Matrix Reloaded* is unprecedented as a set piece of movement and rhythm incorporating visual and aural stimuli.

Contemporary cinema has achieved a virtuosity of the spectacle unparalleled in visual media. It is essential to distinguish between classical representation and a kinetic cinematic sequence that arrests its audience's attention while simultaneously de-emphasizing the narrative. The sequence in which "Bohemian Rhapsody" or "Foxy Lady" is performed in *Wayne's World* functions as a spectacle within the narrative. Once the film is concluded, these spectacle elements have a residual impact on the spectator that surpasses that of the film's narrative, which Richardson rightly calls "perfunctory." Darley appreciates the transcendence of the spectacle in contemporary narrative cinema: "As the corpus of films attached to this rejuvenation of special effects has developed and expanded—from *Star Wars* to the likes of *True Lies* and *Titanic*—so has the narrative element of such films distinctly receded in favor of the stimulation, impact and astonishment that can be produced by new and revamped techniques of image-capture and fabrication."[139] Set pieces in spectacle cinema are at once visually iconic and transposed into a consumer market, there substituted for new aesthetic experiences (in the way that the STAR WARS title screen achieves an autonomy from the narrative—or indeed, from what some have called the "mythology" of the franchise). But these set pieces are also amenable to a series of repetitions. Thus, the "Bohemian Rhapsody" sequence in *Wayne's World* was endlessly repeated on television, music videos, and the advertising media, forming a "series" (Eco) that filtered into pockets of popular culture dissociated from the originality (and authenticity) of the film. The perfunctory story is necessary for the performance of this spectacle in cinema. The CGI sequence in *The Matrix Revolutions* in which a horde of Armored Personnel Units (APUs) take up arms is striking because of its status as spectacle, divorced from the Real, achieving the realization of its reproductive perfection in computer imaging. In relation to the spectacle of contemporary popular cinema (and here I include Kubrick's *2001: A Space Odyssey* and Lucas's *Star Wars* franchise), all "stories" are perfunctory. The "good stories" are told in ages in which authentic artworks and the aura of the real maintain their powerful statuses. How else is one to appreciate Tarantino as one of the most significant filmmakers of the last decade but as a director with a new kind of (meta)cinematic impulse— which is to say, immersion in cinema as spectacle?

This *spectacality* is perhaps the realization of what Benjamin had in mind with his classic formulation of the mechanically reproduced work of art. In the age in which mechanical reproduction has consumed all prior artistic modes (which is to say our age in which cinema dominates the other art forms as mass culture entertainment), the spectacle impulse subsumes the narrative and thematic. And this ontology of the spectacle, which I have argued must form the kernel of any analysis of contemporary popular cinema, is precisely that which has reconciled itself to its status as reproduction. The spectacle acknowledges its *inauthenticity*, and it is this that renders it vital and affecting to its audience. In celebrating its pure spectacle, its pure *textuality*, its status as already reproduced, cinema relieves itself of the burden of a humanist and/or Marxist aesthetic impulse toward authentic art and its failing aura.

Aylish Wood's excellent reading of the opening of *The Matrix* appreciates the centrality of the spectacle aesthetic in the composition of that franchise. "The photography of this sequence gives the impression of time appearing to be both slowed down and speeded up. . . . The subsequent chase scene over the rooftops is captured in a series of shots that accentuate movement, an effect that adds to the vibrancy of the opening sequence."[140] One suspects that Richardson might value *The Matrix* over *True Lies* or *Patriot Games*, but on the basis of the ingenuity of its story, or its finely wrought intertextual fabric (though he fails to appreciate this in *True Lies* or *Wayne's World*, both significant examples of what Collins refers to as the "genericity of the nineties") rather than the merits of its groundbreaking action sequences and innovative special effects. Warner Bros. provided the hundred-million-dollar-plus budget for the film after the Wachowski Brothers had shot the opening action piece, demonstrating their remarkable camera innovation, "bullet-time," and the expertise to convey their complex storyboards on film.[141] By their own acknowledgment, the executives of Warner Bros. could not make sense of the story. It seems that the corporate element of the filmic process better understands the aesthetic of a society of the spectacle (or at least its market value to a contemporary audience) than the cultural theorists who struggle over the mythic or religious foundations of the franchise. I return to a detailed discussion of *The Matrix* franchise in Chapter Three.

Contemporary spectacle cinema presents a challenge to traditional theoretical paradigms. Ultimately, *the spectacle is authentic expression*, and this is something that cultural theory and Marxist hermeneutics has had trouble reconciling with its emancipatory projects. Even I acknowledge that it would be perverse to argue that all cinema is equally worthy of attention, but the nature of this worth cannot be located in traditional aesthetics practiced in outmoded discourses of cultural and artistic elitism, nor in contemporary paradigms in which theorists describe cinema and its various ideologies divorced from an experience of film or an acknowledgment of its profound effect on the spectator. And what a theorist like Jameson fails to appreciate is that, ultimately, his rejection of mass art is as resounding an expression of its authenticity as its acceptance by the masses.

Notes

1. Raymond Williams, *Marxism and Literature* (Oxford: Oxford University Press, 1977), 155.

2. Frederic Jameson, "Reification and Utopia in Mass Culture," *Social Text* no. 1 (Winter 1979), 138.

3. Carroll, *A Philosophy of Mass Art*, 3–4.

4. Frederic Jameson, "Postmodernism and Consumer Society," in *The Cultural Turn: Selected Writings on the Postmodern 1983–1998* (London: Verso, 1998), 2.

5. Anne Friedberg, "The End of Cinema: Multimedia and Technological Change," in *Reinventing Film Studies*, ed. Christine Gledhill and Linda Williams (London: Arnold, 2000), 439.

6. Patricia Pisters, *The Matrix of Visual Culture* (Stanford, CA: Stanford University Press, 2001), 224.

7. Collins, 262.

8. For a lucid account of the Horkheimer/Adorno dialectic of the culture industry, see Douglas Kellner, "Theodor W. Adorno and the Dialectics of Mass Culture," in *Adorno: A Critical Reader*, ed. Nigel Gibson and Andrew Rubin (Oxford: Blackwell, 2002), 86–109. Kellner offers the very useful notion of the culture industry as "administered culture, imposed from above, as instruments of indoctrination and social control" (94). Mass culture, in Adorno's model, is essentially industrialized, externally "produced," administered, and commodified.

9. Jameson, "Postmodernism and Consumer Society," 2.

10. Graeme Turner, "Introduction," in *The Film Cultures Reader*, ed. Graeme Turner (London: Routledge, 2002), 5.

11. Michael Walsh, "Jameson and 'Global Aesthetics,'" in *Post-Theory: Reconstructing Film Studies*, ed. David Bordwell and Noël Carroll (Madison, WI: University of Wisconsin Press, 1996), 481.

12. Mark Jancovich, "A Real Shocker," in *The Film Cultures Reader*, ed. Graeme Turner (London: Routledge, 2002), 470.

13. Jancovich, "A Real Shocker," 471.

14. Jancovich, "A Real Shocker," 477.

15. Paul Schrader, "Notes on *Film Noir*," in *Film Noir Reader*, ed. Alain Silver and James Ursini (New York: Limelight Editions, 1998), 53.

16. See, for example, Mulvey, "Visual Pleasure and Narrative Cinema," 29.

17. Amy Taubin, "The Critics Commentaries," *Reservoir Dogs*, collector's edition two-disc set DVD (Magna Pacific Distributors, 1992).

18. Noël Carroll, "Introducing Film Evaluation," in *Reinventing Film Studies*, ed. Christine Gledhill and Linda Williams (Oxford: Arnold, 2000), 266.

19. Manthia Diawara, "Black American Cinema: The New Realism," in *Film and Theory: An Anthology*, ed. Robert Stam and Toby Miller (Oxford: Blackwell, 2000), 244.

20. John Shelton Lawrence and Robert Jewett, *The Myth of the American Superhero* (Grand Rapids, MI: W. B. Erdmans, 2002), 268.

21. Lawrence and Jewett, 275.

22. Leslie Fiedler, *Love and Death in the American Novel* (New York: Stein and Day, 1967), 25–31.

23. Joseph Campbell, *The Hero with a Thousand Faces* (New York: World, 1956), 30–36.

24. Lawrence and Jewett, 282.

25. Lawrence and Jewett, 275.

26. Ella Shohat and Robert Stam, *Unthinking Eurocentrism* (London and New York: Routledge, 1994), 178.

27. Copeland recognizes this use of intertextuality as central to popular film as early as 1977. See Roger Copeland, "When Films 'Quote' Films, They Create a New Mythology," *New York Times*, Sep. 25, 1977.

28. Peter Kramer, "Star Wars," *History Today* 49, no. 3 (1999), 46.

29. Jane Caputi, "Small Ceremonies," in *Mythologies of Violence in Postmodern Media*, ed. Christopher Sharrett (Detroit, MI: Wayne State University Press, 1999), 155.

30. Caputi, 155.

31. This appeared as a catch phrase on advertising posters when the film was released in 1982.

32. "Meadowlands," *The Sopranos*, season one, episode four, DVD (HBO Home Video, 2004).

33. Carroll, *A Philosophy of Mass Art*, 83.

34. Carroll, *A Philosophy of Mass Art*, 68.

35. Terry Eagleton, *After Theory* (New York: Basic Books, 2003), 190.

36. John Fiske, *Understanding Popular Culture* (Winchester, MA: Unwin Hyman, 1989), 5.

37. For an excellent introduction and overview of the topic, see Thomas Docherty, "Introduction," in *Postmodernism: A Reader*, ed. Thomas Docherty (New York: Columbia University Press, 1993), 1–31.

38. John Fiske, *Reading the Popular* (Winchester, MA: Unwin Hyman, 1989), 1.

39. Fiske, *Understanding Popular Culture*, 11.

40. Fiske, *Understanding Popular Culture*, 14. Fiske is perhaps also drawing on a classic formulation of Althusser's "ideology as unconsciousness." See Louis Althusser, "Ideology and Ideological State Apparatuses," in *Lenin and Philosophy and Other Essays*, trans. Ben Brewster (New York and London: Monthly Review Press, 1971), 127–134 and 141–148.

41. Fiske, *Understanding Popular Culture*, 15.

42. Fiske, *Understanding Popular Culture*, 20.

43. Fiske, *Understanding Popular Culture*, 163.

44. Fiske, *Understanding Popular Culture*, 14.

45. Eminem, "Who Knew," *The Marshall Mathers LP* (Interscope Records, 2000).

46. For a fascinating discussion of the artwork as aesthetically removed from the object, see Steven Rubio, "Inventing Culture," in *The Aesthetic of Cultural Studies*, ed. Michael Bérubé (Boston: Blackwell Publishers, 2005). Rubio discusses Benjamin's notion of the aura as no longer located in the object in contemporary culture: "To be in the presence of great art mattered more than the art itself. The aura had taken over from its source" (181). He also alludes to the importance of personal experience and nostalgia in an aesthetic notion of popular art.

47. John Gaeta, "Commentary," *The Matrix* DVD (Warner Bros., 1999). For one of the best satires on the "evils" of the studio system, see Robert Altman's *The Player*, in which a studio executive hears a pitch for, among other things, "*Ghost* meets *The Manchurian Candidate*" and *The Graduate, Part II*.

48. Rage Against the Machine, "Wake Up!" *Rage Against the Machine* (Album) (Epic, 1992).

49. Fiske, *Understanding Popular Culture*, 6.

50. For a discussion of the "commodification [and aestheticization] of dissent," see Thomas Frank and Scott Weiland, *Commodify Your Dissent: Salvos from the Baffler* (New York: Norton, 1997).

51. Dick Hebdige, *Subculture: The Meaning of Style* (London and New York: Routledge, 1997), 102.

52. Jameson, "Reification and Utopia," 144.

53. Jameson, "Reification and Utopia," 139.

54. Jameson, "Reification and Utopia," 139.

55. Frederic Jameson, *Postmodernism, Or the Cultural Logic of Late Capitalism* (Durham, NC: Duke University Press, 1992), 55.

56. Jameson, *Postmodernism, Or the Cultural Logic of Late Capitalism*, 18.

57. Rita Felski, "The Role of Aesthetics in Cultural Studies," in *The Aesthetics of Cultural Studies*, ed. Michael Bérubé (Boston: Blackwell, 2005), 30.

58. Jameson does not conceptualize false consciousness in the same fashion as Adorno but he does describe a postmodern aesthetic in relation to a prior, *authentic*, art and culture.

59. Jameson, "Postmodernism and Consumer Society," 20.

60. Jameson, "Postmodernism and Consumer Society," 20.

61. Frederic Jameson, "Afterword—Marxism and Postmodernism," in *Postmodernism/Jameson/Critique*, ed. Douglas Kellner (Washington, D.C.: Maisonneuve Press, 1989), 371.

62. See Walsh: "There are also difficulties of internal consistency in the applications of Jameson's periodization" (489). Walsh is suspicious of periodization as a methodology for its inherent lack of specificity. He offers an excellent analysis of Jameson's very broad and, to his mind, incorrect claims about popular film: "To say that genres were repudiated by the mainstream cinema, as Jameson does, is demonstrably not true" (494).

63. See Lyotard, xxiii–xxv.

64. Stuart Hall, "Cultural Studies and Its Theoretical Legacies," in *Cultural Studies*, ed. Lawrence Grosberg, Cary Nelson, and Paula Treichler (New York and London: Routledge, 1992), 278.

65. Jameson, "Reification and Utopia in Mass Culture," 140.

66. Jameson, "Reification and Utopia in Mass Culture," 140.

67. Jameson, "Postmodernism and Consumer Society," 6. Jameson categorizes the "new" subjectivity as a deterioration of the old, and of the loss of an essential self.

68. Jameson, "Reification and Utopia in Mass Culture," 140.

69. Jameson, "Reification and Utopia in Mass Culture," 140.

70. For Jameson's challenge to the Frankfurt School's notion of art as autonomous, see "Reification and Utopia in Mass Culture," 133.

71. Jameson, "Postmodernism and Consumer Society," 20. Consider this also in light of his criticism of Adorno (see previous note), which does not stand up as well in this context.

72. Jameson, "Postmodernism and Consumer Society," 12.

73. The hotel in which *The Matrix* begins and ends is called "The Heart of the City Hotel."

74. Jameson, "Reification and Utopia in Mass Culture," 135.

75. Kennedy, 4.

76. Kennedy, 5.

77. Frederic Jameson, *Postmodernism, or the Cultural Logic of Late Capitalism*, 35.

78. Jameson, "Reification and Utopia in Mass Culture." Jameson suggests that "even ideology has in our society lost its clarity as prejudice, false consciousness, readily identifiable opinion" (139). Here he has found an inventive innovation beyond Adorno: false consciousness has reached a degree of falseness such that it no longer recognizes itself as false.

79. Jameson, *Postmodernism, Or the Cultural Logic of Late Capitalism*, 49.

80. Gabriel, 298.

81. Gabriel, 299.

82. Gabriel, 299.

83. Jameson, "Afterword," 373.

84. Jameson, "Afterword," 373.

85. Gabriel, 299–302.

86. For a reading of Godard's oeuvre as a reaction to traditional cinema, see Peter Wollen, "Godard and Counter-Cinema: *Vent D'Est*," *Afterimage* (Fall, 1972).

87. Jean Baudrillard, *The Evil Demon of Images*, trans. Paul Patton, Paul Floss (Sydney: The Power Institute of Fine Arts, 1987), 13.

88. Baudrillard, *The Evil Demon of Images*, 13.

89. Benjamin, 1172.

90. Baudrillard, *Simulacra and Simulation*, 4.

91. Benjamin, 1184.

92. See Jean Baudrillard, *The Gulf War Did Not Take Place* (Sydney: Power Institute of Fine Arts, 1995).

93. Baudrillard, *Simulacra and Simulation*, 59.

94. Francis Ford Coppola, press conference, Cannes Film Festival, 1979. Recorded in *Hearts of Darkness: A Filmmaker's Apocalypse*, directed by Fax Bahr and George Hickenlooper (American Zoetrope, 1991).

95. Jameson, "Reification and Utopia in Mass Culture," 135. Original emphasis.

96. Roland Barthes, "From Work to Text," in *Image Music Text*, trans. Stephen Heath (London: Fontana, 1977), 158–159.

97. Gabriel, 306.

98. Gabriel, 301.

99. Gabriel, 309.

100. Barthes, "From Work to Text," 158.

101. For a discussion of these trends in recent cinema, see Bruno Lessard, "Digital Technologies and the Politics of Performance," in *New Punk Cinema*, ed. Nicholas Rombes (Edinburgh: Edinburgh University Press, 2004), 102–112. Lessard considers the innovation of contemporary cinema in relation to a history of the image, tracing its origins to Bazin.

102. See Italo Calvino, *If on a Winter's Night, a Traveller* (London: Vintage, 1998).

103. Gabriel, 310.

104. Joseph Natoli, *Memory's Orbit: Film and Culture 1999-2000* (Albany: State University of New York Press, 2003), 32.

105. Walsh: "As Jameson argues at length in *The Political Unconscious*, the critic should read texts symptomatically, looking for the repressed expression of his historical moment out of which they have been generated" (486).

106. Jameson, "Postmodernism and Consumer Society," 7–10.

107. Jameson, "Postmodernism and Consumer Society," 7–8.

108. See David Thomson, "Who Killed the Movies?" *Esquire* 126, no. 6 (1996), 56–57.

109. Jameson, "Postmodernism and Consumer Society," 8.

110. Cited in Rubey, 5.

111. Jameson, *Postmodernism, Or the Cultural Logic of Late Capitalism*, 19.

112. Jameson, "Postmodernism and Consumer Society," 9.

113. Jameson, *Postmodernism, Or the Cultural Logic of Late Capitalism*, 19.

114. Jameson, *Postmodernism, Or the Cultural Logic of Late Capitalism*, 19.

115. Jameson, *Postmodernism, Or the Cultural Logic of Late Capitalism*, 18.

116. For a fascinating analysis of what occurs between Rick (Humphrey Bogart) and Ilsa (Ingrid Bergman) in exchange for the missing transit visas, see Slavoj Žižek, *The Art of the Ridiculous Sublime* (Seattle: Walter Chapin Simpson Center for the Humanities, 2000), 4–8.

117. Jameson, *Postmodernism, Or the Cultural Logic of Late Capitalism*, 20.

118. Gabriel, 312.

119. Jameson, *Postmodernism, Or the Cultural Logic of Late Capitalism*, 19.

120. Jameson, *Postmodernism, Or the Cultural Logic of Late Capitalism*, 15.

121. Jameson, *Postmodernism, Or the Cultural Logic of Late Capitalism*, 15.

122. John H. Duvall, "Troping History," in *Productive Postmodernism: Consuming Histories and Cultural Studies*, ed. John H. Duvall (Albany: State University of New York Press, 2002), 7.

123. Jameson, *Postmodernism, Or the Cultural Logic of Late Capitalism*, 10.

124. See Linda Hutcheon, *A Poetics of Postmodernism: History, Theory, Fiction* (New York and London: Routledge, 1988), 26–27.

125. See Linda Hutcheon, "Irony, Nostalgia, and the Postmodern," http://www.library.utoronto.ca/utel/criticism/hutchinp.html, 6 (accessed Aug. 3, 2005). Original emphasis.

126. Richard Ohmann, *Politics and Letters* (Middletown, CT: Wesleyan University Press, 1987), 91.

127. Eco, "Innovation and Repetition," 179.

128. The spectacle is a field of representation; the engagement with this field engenders a form of consciousness discussed by numerous writers since the interest in new media studies. See, for example, Lev Manovich, *The Language of New Media* (Cambridge, MA: Massachusetts Institute of Technology, 2001), 27–55; for a discussion of a new media culture indebted to Debord, see Douglas Kellner, "Media Culture and the Triumph of the Spectacle," in *The Spectacle of the Real*, ed. Geoff King (Bristol, UK: Intellect Books, 2005), 23–36.

129. Manovich, *The Language of New Media*, 333.

130. Noël Carroll, "The Power of Movies," *Daedalus* 114, no. 4 (1985), 80.

131. Carroll, "The Power of the Movies," 81.

132. Eco, "Innovation and Repetition," 184.

133. Darley, 190.

134. Darley, 179.

135. John H. Richardson, "Dumb and Dumber," *The New Republic*, Apr. 10 1995, 20.

136. Linda Hutcheon, "Irony, Nostalgia and the Postmodern," 4.

137. Richardson, 21.

138. For a discussion of the importance of the action spectacle to contemporary popular audiences, see José Arroyo, "Introduction," in *Action/Spectacle Cinema: A Sight and Sound Reader*, ed. José Arroyo (London: British Film Institute, 2000), xiv.

139. Darley, 52.

140. Aylish Wood, "The Collapse of Reality and Illusion in *The Matrix*," in *Action and Adventure Cinema*, ed. Yvonne Tasker (New York: Routledge, 2004), 121.

141. For principle storyboard art (Steve Skroce and Tani Kunitake) and conceptual art (Geoff Darrow) for *The Matrix*, see Spenser Lamm (ed.), *The Art of* The Matrix (London: Titan Books, 2000).

3

Text and Spectacle in *The Matrix* Franchise

Conceptualizing the Spectacle Aesthetic

Understood in its totality, the spectacle is both the outcome and the goal of the dominant mode of production. It is not something *added* to the real world—not a decorative element, so to speak. On the contrary, it is the very heart of society's real unreality. In all its specific manifestations—news or propaganda, advertising or the actual consumption of entertainment—the spectacle epitomizes the prevailing mode of social life.[1]

Some of my favorite films are made entirely of clichés: *Casablanca, Every Which Way But Loose, The Prisoner of Zenda*. They're clichés, yes, but they have broken free of that problem, because the clichés slide through the narrative at refreshing orthogonal angles. . . . *The Matrix* is a postmodern philosophical movie in which fragments of *philosophy* do this *Casablanca* cliché dance.[2]

I think that in order to transform a work into a cult object, one must be able to break, dislocate, unhinge it so that one can remember only parts of it, irrespective of their original relationship with the whole.[3]

For Eco, cult status and cultural authenticity are not mutually exclusive or contradictory in some sense. Cult cinema (and its impact on what he calls the "cult culture") indicates the great journey culture has undertaken to recuperate some notion of its so-called lost authenticity. For Benjamin, "the uniqueness of a work of art is inseparable from its being imbedded in the fabric of tradition" which finds its "expression in the cult."[4] This chapter is an attempt to draw on Eco's aesthetics of a cult culture to develop the notion of the spectacle as dominant in contemporary popular cinema. Eco speaks more directly and urgently to a popular sensibility in which the authenticity of the traditional cult expression (aura) is appropriated into a plethora of intertextual quotations—a functional metatextuality.

Chapters One and Two theorized a departure from a conventional cinematic realism and the corollary transformations in the cultural sphere. Chapters Three and Four present the various manifestations of the intertextual, hyperreal, discursive, hypermythological, and metacinematic—in short, the triumph of the spectacle aesthetic.

Rather than a purely visual sensibility, the spectacle aesthetic is founded on what I have introduced and will develop in this chapter as textual and cultural "discursivity"; a cultural predisposition that "sifts" the spectacle from story, plot, character, and theme. The spectacle is ultimately the only means of establishing authenticity in postmodern cinema. While traditional elements of the text are maintained, and are indeed crucial to any reception of mainstream film, the dominance of the spectacle has reorganized the relation between realism and its representation on the screen. I suggest also that the triumph of the spectacle aesthetic requires a transformation in the ontology of the traditional film or cultural theorist, a notion I will explore at some length. I focus primarily on a reading of several mythological structures in *The Matrix* franchise. However, I conclude the chapter with a discussion of various alternatives to Bazin's realist image strategies of classical cinema, drawing on the advent of digital cinema and, more specifically, what I term the "ontology of bullet-time."

Further Musings on Authenticity and the Spectacle

Contemporary theory presents a challenge to textual analysis; the endeavor to analyze text in the traditional way, as Barthes has argued, is anachronistic.[5] Rather, in a standard post-structuralist substitution for interpretation, one "plays" the text. But even playing an open-ended text is not perfectly satisfactory, fraught as it is with open-ended meanings and post-structuralism's perpetual displacement of signifiers. The open-ended text is useful in demystifying the traditional bourgeois subject, and thus the author, to affirm which "is to impose a limit on that text, to furnish it with a final signified, to close the writing."[6] But without authors and conclusive meanings, the reader (and spectator) is dissociated from the meaning-making process. In being fully liberated, born anew as the reader,[7] the subject realizes that perfect liberation is akin to perfect stagnation. This is the kind of stagnation Shohat and

Stam perceive in post-structuralist discourse: "Post-structuralist theory reminds us that we live and dwell within language and representation, and have no direct access to the 'real.' But the constructed, coded nature of artistic discourse hardly precludes all reference to a common social life."[8] In Chapter Two, my analysis of Jameson's position was founded on his recuperation of the authorial and evaluative eye (a nostalgia for a lost realism and, despite his occasional arguments to the contrary, modernism), and the reinstatement of critical distance. The cloying paradox for Jameson lies in his pronouncement of the dissolution of critical distance while accepting that this pronouncement is made from beyond the same critical distance he has dissolved.

I suggest that popular culture requires a transformation in the theorist's sensibility (or ontology, which is nearer to the nature of the transformation that is required). It has always been perfectly acceptable to address Shakespeare's works as a benchmark in humanist art, and equally as representing the inception of a "modern" aesthetic.[9] The same can be said for the literary canon, though this distinction has more recently been shown to be problematic.[10] I argue that a problem endemic to critical theory is not only *how* to read popular culture (that is, whether to privilege the ideological/structural over the affective/aesthetic), but even more critically, where to locate the cultural coordinates in which the theorist must position herself. In a superb piece about the youth response to George Lucas's *Star Wars, Episode 1: The Phantom Menace*, Tara Brabazon describes this deficiency in the influential Birmingham School of cultural studies:

> Cultural studies theorists carry the baggage of the Birmingham Centre into any history of youth culture. The taken-for-granted "youth as resistance" mantra, embodied in *Resistance Through Rituals* (Hall & Jefferson, 1976) and *Subculture: The Meaning of Style* (Hebdige, 1979), transformed young people into the ventriloquist's puppet of cultural studies.[11]

While Brabazon does not explicitly address the position of the theorist in relation to the "culture of resistance," her argument is founded on this perceived lack of communication, or disparity, between the theorist and the individual (and collective) subjectivity of popular culture. For example, Hebdige considers the aesthetics of punk, among other things, as a ritualized, though strategic, resistance to hegemony, suggesting that to classify subcultural production as "high art" is to miss the point: "Subcultures are not 'cultural' in this sense, and the styles with which they are identified cannot be adequately or usefully described as 'art of a high degree.' Rather, they manifest culture in the broader sense."[12] Hall perceives something very similar for the project of popular culture: "Popular culture is one of the sites where this struggle for and against a culture of the powerful is engaged. . . . It is not a sphere where socialism, a socialist culture—already fully formed—might be simply expressed. But it is one of the places where socialism might be constituted. That is why popular culture matters. Otherwise, to tell you the truth, I don't give a damn about it."[13]

But to whom does popular culture matter in this way? If Hebdige can be accorded some latitude in constructing an aesthetics of punk as resistance to hegemony (a resistance which, in any case, is limited), Hall's popular culture as a mechanism for socialist change misses the point entirely. Most popular culture is not practiced in service of an emancipation project conceived by intellectual theory. In this sense, I concur with Felski that "the problem with literature departments . . . is not that they study literature, but that they often see themselves as having a monopoly on what counts as aesthetic experience."[14] For Hebdige and Hall, the aesthetic of high culture is exchanged for a social and political theory of the popular. For aesthetic beauty and truth, literary and cultural theorists rarely look to popular art forms.

Brabazon suggests that "to discuss a Lucasfilm's conspiracy of slick marketing is to completely misread the event. The uncomfortable recognition that too many journalists seem unable to grasp is that millions of men and women possess an emotional investment in this film."[15] I would argue that Brabazon's journalists and the majority of film theorists could be classified in much the same way. The contemporary film theorist struggles not only to make sense of *what* popular cinema means to its audience, but *how* this product makes its meaning. Recall Lawrence and Jewett's reading of a "quotation" of Riefenstahl's *Triumph of the Will* in the last scene of *Star Wars*. The authors suggest this quote reflects the film's fascist tendencies. I argue that this is a categorical misreading based on a failure to appreciate the way popular cinema is composed of prior myths and texts, and the way it addresses its spectator. Even if the authors wish to argue that Lucas is a closet fascist, the Riefenstahl quotation is not satisfactory textual evidence.

Conceptualizing this disparity in affective (and indeed, critical) distance between the theorist and the popular culture spectator is increasingly difficult because of what I have described as the inherent discursivity of popular culture. Redressing this disparity must be done in a series of tentative gestures. One such gesture that reverberates *within* popular culture is Brabazon's confession that popular cinema has a powerful personal appeal and a currency that demands critical attention. The anecdotal (and confessional) opening to her piece is disarmingly real:

> A few Saturdays ago, my 71-year-old father tried to convince me of imminent responsibilities. As I am considering the purchase of a house, there are mortgages, bank fees, and years of misery to endure. Unfortunately, I am not an effective Big Picture Person. The lure of the light saber is almost too great. For 30 year old Generation-Xers like myself, it is more than a cultural object. It is a textual anchor, and a necessary component to any future history of the present.[16]

While *The Phantom Menace* does not have quite the same appeal for me, I confess that I have a thousand such "textual anchors" to popular culture, and few are founded on a personal or collective project of resistance to a hegemony. Following Brabazon's lead, then, I will approach popular cinema as a subject immersed in its textual, mythological, and cultural strategies, acknowledging that this culture exists as a system of meanings of which I am an integral part. I am not privileged with Jameson's critical distance to assess the relative advantages or disadvantages of this position. I accept that culture is suffused with a plethora of ideological positions actively engaged with my own response as theorist, spectator, and consumer. But though I may locate myself in opposition to these ideologies, I am in much the same position as John Gaeta, who claims (futilely) that the desecration of a Warner Bros. logo enacts a rejection of the studio system by the creative and artistic minds under their control. As I have argued, the transposition of this symbol as ideology is mediated by several strata of cultural meanings, and conceivably affirms the pervasiveness of the studio system. It is what Fiske might call the *incorporation* rather than the *excorporation* of the symbolic logo, ultimately leaving the hands (and corporate minds) of the studio executive, destined to return to its ideological point of inception after a circuitous textual route. The fact that Tom Cruise can demand 25 million dollars in a 150-million-dollar studio production because he constitutes a product for consumption in the marketplace (and is thus deserving of the fee—economic rationalism has always been the cornerstone of the Hollywood star system) seems absurd. And yet as a spectator I am immersed in the performance of the star system, which is only one corollary of the studio system that has dominated Hollywood since the 1930s. Popular audiences are emotionally and psychically invested in the "spectacle" persona of a Tom Cruise or Angelina Jolie. The spectacle aesthetic requires iconic stars to function affectively; iconicity requires consumptive leverage in the marketplace. How else can one explain the fascination with "Hollywood's Hundred Richest" lists except by attaching the icon to its consumptive value? This is to say, simply, that Tom Cruise is not Tom Cruise without the eight-figure salary freely available as information (merely another means of consumption) to the interested consumer. Butler is correct to suggest that

> the star's *image* dominates movie posters and appears on dozens of magazine covers; it is clearly one of the principal commodities that is used to market a film to an audience—equal in importance, in the minds of film producers and film viewers alike, to a compelling story or majestic scenery or a trendy director.[17]

But while trendy directors occasionally have an art-house hit that pleases the studio (*Reservoir Dogs* [Tarantino], *Sex, Lies and Videotape* [Soderberg], *Eternal Sunshine of the Spotless Mind* [Gondry/Kaufman]), Leonardo Di Caprio can bolster what is in my opinion a turgid romantic melodrama (*Titanic*) into a billion-dollar economic franchise.

Gabriel's celebration of the political aesthetic of Third World Cinema and his critique of mainstream Hollywood, in these terms in which "consumption can be its own aesthetic reward,"[18] is absurd. I cannot fathom a way in which Third World Cinema offers an alternative yet viable aesthetic in the cultural arena without altering the economic and social fabric of that arena. Of course, for Gabriel (as for Jameson, Hall, and Hebdige), such an alteration is precisely what is required to find something of aesthetic worth; but this approach will always be profoundly limited, even self-defeating. I do not wish to reject the ideological nature of the arena in which this affectivity is expressed, but to suggest that ideological analyses divorced from the affective are conceptually simplistic and generalized. This kind of analysis often results in theory prescribing the analysis of texts, which occurs frequently in psychoanalytic readings of popular cinema[19] or so-called scientific studies of the impact of cinematic violence on the spectator.[20]

A Brief Note on (Mis)Reading Cinema

What I am suggesting is a return to the screen as a spectator (whether a television, movie theater, computer monitor, or some other site of representation) as the initial point of contact between film and theory. In a piece devoted to the study of the serial killer sub-genre, Barry Keith Grant suggests that "the structural repetitions inherent in the act of serial killing seem to echo the repetition compulsion in our own intensive consumption of narratives about it."[21] Preceding this paragraph, Grant opens his piece with the claim that "Jonathan Demme's *Silence of the Lambs* won several Academy Awards and brought serial killing squarely into the mainstream. In short, as Martin Rubin has noted, fin-de-siècle America seems especially obsessed with the figure of the modern multiple murderer."[22] The implication is that *Silence of the Lambs* constitutes a phenomenon in the serial killer sub-genre, conforming to a general narrative structure (a killer stalking and then killing women) as well as the more recent "repetition compulsion" of popular society. But if Grant looked closely at *Silence of the Lambs*, he would notice that all the female victims are killed *before the film begins* (they are literally back-story—Catherine Martin is abducted but rescued by Clarice Starling [Jodie Foster]), that violence is implicit rather than overt (the act of violence is almost never shown; rather the film seems interested in the image of the *consequence* of graphic violence), and that serial killer films such as Michael Mann's *Manhunter*, Demme's *Silence of the Lambs*, or even Powell's earlier *Peeping Tom* do not instantiate a new approach to violence that is pervasive, or even broad-based.

It is astonishing that Grant can make a claim such as: "The scene in *Pulp Fiction* (1994) where two hapless hit men must deal with the splattered blood and brains of their dead hostage Marvin demonstrates that we are more likely to laugh at blood on the upholstery than to be shocked."[23] Surely this oft-discussed scene demonstrates nothing of the kind. On one level, we can say simply that violent acts take their "meaning" from the context in which the violence appears on screen. Marvin's death is funny not because we (whoever "we" are in Grant's analysis) are desensitized to violence *per se*, but because the situation involving Vincent (John Travolta) and Jules (Samuel Jackson) is patently absurd. The humor is created not because the spectator can't appreciate the horrible "reality" of physical violence but because the *situation* constructed by the narrative is overtly humorous. Marvin's death is a brilliant example of postmodern absurdism divorced from the Real. If we contrast Marvin's death with a similar unintentional shooting in *Reservoir Dogs*,[24] it becomes clear that the coding of the violent act on screen is contingent on its narrative context. We can also say that a Jules/Vincent situational absurdism was certainly not the norm in mainstream cinema in 1994 any more than it is in 2006.

Spectacle and Technology

Investigating the spectacle aesthetic requires an alteration in the theorist's ontology. Grant's position on *Silence of the Lambs* is exemplary of a criticism that employs popular art in the service of an ideological agenda without a close analysis of that art. But more significantly, if a response to cinema is indeed fundamentally affective (as I have argued), the analysis must begin precisely by collapsing the critical distance treasured by traditional theory rather than by constructing some ideological project at the outset. Rejecting the Utopian (and equally nostalgic) impulse, as Hutcheon does, makes some headway toward this new ontology. Hutcheon's notion of nostalgia—or in a broader sense, history—in the postmodern world is radical in light of Jameson's rejection of a postmodern historicism. To this, Hutcheon retorts: "The view that postmodernism relegates history to 'the dustbin of an absolute episteme, arguing gleefully that history does not exist except as text' (Huyssen 1981, 35), is simply wrong. History is not made obsolete; it is however being rethought—as a human construct."[25]

Accepting that the plethora of new technologies is a meaningful contribution to—and thus substantial alteration in—the way cinema is viewed and the impact it has on popular audiences is also a crucial step in the process. I disagree with John Belton that digital cinema is a "false revolution" because it can do no more than "elmina[te] jitter, weave, dirt, and scratches from the projected image."[26] Rather, the gradual acceptance of digital cinema, which has come only after a lengthy trial period in the use of special effects, has affirmed the centrality of spectacle cinema to popular culture. In adapting the graphic novels of Dennis Miller, Robert Rodriguez's "digital aesthetic" in *Sin City* is compatible with the hyper-reality of the graphic novel. Rodriguez could have shot *Sin City* on 35mm, but the use of digital technology offers a new kind of cinematic realism.

While Belton is correct to say that digital films do not look substantially different from 35mm, he fails to appreciate the significance of the phenomenon of digital technology as an innovation on, and departure from, the traditions of cinema that preceded it. Discussing influential U.S. critic Roger Ebert, Belton writes that he is "one of the few people speaking out against digital cinema. Ebert's chief objection is that digital projection cannot duplicate the *experience* of 35mm film. In this respect his argument is much subtler than my own."[27] But their respective arguments are less a question of subtlety than conception. For Ebert, the distinction between 35mm and the digitally filmed image is fundamental; Ebert acknowledges a profound disparity between the product of a digital camera and 35mm film stock. One might speak of the "glorious Technicolor" of *Gone with the Wind* as an innovation *toward* realism in the early use of color in the Hollywood studio film (though I would argue that the color saturations of David Lynch and those of *Gone with the Wind* have a great deal in common), and of the washed surfaces of *Sin City* as a deliberate aestheticization of the film image.

The Matrix Phenomenon

Before proceeding, let me say a brief word in defense of *The Matrix* franchise, which is perhaps necessary in light of the largely negative reviews of *The Matrix Reloaded* and *The Matrix Revolutions*.[28] I argue simply that the discursivity of popular culture is reflected in "orthogonal angles" (to use Sterling's interesting phrase describing the use of cliché in cinema) in *The Matrix* franchise. The heteroglossic utterance of a young Aboriginal boy wearing an Eminem tracksuit finds some form of expression in a popular film that traverses Plato, Descartes, Baudrillard, Marxism, late capitalism, the poetics of postmodernism, and a new and interactive media. The additional interpretive frame in which the film (or trilogy) is received by popular culture as a *franchise* is equally significant. The performance of the text does not end when the credits roll. Rather, *The Matrix* finds expression in corporate advertising and product placement (Samsung mobile phones, Energizer batteries); action figures; leather jackets and boots; DVD box sets with additional features; tie-in comic books that delve into the "Zion Archives" (and thus also the textual archive of the franchise); film soundtracks; sound bites on TV advertisements; the console game *Enter The Matrix* (available on PC, Sony PlayStation, and X-Box); the interactive website and associated blogs; the star system (Keanu Reeves, Carrie-Anne Moss, Lawrence Fishburne) and its culture of celebrity; the recuperation of Rage Against the Machine as resistance not to social hegemony in the United States or contemporary late capitalism, but to the Matrix. *The Matrix* franchise is less a cinematic text than a popular culture entity as *Star Wars* once was and is again in the wake of the recent "prequels." On a narrative level, the franchise is incomplete, subject always to revolution: at the end of *The Matrix Revolutions*, the shot immediately after Neo's "death" shows the Matrix rebooting, the simulation reforming, its dialectic opposition to the Real reconstituted. This is what Eco means by repetition, which equates not only to the repeat performances of the serial or soap opera, but to the sophisticated *recycling* of the product in the cultural arena, and the complementary coming to awareness of the cult status of popular culture:

> The required expertise is not only intercinematic, it is intermedia, in the sense that the addressee must know not only other movies but all the mass media gossip about movies. This third example presupposes a "*Casablanca* universe" in which cult has become the normal way of enjoying movies. Thus in this case [the case of *Casablanca*] we witness an instance of metacult, or cult about cult—a Cult Culture.[29]

What is also remarkable about *The Matrix* franchise is its reception in academic and literary (referring to an arena in which literature is discussed, rather than the self-conscious literariness of the *New Yorker* or *McSweeney's*) circles. In addition to its acknowledged status as film and pop cultural phenomenon, "in 2002 no fewer than six full-length scholarly books were published with *The Matrix* as their primary subject matter."[30] Several more have been published since. Cyberpunk aficionados Bruce Sterling and William Gibson have praised the film's technical and thematic richness.[31] Baudrillard, who perceives in *The Matrix* and *The Matrix Reloaded* a conflation of the Platonic illusion and the simulation, has felt the need to forge his own position in relation to the franchise.[32] Esteemed film and literature scholar, Slavoj Žižek, has published a piece postulating the Matrix as "the big Other."[33] Chris Seay has written an entire book describing the essence of *The Matrix* as "belief": "The *Matrix* films call us to a spiritual life beyond simple cause and effect, beyond what can be measured by our senses, sometimes even beyond what makes sense."[34] Andrew Gordon suggests that "*The Matrix*, like the *Star Wars* and the *Star Trek* series, has spawned dozens of articles and even a few college courses exploring its philosophical, religious and scientific dimensions. A science-fiction film like *The Terminator*, with similar action and complex themes, did no such thing."[35]

I employ *The Matrix* franchise in this chapter as the nearest approximation to the performance of the spectacle aesthetic. The text of the franchise functions as a self-aware exploration of the postmodern consciousness, schizophrenic and fragmentary, vacillating between political and social conservatism and romantic radicalism, realist authenticity, and simulacral reproduction—in short, a variation on what Baudrillard has called the hyperreality, or Collins the "hyperconsciousness," of the postmodern spectator.

Toward a Notion of Textual Discursivity

I argue that the notion of discursivity to which I alluded in Chapter Two is necessary to traverse the gulf that separates theory *about* popular culture and the consumption experience of *partaking* of that culture. Partaking of culture is, as Brabazon says, "an emotional investment."[36] Culture is constituted by a process in which texts affect the spectator; it is less a system of signs that cohere as meaning than a site of interaction, or *engagement*, with the text. Simply put, what films, books, or comic strips *mean* is only one component of the way they are consumed.

To experience the text, I argue that the spectator must appreciate it as a reproduction, or simulation, of prior textual forms. This is perhaps the most crucial aspect of the spectacle aesthetic, and it is what makes discursivity central to any notion of contemporary cinematic culture. Whereas Barthes's distinction between the Text and Work offers something very similar about the incompletion of the Text and the finitude of its production in the Work,[37] Barthes was not writing about a filmic franchise that acknowledges its status as "already reproduced," or what I have referred to as nonauthentic. In a very real sense, *The Matrix* is a film about the perpetual displacement of textual authenticity. "What is Real?" in the franchise reverb is just as easily "What is the Real interpretation?" for the spectator. The franchise offers an investigation of how the postmodern spectator might discover an aesthetic value in a text that practices a revision of such values. Ultimately, what *The Matrix* franchise means is contingent on how the spectacle aesthetic makes meaning.

The spectacle aesthetic appreciates textual meaning as "displaced," or perhaps more correctly, it appreciates text as a site of "displaced meaning." The spectator experiences what Bauman calls "ambivalence" to the text.[38] While several theorists have posited a traditional "grand narrative" of *The Matrix* franchise,[39] I argue that the franchise embodies an aesthetic in which various grand narratives are reconstituted as simulacral tropes, or cinematic quotations. This aesthetic is necessarily one in which the text is reconstituted through spectator engagement with it as a commodity in the market. I have termed this notion of engagement "consumption."

Discursivity is essentially a cultural aesthetic. This formulation is indebted to Jameson's notion of postmodernism as a cultural aesthetic. Postmodernism is for Jameson more than a system of ideas, or an adjunct to poststructuralist discourse. It is rather a sense of individual and collective cultural "being," incorporating art, values, and ideals that are coherent only in the late capitalistic market. Discursivity, in my usage, connotes something similar, a cultural aesthetic rather than a singular practice or process, but without the pejorative slant. The necessary abstraction of discursivity is something akin to Barthes's distinction between the Text and a Work in which the Text *decants* the Work. For Barthes, the Text is discursive and unfinished, the Work its tactile expression, perhaps a volume in a library: "*The Text is experienced only in an activity of production*. It follows that the Text cannot stop (for example, on a library shelf); its constitutive movement is that of cutting across (in particular, it can cut across the work, several works)."[40] For Barthes, the Text is engaged in a process of displacement; it cannot be read because it is engaged in an open-ended itinerary.

Hall says something similar about the "textuality" of cultural theory. This is why the cultural theorist cannot posit a "theory" without having an awareness of its immersion in "theoretical legacies,"[41] and without being suspicious of its veracity in relation to a real, living culture. Theory is equally commentary and an inscription of something altogether new. For Hall, theory is implicated in the pluralism of the Text, being itself subject to plurality and open-ended meanings; thus, negotiating the plurality of the Text and the politics of cultural theory is a very real and necessary tension.

A notion of Barthes's Text is necessary to conceptualize the Work. It is possible in this sense to say that a discursive culture decants its subjective expression. The Text decants a closed interpretation, but its discursivity remains intact. For Barthes, this is a textual reality, a veritable life of the Text. I argue that *The Matrix* franchise performs this abstract relationship between the Barthesian Text and Work.

It should be said here that the distinction between the Text and the Work is hardly new; it is perhaps the foundation of post-structuralism. Culture, in fashionable theoretical models, is a site in which "science, for all one knows and can know, is one story among many."[42] For Barthes, the distinction is crucial precisely because it recuperates some notion of the authenticity in the contemporary work: "In particular, the tendency must be avoided to say that the Work is classic, the text avant-garde; it is not a question of drawing up a crude honours list in the name of modernity and declaring certain literary productions 'in' and others 'out' by virtue of their chronological situation."[43] For Barthes, the Work that is decanted from the Text is an authentic cultural artifact.

However, acknowledging a relationship between textual discursivity and a subjective interpretation does not assist in understanding *how* the textuality of a film franchise impacts on the spectator. Knowing that a story is merely *one story* seems inadequate as a way of understanding how postmodern culture, or a new aesthetics of spectacle cinema, might work. Knowing the limitations of the discursive text in abstract theoretical terms is perfectly feasible. We can agree that Text is "open," or that it "cuts across" the Work, laying bare a plethora of interpretive positions. But how do spectators continue to engage with a spectacle cinema that is no longer an authentic (or classic) art form? In the Barthesian model, what stands in for authenticity?

Intertextuality and Discursivity

In response to the challenge of the pervasiveness of intertextuality in popular culture, Eco suggests that popular cinema must compensate for the consumer who cannot recognize the cinematic quotation.[44] If one criterion of Eco's cult cinema is intertextuality, the spectator oblivious to the cinematic quotation must find some other aesthetic charge. But between the spectator who recognizes the quotation and the spectator who remains ignorant, there is surely a vast array of interpretive positions. Compensation for the "ignorant spectator" does not equate with an understanding of the way cinematic quotations impact on an audience. Eco merely assumes that some will "get the message" while others will miss it. He assumes also that there is a single message to get, which it seems to me is not the case.

How can the theorist be sure that the discursive textuality of *The Matrix* franchise is appreciated, or even dimly recognized, by the spectator? To some spectators, a first viewing of *The Matrix* might "give up" its intertextual debts to Sergio Leone or James Cameron's *The Terminator* and *Aliens*. But it is left to the theorist to speculate about the reverberation of these quotations on a culture at large. This is where the analysis invariably suffers, because intertextuality, contrary to Jameson's belief that "it seems at best to designate a problem rather than a solution"[45] (and can therefore be disregarded altogether), is perhaps the most fundamental component of the spectacle aesthetic. Film theorists must appreciate how popular texts function as *Text* in a discursive culture; how the Text is read, and by whom. Popular cinema audiences are resistant (or oblivious) to theory and the intellectualizing of popular art. In the popular culture sphere, theory is hardly necessary for the majority of spectators to engage with mainstream cinema. I would also argue that theorists are largely oblivious to the mainstream response to popular cinema. To my knowledge, very little work has been done to actively investigate the impact of intertextuality on film audiences, particularly at cinema multiplexes where the box office takings first register. This is precisely why Chris Rock's interviews conducted at a multiplex in Los Angeles are something truly innovative and increasingly necessary.

To speculate on the relationship between the discursive culture and the response to the intertextuality of a film franchise, the theorist must attempt, first and foremost, to speak for herself as *incorporating* (in the Fiskian sense of the incorporation of the commodity) this cultural discursivity, embodying all modes of thought, all ideological utterances, and a comprehensive version of what Eco calls the "encyclopedia" of the spectator.[46] (Of course, the imaginary encyclopedia can never be comprehensive, but the belief in its comprehensiveness is necessary for an appreciation of the intertextual utterance.) The theorist must address the text with an inherent "full" awareness of its strategies and impact on the audience. While this is in one sense perfectly obvious, this approach serves to shrink the critical and affective distance between the theorist and the imaginary spectator. The theorist is thus implicated in the nonauthentic culture, simultaneously theorist, spectator, and consumer; there must be a sense in which the theorist and the consumer share a "collective consciousness."

What is crucial in this "speaking for oneself" is the positioning of the theorist *within* popular culture. The theorist is simultaneously aware of the text as ideological utterance *and* incorporated commodity. This is essentially what Eco means by the Cult Culture, which is maintained only through the collapse of the distinction between high and low culture, and more specifically in this argument, theory and spectacle. Eco's formulation is a significant advance on Jameson's notion of a postmodern culture described in Chapter Two. For Jameson, such a transformation is a diminishment of an earlier aesthetic system. While he describes postmodernism as having collapsed this critical distance through the convergence of high and low art, the inherent nostalgia of his position reinscribes the critical distance into his paradigm. While he argues for the loss of critical distance, his mode and strategy of argumentation is founded precisely on the critical distance he claims has vanished. In this model, the theorist is doomed to observe (and abstractly theorize) culture from beyond its borders—from a perceived cultural fringe that resists commodification. This is precisely the approach to culture and cinema that must cease to function as having a monopoly on authenticity.

Eco distinguishes between two forms of quotation in popular cinema, one of which "the author is aware but that should remain ungraspable by the consumer," and the other occurring when the quotation "is explicit and recognizable, as happens in literature or post-modern art, which blatantly and ironically play on intertextuality."[47] The deliberate intertextual text for Eco is something akin to Kevin Williamson's *Scream*, in which the film's narrative functions as a commentary on the horror or, more specifically, the slasher film genre. The intertextual quotation is foregrounded and explicit. The conventions of the genre dictate—and indeed *construct*—the course of the narrative: "Only virgins survive horror films" dictates that the chaste and morally worthy Sidney (Neve Campbell) will survive the film, while the flirtatious (and, we assume, promiscuous) Casey (Drew Barrymore) is disemboweled in the opening set piece. In another scene, a janitor (played by Wes Craven, director of both *Scream* and *A Nightmare on Elm Street*) clad in Freddy Kruger's tattered clothes, mops a bathroom floor.

Eco argues that this form of intertextuality is typical of postmodern textual practices, and he is no doubt correct. He suggests, for example, that the scene in Spielberg's *Raiders of the Lost Ark* in which Indiana Jones is confronted with a "giant Arab" engages with "original *topoi*. In the case of the giant, it is a situation typical of the genre."[48] "In both cases the topoi are recorded by the 'encyclopedia' of the spectator; they make up part of the collective imagination and as such they come to be called upon."[49] What we should bear in mind here is the intriguing notion not of a single but a *collective* imagination, which is intrinsic to the performance of intertextuality in cinema.

What interests Eco less is "stylistic quotation, in those cases in which a text quotes, in a more or less explicit way, a stylistic feature, a way of narrating typical of another author."[50] However, in so doing, I feel that Eco underestimates the pervasiveness of intertextuality in popular film. I would argue that stylistic quotation is often no less intended nor less explicit than Eco's notion of a literal "play on intertextuality." One could consider Scott's *Blade Runner* as a stylistic cinematic quotation from beginning to end, visually and aurally recuperating *film noir*, cyberpunk, and European existentialism. The stylistic quotation becomes literal, for example, in the use of the Millennium Falcon set (of *Star Wars*) in several interior shots of *Blade Runner*. Fincher's *Se7en* establishes its lineage to classical *film noir* in a number of stylistic tropes: wet streets, low lighting, low camera angles. It is not as explicit as Jean-Paul Belmondo's (*Breathless*) fidgeting with his earlobe to recall Bogart's Phillip Marlowe in *The Big Sleep*, but the issue of the relation between an intertextual stylistics of cinema seems to me as vital, if not more vital, than the traditional (literally inscribed) intertextuality that Eco has so thoroughly explored.[51] It is this stylistic intertextuality that is most obviously compatible with the spectacle aesthetic and finds unique expression in *The Matrix* franchise. The opening sequence of *The Matrix* establishes an intertextual reference frame to classical *film noir*, yet the green color tinge over the image recalls the hard chromatic visuals of a cyberpunk world. The stylized dress (notably Trinity's black leather outfit and pale features) establishes a broader stylistic (and intertextual *mise en scène*) of neo-Gothicism and cyborg androgyny. These "quotations" are in every sense stylistic rather than literal. It is this stylistic intertext that establishes the cinematic text as a quotation drawing on Eco's encyclopedia of references.

In assessing the impact of intertextuality in the consumption of film, whether it is in the form of subtle stylistic quotation (*Se7en*) or an explicit textual reference (*Scream*[52]), it is necessary to distinguish between the "potentialities" and the "actualities" of spectator response. In coming to terms with popular cinema franchises and the spectacle aesthetic, surely the most pressing question must be: Exactly *how* is a discursive text received by its audience?

Although I will return to a close analysis of the film, for the moment let us consider the sequence in *The Matrix* in which Neo is reborn. Recall that the Matrix is a cyberspace, modeled on our contemporary world, that can be entered, negotiated, and lived within. The human mind "jacks" into the Matrix (the subjective consciousness is literally downloaded into the computer-generated simulation), leaving the body behind, docile, ineffectual, and obsolete. For those of humanity (indeed, the multitude imprisoned in "fields of pods") living inside the Matrix, "the Matrix is [literally] everywhere. . . . You can see it out your window or on your television. You feel it when you go to work, or go to church or pay your taxes." Prior to Neo's death and rebirth, the Neo of the Real is seated in a chair on board the Nebuchadnezzar, jacked in to the Matrix; the Neo of the Matrix, clad in black coat and leather boots, is killed by Agent Smith in the Heart of the City Hotel. These two actions take place simultaneously. Death in the Matrix is contiguous with death in the Real. In assessing potential and actual responses to the film's intertextual fabric, I want to consider the impetus for Neo's resurrection. Precisely what brings him back to life?

According to Eco's model, this sequence fits into the "explicit and recognisable" quotation.[53] A number of intertextualities imbue Neo's death and resurrection with an extratextual knowledge.[54] The sequence is connected to an encyclopedia of cinematic references that have accrued up to this point in the film: *Vertigo* (the medium shot of Trinity pursued over a rooftop), *The Terminator* (the image of an agent landing on a rooftop in the same pose as the Terminator when he materializes in the present), a face-off in a subway station reminiscent of Leone's *Fistful of Dollars* or Woo's *Bullet in the Head*, *film noir* (stylistic), classical Hollywood melodrama (stylistic), cyberpunk and postmodern apocalyptism (stylistic). While Eco argues of *Raiders of the Lost Ark* that "there remain plenty of possibilities for the naïve spectator, who at least can always enjoy the fact that the hero gets the best of his adversary," this sequence in *The Matrix* requires the spectator to appreciate the network of textual references (or at least a healthy proportion of them) to make sense of a critical moment in its plot: the resurrection of the hero. The narrative cannot explain the resurrection of the One without recourse to a stream of textual quotation.

The resurrection partakes of the narrative of the death and resurrection of Christ. The textual precursor (the Christian narrative) is a license to transgress what the audience expects. Reality (even the "reality" of the Matrix) dictates that Neo is dead, destroyed finally by his nemesis, Smith. While the Matrix is a simulation, it is still subject to the rules of an external reality. Nothing in the film thus far has permitted the resurrection of Neo. Morpheus is explicit on the point that death in the Matrix is contiguous with death of the mind and the material body. Therefore, the quotation of the resurrection of Christ is necessary to transgress the cinematic boundaries of a conventional cinematic realism. Rather than an explicit quotation, the Christian mythical frame functions as a separate stratum of meaning altogether.

After Neo's death, Trinity leans over Neo's lifeless corpse and murmurs: "Neo, I'm not afraid anymore. The Oracle told me that I would fall in love, and that that man, the man I loved, would be the One. So you see, you can't be dead. You can't be . . . because I love you. You hear me . . . I love you." She kisses him as the sparks from the acetylene torches of the sentinels rain over the ship in an ethereal fireworks display. A romantic theme rises as Trinity says: "Now get up." Neo's life returns with the sound of a heartbeat on a monitor. The scene cuts to the Matrix as Neo is "reborn," then cuts back to the Real as Morpheus (in close-up) says: "He is the One." There is a final cut to the Real, where a generic religious score rises and Neo confronts Agent Smith in a corridor of the Heart of the City Hotel.

The significance of the two pieces of music is crucial as an indication of two separate intertextual streams that permit the resurrection of the One.

The Christian narrative constitutes one stream, the classic Hollywood romance constitutes the other. The spectator/theorist is something of an intertextual "spotter." The kiss of life is no doubt immediately recognized by some spectators as a recuperation of the *Sleeping Beauty* story. In this case, the gender roles are reversed. Neo is rescued from an archaic form of religious martyrdom and brought back to life; Trinity is the agent of this rescue operation. (Of course, in the broader scheme of the narrative, the male ultimately rescues the female [insofar as Neo rescues all of humanity], and Neo does in fact bring Trinity to life at the end of *The Matrix Reloaded*.[55]) Unlike the specifically intended quotation, these two levels of intertextual meaning are as central to the narrative as the storyline: Neo *needs* to be Christ for the resurrection to take. The superhero, alienated youth, anonymous monomythic quester, must make room for the Christian referential frame. But he must simultaneously take his position as the sleeping "Prince," awakened by the kiss of a knight in shining armor (who wears Spartan clothes in the Real and black leather in the Matrix), Trinity. The One is thus resurrected through two separate though simultaneously functioning referential frames. Within the levels of meaning are specific intertextual quotations that inform the whole. Thus, the sparks from the sentinel's acetylene torches constructs on one level a generic romance scene in which love is confessed and requited.[56] On another level, the ethereal light shower recalls specific cinematic romances back-dropped by fireworks, such as the scene in which Grace Kelly and Cary Grant kiss in Hitchcock's *To Catch a Thief*. I am not suggesting here that the Wachowski Brothers contemplated this sequence as a quotation of Hitchcock's film (though this may very well be the case). Rather, it is born of a wellspring of cinematic references, Eco's collective encyclopedia. Similarly, at the film's conclusion, I cannot say that the newspaper that flutters across the deserted train station like tumbleweed recalls Leone's theatrical precursor to a duel in *Once Upon a Time in the West*, yet the "quotation," less than explicit on screen, is no less potent as textual performance.

The potential responses to this sequence can surely not equate with the dominant subjective response in mainstream popular culture. How much of this sophisticated intertextual network is consumed by the spectator? I perceive three potentialities. Perhaps the "naïve spectator" does not appreciate either of the intertextual levels of meaning: Neo as the resurrected Christ or Neo/Trinity as Sleeping Beauty/knight in shining armor (and the corollary Neo/Trinity as Hollywood romance). This spectator does not pause to reflect on the conspicuous use of an extreme close-up on Trinity's face during her speech. The close-up and extreme shallow focus give the fireworks a benignly ethereal quality (the spectator thus holds two separate symbolic images simultaneously: hostile acety-lene torches, ethereal shower prefiguring the "consummation" of love). It appears as if the sparks are descending to the floor in a dreamlike slow-motion, but it is merely a contrivance of the close-up and focal length. In this case, what is *not* central to the shot is indeed as crucial to its meaning as what is. This spectator does not immediately connect the resurrection of Neo with the resurrection of Christ, nor the kiss of life. Perhaps for this spectator, it is merely enough that Morpheus's unfailing belief in the One and his incredulous murmur, "It can't be," are enough to authorize the resurrection.

Another spectator perhaps recognizes the intertextual quotation, both in specific form and in the broader textual scheme: Christian death and resurrection, Sleeping Beauty brought back to life. The quotation is aesthetically charged and permits the spectator to reflect on her own awareness of its textual sophistication. The quotation also permits the resurrection and thus furnishes a credible conclusion to the narrative. For this spectator, the resurrection is not only permitted, but a sophisti-cated method of advancing the narrative and bringing the story to a point of closure (the two sequels were not originally intended).

A third spectator recognizes the quotation, the two levels of mean-ing that furnish the narrative with a conclusion, but *also* an inherent intertextuality of the sequence as narrative, image, trope, motif, and symbol—a *metatextuality*. This spectator considers the implication of the sequence as "pure" intertext, and its inherent discursivity: that is, as drawing upon an encyclopedia of textual references of which her own set is merely a component. This spectator appreciates that an intertextual stylistics is operating alongside Eco's explicit quotations—for example, the filter that provides a green tinge to the sequences in the Matrix recalls the use of a yellow filter in Polanski's *Chinatown* (which in turn recalls the sepia/nostalgized color tones of a "cinematic" representation of the 1930s)—which in turn operates in accordance with plot, character, and theme. Intertextual quotation operates upon the "interior" coherence of the work.[57]

I am not suggesting that *The Matrix* is beyond any concrete interpre-tation because of its intertextuality. I am not arguing for a reversion to infinite pluralism and the uninterpretability of all texts. Popular culture texts (and certainly *The Matrix* franchise) are profoundly *engaging*; the spectator is involved in forging a meaning out of its intertextuality. But an awareness of the possibilities of its intertextual frames of meaning reveals its inherent discursivity. There is no "authentic" (or literal) reading of

Neo's resurrection; the literature published on the franchise has certainly not arrived at such a consensus.

Theory, in applying a methodology to an investigation of popular culture, must engage with the phenomenon of intertextuality and its challenge to traditional modes of interpretation. This is equally a strategy of abstract theorizing and an empirical study of audience response to popular culture, which is only now being seriously investigated as a component of cultural theory and/or film studies.[58] I have not attempted here to provide a theoretical model that provides a solution to the challenge of intertextuality, which is, as Jameson acknowledges, a very real problem to current and future investigations of popular culture. As Eco suggests, the contemporary spectator (or better still, theorist/spectator) draws on a wealth of cinematic references and simultaneously, and as significantly, on a range of mass (and other) media that commentates on cinema and culture. The spectator/theorist is thus immersed in a spectacle that recycles prior textual modes (but in which cinema is indisputably the dominant), forming its own discursivity while aware of (or naïve to) the inherent discursivity of popular cinema. Yet I concur with Eco that the textual "awareness" of audiences, and the consequent challenge to traditional hermeneutics, is ever more apparent: "It will be a sad day when a too smart audience will read *Casablanca* as conceived by Michael Curtiz after having read Calvino and Barthes. But that day will come. Perhaps we have been able to discover here, for the last time, the Truth."[59]

The discursivity of text is manifested in *The Matrix* franchise as a metatextuality. *The Matrix* is about the performance of the Text; but it is equally a performance of this vital new aesthetic. The franchise foregrounds its immersion in prior texts, prior cinematic *mise en scène*, realizing a spectacle that comprises a popular "consciousness" rather than an interpretive "mind." For contemporary popular culture, perhaps Calvino and Barthes are only vaguely felt, if at all—*If on a Winter's Night, a Traveller* is hardly the same publishing phenomenon as *Harry Potter*. But perhaps J. K. Rowling's intertextual universe can substitute just as easily for Calvino's, albeit without the degree of authorial awareness of the theoretical implications of intertextuality. Equally, one does not need Roland Barthes to appreciate that the integrity of "The Real" is being challenged in *The Matrix*.

Myth and Text in *The Matrix* Franchise: Gorging on the Sacred Past

But, whether true or false, my opinion is that in the world of knowledge the idea of good appears last of all, and is seen only with an effort; and, when seen, is also inferred to be the universal author of all things beautiful and right . . . and the immediate source of reason and truth in the intellectual.[60]

However it be defined, contemporary literary interest in myth indicates an emphasis upon content in addition to literary form, quite in contrast to the Aristotelian *mythos*, which referred essentially to the formal sequence of thematic units (*topoi*) or to what subsequently was called plot.[61]

Doty defines the primary organization of myth as twofold: content and form. He suggests, furthermore, that literary theory emphasizes the importance of the content of the myth rather than its mode of organization (a system of themes or ideas). In contrast to this dialectical approach, Bruce Sterling refers to the presentation of myth in *The Matrix* as "brain salad,"[62] suggesting that it is both intellectual food for the brain and an eclectic array of myths, texts, and pop culture clichés tossed together like a mixed salad. He is blasé about the "value" of such a textual (or franchise) strategy—"True, it veers perilously close to another [H. G.] Wells problem: 'If anything is possible, nothing is interesting'"[63]—but concludes that "you get all the intellectually sexy head-trip kicks of philosophizing without any of the boring hassles of consistency of rigor."[64]

Between Doty's functionality of myth and Sterling's "brain salad," a profound transformation has occurred in the way popular culture approaches textual mythology. The conclusion of *The Matrix*, which I have discussed in terms of the resurrection of the One, is simultaneously a thinly veiled performance of the coming to full consciousness in Plato's Allegory of the Cave. The film's narrative establishes a dialectical opposition between the Real and the illusion, its inauthentic reproduction. The individual is "woken up" (indeed, the film's concluding shot in which the One ascends into the heavens of the Matrix is accompanied by Rage Against the Machine's "Wake Up"[65]) from the "prison for the mind" and springs alive to enlightenment and full awareness of the controls of the Matrix. Neo reads the simulation as the coded artifice or simulation of the Real[66] as Plato's prisoner realizes the disparity between the illusion and the Real.

I argue that the purity or *authenticity* of Plato's allegory is challenged by the mode in which it is *performed* in the conclusion of *The Matrix*. Neo's coming to full consciousness is indeed a performance of the allegory, but setting it alongside the redemption of the One based upon faith (which is to say, drawing on the Christian frame of reference discussed earlier) renders the allegory as merely one fragment in a sprawling collage. Analyzing the play of mythic representation in *The Matrix*, Sterling suggests that "small wonder that Neo runs back into the fantasy. He's living in the pixels [of the digitized collage], stepping out of a phone booth, and flying. That is his victory, limited and illusory though it is. The cyber-messiah didn't change a thing, not really; when it came to the crunch, it was all smoke and mirrors."[67] For Sterling, the Matrix is indeed a place to hide from the Real, *experiencing* rather than understanding the simulation.

Doty's distinction between a classical (Aristotelian) *mythos* (a formal mythic pattern) and *content* cannot be applied to the performance of myth in *The Matrix*. On one level, the spectator responds to the Allegory of the Cave and *simultaneously* what is, at least on a philosophical level, the dialectically opposed allegory of the resurrection of Christ. On another level, the spectator appreciates the confrontation between—and/or synthesis of—the two. An analysis of *The Matrix* franchise must consider the relationship between the reproduction (the text and its performance as franchise in the cultural sphere) and the original—or, to use its own terminology, between the simulation and the Real. Both the Christian and Platonic mythic frames are *revisions* of an original utterance that now finds itself played in the discursive textual arena of the franchise. Such an analysis is invariably implicated in concerns of authenticity, textual value, ideological function, and the impact of the reproduction on a society that has lost its memory of the original utterance. A traditional literary theorist like Harold Bloom would consider the bricolage of the reproduction as another phase in the "shocking process of dumbing down *our* cultural life."[68] It is thus the duty of the spectator/theorist to conceptualize the way classical myth works in a wholly anachronistic film medium.

Cinema and the Contemporary Mythology

The Matrix franchise offers neatly formed parcels of traditional mythology, accessible and eminently recognizable to a contemporary popular culture audience. When Morpheus declares, "Now do you believe?" and the aphoristic, "He is the One," this audience silently cheers at a performance of a popular, age-old confluence of narratives of destiny and individuality. We recall the plight of the young Luke Skywalker in *Star Wars*, the boy from a backwater town who saves the galaxy; his twin sister Leia may stem from a royal upbringing and noble patronage, but it is crucial for the monomythic presentation of the One that he arise from obscurity and ascend to a position of centrality (of the village, town, city, country, or universe). Campbell describes the monomyth as central to Western cultural myths;[69] Jewett and Lawrence trace in detail its recuperation by Hollywood and popular culture.[70] While I would argue that the particularities of the myth are crucial in differentiating one text or franchise from another (the monomyth performed through the maturation process of Luke Skywalker is not *identical* to the process of maturation for Neo), there is a resemblance in the narrative structure of the major popular film franchises that conforms schematically to the monomyth: *Star Wars*,[71] *Indiana Jones, The Terminator, Alien/s, Back to the Future, The Matrix, Harry Potter, Independence Day*. The narrative/thematic structure as monomyth is connected to cinema as a popular culture phenomenon. A recognizable mythic foundation requires a paring down of plot and character and a sophisticated development of the visual aspect of cinema. It is thus significant that each of the franchises mentioned above are stylistically innovative and technologically pioneering; *Indiana Jones* could perhaps be considered an anomaly, but the emphasis on visual and aural spectacle is everywhere apparent.

The Matrix locates itself in this lineage of film franchises. It presents a clear Christian mythological foundation—the One is killed and resurrected, only to be killed again at the conclusion to *The Matrix Revolutions*. Yet even this death is not final as the Oracle suggests that Neo will indeed return—the One is resurrected a second time, though the nature of this resurrection is withheld. Larry Wachowski suggests that "we're [the Wachowski Brothers] interested in mythology, theology and, to a certain extent, higher-level mathematics. All human beings try to answer bigger questions, as well as The Big Question."[72] The narrative is attuned to the staple mythic and textual elements of contemporary popular culture, yet it is hardly the stuff of esoteric intellectualism.[73] The shooting script of *The Matrix* includes a scene in which Morpheus explicitly references Baudrillard when explaining the Matrix to Neo, but this sequence was omitted from the film.

The characters that enter the mythological structure are archetypal, though not caricature—a mythic resonance invests the characters with a quasi-profundity. Morpheus, a god of dreams in a Greek mythological structure, foregrounds the mythical aspect of his character at the end of *The Matrix Reloaded*: "I have dreamed a dream, and now that dream for me is gone." Adopting the Greek mythological structure is merely an interim position, perhaps what Stuart Hall would refer to as an arbitrary closure on the ever-expanding bricolage of the text.[74] Morpheus simultaneously partakes of the Christian mythical structure as a refashioned John the Baptist, of whom it is prophesied that he will find the One. Leather clad, wearing rimless mirror shades (an old cyberpunk trope[75]), Morpheus speaks in the highly clichéd, stilted dialogue of a Master Yoda or Obi Wan Kenobi: "Neo, I can only show you the door. You're the one that has to walk through it." Or consider the exchange:

> Neo: I know what you're trying to do.
> Morpheus: I'm trying to free your mind.

The archetypal and clichéd resonates because it is contrived and recognizable to the spectator. Familiarity breeds a pop accessibility.

While Neo sees (no doubt through a glass darkly) the path of the One, a separate stratum of mythologies is gradually set on his shoulders, reconfiguring the prevailing mythic structure. *The Matrix* opens outside the Heart of the City Hotel, connoting a centrality of the contemporary postmodern space, a realm of similar textual and cultural legacy to that which spawned the dystopias of *Blade Runner*, *Se7en*, *The Terminator*, and *Akira*. The notion of a "heart" or essentiality of the postmodern is rejected; the postmodern center is ultimately an imaginary construct in the Heart of the City Hotel, cohering spatially and temporally only in the simulacrum. "Viewed" from the perspective of the Real, the city exists in a perpetual present, subject to resimulation, or rebooting. Hugo Weaving's first appearance as Agent Smith outside the hotel recalls the hard-boiled, stylized dialogue of Chandler's Phillip Marlowe or Hammet's Sam Spade. The conspicuous use of high contrast recalls classical *film noir*; the recuperation of the *noir* city in the simulacrum is thus a literal reproduction that antecedes the Real.[76]

The spectator is introduced to Thomas Anderson in a studio apartment "overgrown with technology" in which "weed-like cables [coil] everywhere, duct-taped into thickets that wind up and around the legs of several desks."[77] Anderson is recognizable as the contemporary alienated man (recalling Chuck Palahniuk's nameless narrator in his cult novel, *Fight Club*[78]), a cyborg in his relationship to a technology of which he is a part, the creator and construct. He inhabits a body dislocated from the digital realm of cyberspace. It is the body that is alien, the mind splintered by the absurdity of physical effort. Donna Haraway discusses the literary (and cinematic) cyborg as "resolutely committed to partiality, irony, intimacy, and perversity. It is oppositional, utopian, and completely without innocence."[79] The cyborg is a textual trope that is a confluence of intertextual subjectivities. Interestingly, Haraway's attempt to mold a cyborg identity that transgresses a Western patriarchal subjectivity does not at all accord with Thomas Anderson/Neo as cyborg. Indeed, Haraway would perhaps view Neo less as radical political agent than reactionary, an agent of the political hegemony of the times even while superficially engaged in resistance. If the Cyborg offers a rupture from patriarchal modes of subjectivity, Neo's "coming to awareness" might be read as a reinscription of patriarchal values, particularly in relation to the Neo/Trinity romance. This would perhaps accord with the conclusion of the *The Matrix Revolutions*, suggesting that Neo is a synthesis of human and machine, issued of a "Source," which is of course also absent from Haraway's postmodern-inclined cyborg world.

Existential alienation meets the collective in millennial angst, apocalyptism, eschatology. In the Matrix, it is 1999, "the peak of human civilization." In the Real, "it is closer to 2199." Both epochs are at the turn of the century, both demand revolution. The conclusion to *The Matrix Revolutions* recalls a fascination with pyrotechnics in a pointed *homage* to *Akira*: archetypal good and evil collide, producing a mushroom cloud that resembles the catastrophic birth of Neo-Tokyo in *Akira*. Theology, contemporary existentialism, and apocalyptism are commingled with healthy doses of Hollywood blockbuster populism—hyperbolic action, stylized depictions of violence, clichéd romantic melodrama. In *The Matrix Revolutions*, Neo finds himself stranded in a Mobil station, a less-than-subtle anagram of Limbo, installing a Buddhist mythological structure that was vaguely apparent in the first two films.[80]

The challenge to the theorist/spectator is to assess the various ways in which these mythic structures resonate within the franchise and within the discursive culture that actively engages with these mythic structures. The task is thus twofold. First, it is to consider the way in which mythic structures are incorporated in the text (the formal arrangement, or what Doty refers to as the classical *mythos*). Such an analysis would consider the structural coherence of the whole—a "mythical narrative" that informs the text—as well as its accessibility to a wider audience. Second, it is to assess the impact of the "original" mythic utterance on a contemporary spectator and culture (content). Doty offers a broad definition of mythology as "narrative fictions whose plots read first at the level of their own stories and then as projections of immanent transcendent meanings. Such plots mirror human potentialities, experiences with natural and cultural phenomena, and recognition of regular interactions between them."[81] In these terms, the function of myth is essentially communicative at the literal, or intratextual, level. Myth enables the spectator to incorporate the original content, or initial utterance, into the reproduction. Thus, the spectator draws on Plato's Allegory of the Cave in its essentiality, that is, in its embryonic mythic form. Neo is substituted for the prisoner in shackles who is freed and brought to full consciousness in the light of goodness and truth. He is equally substituted for Christ in death and resurrection and must *believe* he is the One before he can realize it. He is also Sleeping Beauty on board the Nebuchadnezzar. These mythological narratives are transposed on a literal, explicitly communicative level.

However, the limitation of Doty's paradigm becomes apparent when assessing the mythological structure holistically. If, on a literal level, the mythic *content* of the franchise is at least problematic (if not incoherent), the prevailing mythic structure of the narrative is a site of contestation rather than a literal transposition of myth to spectator. The original utterance is reconfigured by its association with—and position in relation to—separate mythic structures. When reproduced, a mythic (or textual) utterance is aestheticized and simultaneously severed from an original mythic form. Myth is reconfigured as spectacle; the eclecticism of mythical narratives is invigorated with life and meaning in popular cultural practices. This is to say that the ontology of myth is fundamentally altered in the spectacle presentation. Popular culture does not receive mythic narratives in a traditional unmediated, and thus uncontaminated, form. The discursivity of culture finds expression in, and indeed is reliant upon, the discursive formation of mythic and textual narrative. Eco's tentative conclusions toward a "cult culture" are indeed prescient: "Thus in this case we witness an instance of metacult, or of cult about cult."[82] However, what is more significant than a "cult *about* cult" is a cult that is *always already* cult. Popular culture cannot dissociate itself from the myth as cult text. In fact the desire to reflect on idealistic mythic messages has well and truly expired. Film theory requires that cult cinema be *about* the status of cinema as reproduction. But this form of creative self-awareness, so fashionable in the work of Calvino, Borges, Eco (*The Name of the Rose* is a particularly fine example of the text as post-structuralist labyrinth[83]), Paul Auster, and others, has less currency in the pop culture arena in which myths have residual or spectacle resonance without the required sophistication of postmodern pastiche.[84] Pastiche operates in popular cinema as a form of commentary on prior myths, narratives, and textual forms—and this without a necessary recourse to the theories of irony and nostalgia that have informed a great deal of writing on the topic. This is ultimately what Jameson fails to appreciate in his reductive assessment of postmodernity: that pastiche is not an aesthetic destruction but rather a profoundly new and vital creative impulse.

Conceptualizing the Hypermyth

The performance of myth and text in a media-savvy culture is divorced from traditional myths and their importance to the individual. I have suggested that myth is divorced from its first-order, or denotative, message—a literally transposed idea drawn from a mythic structure. I have also argued that myth is divorced from what would be conventionally considered its second-order, or connotative, message—a myth reworked into a contemporary context but maintaining the veracity of its original utterance, its indissoluble and unaltered "truth." In this way, myth is often considered a timeless part of the maturation process for the individual and culture—this orthodoxy is assumed to persist for contemporary cultural receptions of myths and texts. For example, consider Anne Lancashire's reading of the *Star Wars* franchise in which "the overall message of the *Star Wars* trilogy—that life's ordeals, and even death itself as fearful, can be overcome through human growth toward mature and compassionate love and self-sacrifice . . . is in part the message of some of the world's most successful religions."[85] While Lancashire's reading of the narrative of the *Star Wars* franchise as a traditional mythic/religious structure is persuasive, the analysis does not take into account the performance aspect of the mythic structure, that is, the way in which it is reconfigured at the point of expression (on the cinematic screen) and reception (by the mass culture spectator in a movie theater). Myth recuperated as spectacle initiates a third-order, or *discursive*, message.[86] I designate this alteration the transition from myth to hypermyth, an ontological position in which "a viewer is no longer referred to a world outside the image" but a "crystalline representation [that] refers only to itself."[87]

Baudrillard and a Simulated Mythology

Rather than disorientation, these strategies of rearticulation that reflect a hyper-consciousness about the impact of images on social categorization are a process of fundamental *reorientation* conducted on and through that double referentiality.[88]

An early scene in *The Matrix* depicts Thomas Anderson (Neo) awaking from sleep to a message on his computer screen: "Wake up Neo. . . . The Matrix has you." A knock sounds at the door and Anderson exchanges illicit software for money. He removes the software from a hollowed-out copy of Baudrillard's *Simulacra and Simulation*. The copy appears to conform to Baudrillard's book, displaying the eleventh chapter, "On Nihilism."

The book is closed and returned to the shelf. Morpheus, when attempting to explain the Matrix to Neo, returns to a Baudrillardian model of the simulation of the "desert of the Real"; the simulation, once functional, destroys the oasis of the Real and installs a wasteland in its place.

The relation of the copy of *Simulacra and Simulation* stored on a shelf in the Matrix to the one currently resting on a desk before me mirrors the relation between the Real and the simulation in the narrative of the film. What is the status of the "real" object inside the simulacrum? And of greater interest is the ontological status of Baudrillard's book when *inserted into the Matrix*. I distinguish here between a work and the Text, drawing again on Barthes. The infinitely discursive Text remains an abstract theoretical consideration that implicates the Matrix in its performance; indeed the polysemal Text knows no boundaries. But the work is cordoned off, subject to "arbitrary closure" and a reading/molding of its contents into a semblance of form. What would a reading of a work (rather than Text) *within the Matrix* produce?

Baudrillard suggests that the Wachowski Brothers conflate simulacrum with illusion in the narrative structure of *The Matrix* and *The Matrix Reloaded*.[89] According to Baudrillard, Neo represents the prisoner in shackles in the Allegory of the Cave, who comes to enlightenment and a discovery of the essential Truth above and beyond the perversion of the simulation. This is ultimately the metanarrative of the franchise: that the One is destined to discover the inherent artifice of the simulation, rendering it obsolete and the Real eminently visible. The Wachowski Brothers thus bear recourse to a Platonic philosophical paradigm in which the Real and its simulation are distinct and dialectically opposed.

Conversely, Baudrillard says, his theory of the simulation (as opposed to illusion) is a performance of a once indissoluble truth that simultaneously erases that truth through its performative aspect. Accepting the performance reveals the absence of the Real; there remains only the apparition, the phantasm. Whereas in *The Matrix* the Real and the simulation are contiguous and dialectically opposed, the inception of the simulacrum in Baudrillard's conception severs the connection with the Real and destroys memory (history and time) and geography (space). The crucial distinction lies in the resultant *precession* of the simulacra: the simulation of the Real erases the Real and installs the simulation as the only point of origin. In this reading of *The Matrix*, Baudrillard seems to concur with Bartlett and Byers's claim that *The Matrix* is "Pomophobic," or avoidant of postmodern tenets, attaining only a neoconservative dichotomy that esteems transcendental truth over a system of authoritarian-controlled lies.[90] Radical postmodern polemic, in Baudrillard's estimation, is merely a façade in the film for a run-of-the-mill blockbuster action film.

I disagree with Baudrillard's reading of *The Matrix*. I will argue this point only to suggest that the status of the object in the simulation is irretrievably *simulated*. This is a crucial point because the effacement of the dialectic between Real and simulation is necessary for the performance of the hypermyth. The Wachowski Brothers are aware of Baudrillard's reputation as a radical post-structuralist. Norris describes Baudrillard as a "cult figure on the current 'postmodernist' scene,"[91] whose ideas are "picked up from the latest fashionable sources." "And so it has come about that a thinker like Baudrillard can proffer his ridiculous 'theses' on the Gulf War with every confidence that they will gain wide attention among watchers of the postmodern cultural scene."[92] In the context of the film, we are not dealing with a matrix, but *the* Matrix. The copy of *Simulacra and Simulation* that appears briefly in the film constitutes a manual for reading the Matrix. But, crucially, its status as already simulacral strips the work of its political and ideological agency, as well as its descriptive power. Appearing inside the simulation effaces its status as Real object. Suggesting that the Matrix is ultimately subservient to the Real in the first two films, Baudrillard fails to appreciate the simulation as a postmodern *condition* rather than a textual "reality." The simulation *contaminates* the Real, compromising its integrity, eradicating its authenticity, decanting a once indissoluble Real into a stratum of residual mythic and textual images. The appearance of *Simulacra and Simulation* in the Matrix of the film affirms ultimately that the Real (including subversive theories of the simulation postulated by Baudrillard in his book) is always already simulated. The manual that the spectator/theorist draws on to "lay bare" the reality of the simulation is itself trapped within the simulation. The work is thus hollow, bereft of content. The conclusion to *The Matrix Revolutions* is less an ending than a reversion to the start, a cycle in which the narrative and mythic structure is eternally returned.

Thomas Anderson (Keanu Reeves) and a hollow Simulacra and Simulation.

Accepting the contamination of the Real by the simulation does not, however, equate with a *rejection* of the Real. This is a crucial point on which Baudrillard and I disagree. The notion that the simulation literally precedes the Real borders on the nonsensical. Baudrillard suggests that the subject "require[s] a visible past, a visible continuum, a visible myth of origin, which reassures us about our end. Because finally we have never believed in them."[93] But wouldn't the opposite be the case? That we require a visible past to affirm the *reality* of our belief over and above its simulation? I find it difficult to make sense of myself without a visible past (which I acknowledge is subject to its simulated form, but yet maintains a striking resemblance [and relation] to the Real). Baudrillard acknowledges this resemblance—"Everywhere we live in a universe strangely similar to the original—things are doubled by their own scenario"[94]—but seems to view the simulation as inherently sinister and a deterioration of the ideal Real. He does not explore the possibilities of self in the simulation as much as revel in the decadence of the destroyed Real.

For Baudrillard, the "awareness" of the precession of the simulacra is commensurate with the effacement of the subject as theorist and spectator. This is clearly premature. The Matrix, after all, functions according to "rules that are no different from the rules of a computer system. Some of them can be bent. Others can be broken." I have argued that popular culture offers a site of engagement with its mythic and textual legacies. This engagement, to my mind, requires at least the *semblance* of subjectivity, and such a semblance precludes the precession of the simulacra. The nature of the work within the simulation presents a point of mediation between the simulacral precession and the Platonic ascent to truth. I have designated this a realm of the *hypermyth*, in which myths are transposed from their origin into a *simulated* form. The relation of myth to hypermyth corresponds to Baudrillard's abstract relation between the Real and the hyperreal, in which the simulation is *more* than the Real. "Hyper" connotes an increase or energizing of the object exhausted of its potential as concrete referential. The Real in Baudrillard's conception is a tired form, stripped of its capacity to describe a contemporary culture founded on its erasure. The subject no longer engages with the Real object, but its simulated reflection. I wish to employ Baudrillard's theory of the precession of the simulacra as a defense of the spectacle in popular cinema. The attachment of "hyper" to "real" in the simulacrum implies a transformation of the Real. But what precisely is Baudrillard suggesting has become of the Real once the simulation has taken hold and become the dominant aesthetic?

The hypermyth reflects a cultural and subjective discursivity, a capacity to engage with what Barthes calls the infinitude of Text while permitting the arbitrary closure Hall demands of contemporary cultural and aesthetic practices. If the Real is contaminated into obsolescence, Baudrillard's theory of the simulacrum comprises merely another abstract reflection on the lost authenticity of the Real; it is merely another form of nostalgia disguised as radical nihilism. Ultimately it is the latest incursion into the dominance of the popular (which is perceived as a deterioration of aesthetic value) as well as a plea for the usefulness of the theorist after the collapse of critical distance. This mode of nostalgia is thus equally a strategy of self-preservation. Castigating the contemporary for its aesthetic fall from grace affirms tradition and forms commensurate with an earlier age. Vanquishing the Real enacts the coming into being of the sinister simulation, the omnipresence of a Disneyland space and time of images.

Rejecting the contamination of the Real altogether is an act of denial in the face of evidence of the pervasiveness of the mediated image. "Real" connotes the uninterrupted means and ends of contemplation, a transposition of the message without mediation by the carrier. This is clearly not the way meaning is disseminated in the cultural sphere, as even the most tenaciously political theorist would acknowledge. Culture is a mediated field. Mediation is fraught with epistemological and ethical problems illuminated by Marshall McCluhan in the 1960s and tacitly accepted ever since.[95] Post-structuralism offered a paradigm in which to explode the act of mediation in such a way that it constituted the centrality of textual theory. Thus, post-structuralism privileges form over content, which is to say, content *as* form. This is surely only a single step to Baudrillard's precession of the simulacra. Norris, one of the sternest critics of Baudrillard's radical epistemology, concedes that the Gulf War

> [was] indeed in some sense a "postmodern" war, an exercise in mass-manipulative rhetoric and "hyperreal" suasive techniques, which does undoubtedly confirm some of Baudrillard's more canny diagnostic observations. How else could one explain the extraordinary inverse relationship between extent of coverage and level of informed public grasp.[96]

The contemporary cultural theorist does not set her sights so much on the radiance of truth and beauty as merely on the most perfect semblance of it. Classical Platonic forms are less than fashionable in cultural studies. For Lyotard, this analytical foundation has profound limitations:

The fact is that the Platonic discourse that inaugurates science is not scientific, precisely to the extent that it attempts to legitimate science. Scientific knowledge cannot know and make known that it is the true knowledge without resorting to the other, narrative, kind of knowledge, which from its point of view is no knowledge at all.[97]

There is no recourse to a knowledge that does not compromise its own status as scientific. Baudrillard's simulation bears much the same resemblance to the imaginary Real. Yet, if as for Norris the mediation of images does not preclude "argued critical resistance,"[98] then neither does the awareness and acceptance of the simulation as a dominant aesthetic form render the Real unintelligible. Rather it incorporates the reflection of the Real into the simulacral image, the vestige of reality into the hyper-real representation. Hypermythology connotes a *reorganization* of the original mythic utterance and a transformation in the ontological status of myth such that the Real is merely a template for the "residual mythic image"[99] performed within the simulation. The hypermythologizing of myth is necessary to function affectively as a discursive aesthetic in which myth is merely textual quotation. Without recourse to an abiding Truth or reality, the spectator must find aesthetic worth in the recuperation of myth into new forms.

What coheres ultimately in the internal logic of *The Matrix* franchise is a panorama of residual mythic images. The tools required to decode these images (a component of which is Eco's encyclopedia of film references) are as much a part of contemporary postmodern consumption practices as traditional textual interpretation. The spectator/theorist is aware of the parameters of the construct/simulation in which the text is played. There is thus a necessary ambivalence in aesthetically responding to the simulated myth as *artificial*. A hope lingers to partake of the original, the true One whose replication is that which Plato considered a "familiar," merely the paltry reflection of an ideal and radiant form. It is this ambivalence that forms the emotional core of the discursive subjectivity. The hypermyth, divorced from an originary mythic truth, enables the simultaneous performance of separate and contradictory mythic structures that resonate for a subjectivity immersed in the simulation.

Screening the Hypermyth

Hypermythology finds expression as performance. It is the performative aspect that revises the prior mythic form (a mythic Real) into a simulated textual utterance. To demonstrate this performance, consider the following textual itinerary of the grand finale of *The Matrix* franchise.

The romantic hero (Keanu Reeves is a useful combination of tough guy and effete male) departs from his destined Love in an excruciating and wonderfully sentimental exchange, demonstrating what Jewett and Lawrence call the "sexual segmentation" of the monomythic hero.[100] This segmentation is necessary to establish the plight of the One as heroic individualist. Physically blinded, he confronts a heavenly simulacrum, a realm of "white on white,"[101] or in this case, light on light. Heaven is a construct, a mechanically functioning simulation. The artifice is maintained in the quasi-God figured Deux Ex Machina, a construct of component sentinel parts.

Upon jacking into the Matrix, the hero dons the cinematic ethos of the anti-hero in a second re-presentation of a Sergio Leone Western showdown (the first takes place in a subway station in *The Matrix*). The Wachowski Brothers tip their hats to Leone's films, acknowledging their presence on screen and their revised performance within the Matrix. Neo's flowing coat is as suitably a religious cassock as the dust jacket of the Cheyenne romantic bandit in *Once Upon a Time in the West*.

The anti-hero is further inscribed by the mirror shades. The Wachowski Brothers use the motif of images reflected in mirror shades several times in the franchise. The reflection draws attention to the image as refracted in a cyberpunk trope; the spectator perceives the image in the simulated Matrix through a lens. The camera that rests on Neo's black boots (which are configured elsewhere in the series as sexual fetish) and ascends his body recalls Cameron's *The Terminator*, a film that looms gargantuan over this franchise. The opening shot of the confrontation between Smith and Neo replicates the entrance of Schwarzenegger in *The Terminator* and is the crucial indication that the spectator is watching a performance of a prior cinematic piece.

Performance as an aesthetic value permeates this sequence. Indeed, Reeves as actor steps aside to admit *Neo* as actor. The sentimentalism of the contemporary leading man ("Trin, you can't die!") is *refigured into* stoic, transcendental heroism. "It ends tonight" functions as a depthless (to be sure, hollow, as in Baudrillard's bible of the simulacrum, and infinitely regressing, as in Barthes's inexhaustibility of the Text) reverberation of every line prefiguring a confrontation. The archetypal Good versus Evil confrontation is reconfigured as a stylized *homage* to Hong Kong kung fu cinema of the 1970s. The spectator recalls Neo's impersonation of Bruce Lee in a sparring duel with Morpheus in a simulated dojo. The silhouetted shot of the fighters in an abandoned warehouse (which seems miraculously to appear within the simulation) is a familiar trope of classic Hong Kong cinema and, incidentally, is used to astonishing effect in Tarantino's *Kill Bill, Volume 1*.

Three other significant cinematic references operate to construct a discursive, performative frame of reference. The midair tussle between Neo and Smith is reminiscent of the climactic duel between Superman and General Zod in *Superman II*; the Christ figure partakes of the Marvel Comics heroic tradition. The second, and more obvious, *homage* is the circular energy field that explodes from the confrontation between Neo and Smith, replicating the shot of the nuclear explosion in *Akira* that leads to the formation of the futuristic dystopia of Neo-Tokyo. More distantly, the general visual style recalls *Dragonball Z*, a cult animé series popular both in Japan and the U.S.

This reading of a sequence in *The Matrix Revolutions* offers a conception of the franchise as a cinematic simulacrum—a discursively performed metacinema—that inscribes Neo simultaneously as the apotheosis of the monomythic figure *and* its redundancy. The risen Christ is equally a superhero inhabiting a textual realm drawn from classical mythology, comics, animation, and popular cinema. The franchise functions as mythology in flux, simultaneously locating and then displacing textual utterances. As spectacle, the franchise consumes its textual precursors, gorging on a sacred past, so to speak, but without the disparaging and debilitating recourse to Jameson's cinematic pastiche. Instead, the redundancy of the monomyth takes place at an acceptance of the text as discursive and constructed—a simulacrum functioning onscreen and off.

The Discursivity of the One

Morpheus
Residual Self Image: it is the mental projection of your digital self.[102]

Neo
I believe that the Matrix can remain our cage or it can become our chrysalis, that's what you helped me to understand. That to be free, truly free, you cannot change your cage. You have to change yourself.[103]

The Matrix as *chrysalis* suggests a space of transformation of the consciousness with profound implications for the conception of the Matrix in the franchise. Rather than Baudrillard's sinister simulacrum, the Matrix presents a possibility for the subject to evolve beyond the parameters of the Real: authenticity, truth, right, purpose. Remarkably, this passage in the shooting script was omitted because preview audiences did not know the meaning of the word "chrysalis." Instead, Neo informs the machines that humanity wishes to reclaim its freedom *outside* of the Matrix. At least this is the implication with the omission of "chrysalis": "Where we go from here is up to you." The inclusion of chrysalis in the passage implies that freedom is ultimately attainable only *in relation to* the Matrix, that is, after understanding the contours of the simulation in relation to the Real. This notion is borne out in *The Matrix Reloaded* and *The Matrix Revolutions*. Neo is a cyborg, a machine/human synthesis issued from the "Source," an original mythical point that draws equally on Christian, Buddhist, Agnostic, Manichean, technological, cyberpunk, and pop culture narrative structures. However, "cyborg" in *The Matrix* franchise

Replicating cinematic nuclear destruction: The Matrix Revolutions.

implies more than the machine/human combination that allowed Arnold Schwarzenegger to resist bullets and yet express a human emotion through tears in *Terminator 2: Judgment Day*. The cyborg in *The Matrix* universe is a conduit between the Real and the simulation, a native to each imaginary plane. *The Matrix* shows Neo's gradual control over the rules of the Matrix; *The Matrix Reloaded* extends this control to include a control over the Real. At the conclusion to *The Matrix Revolutions*, Morpheus's rhetorical final question, "Is it real?," uttered while gazing upward at a heavenly glow, subverts the project to recuperate the Real through the destruction of the Matrix. The question resonates as a repetition of Schwarzenegger's final line in Verhoeven's *Total Recall*. Standing beneath a Mars sunrise that recalls an image from a Hollywood Techni*color* production, he murmurs, "What if I'm dreaming?," to which his love replies, "Then kiss me before I wake up." The Sleeping Beauty/Prince tale is reworked here to dazzling effect. Morpheus's recuperation of the sequence in *Total Recall* is thus an incursion into the internal logic of *The Matrix* narrative. The textual fabric that touches *The Matrix* franchise and *Total Recall* draws also on the classic metaphysical conundrums of Philip K. Dick, upon whose "We Can Remember It for You Wholesale"[104] *Total Recall* was loosely based. Dick's open-ended, often self-effacing metaphysics[105] pervade the textual play of *The Matrix* franchise.

Morpheus's suggestion that an awareness of the Matrix (or the ability to recognize its parameters) allows a heightened appreciation of the *nature of the Real* is thus misguided. Rather, the "residual self image" of the One, initiated within the Matrix, offers a "consensual hallucination," to quote William Gibson in a very similar context.[106] The subjective consciousness evolves, immersed within the simulation, partaking of the Real *as* residual mythic image in which Real self and simulated Other are conjoined in a symbiotic relationship. Neo, simultaneously of the Real and the post-historical, a functioning recuperation of the original mythic form as simulated spectacle, is a "child of the Real." He is "irrevocably human," to quote the Architect in *The Matrix Reloaded*, but equally the progeny of the virtual.

Motifs of fractured identity (machine/human, male/female, real/virtual) appear throughout the franchise. In the scene in *The Matrix* in which Neo and Trinity enter a government building to rescue Morpheus, the two forms are androgynous reflections, almost identical in clothing, makeup, and movement. Reeves and Moss look uncannily alike. In her reading of the first film, Martina Lipp does not appreciate the significance of the androgynous sexuality of the One, preferring instead a masculinization of the "female hero."[107] The neofascist motif of leather boots functions as a symbol of deviant sexuality, sadomasochism, and neo-Gothic grunge culture. After the destruction of the building in perhaps the franchise's most impressive visual sequence, the camera offers a close-up of Trinity's leather boots (emphasized with a squeak on the floor tile), installing the simulated Trinity as masculinized hero, feminine sidekick, and cultural deviant.

The image in the machine city of a fleshlike organic tube attached to a mechanical/organic womb is an explicit quotation of the confrontation between Ripley (Sigourney Weaver) and the Queen alien in Cameron's *Aliens*. In *Alien: Resurrection*, Ripley is reborn as an alien-human hybrid, which resembles Neo's symbiotic form of human and machine, real and virtual, at the conclusion of *The Matrix Revolutions*. In terms of the franchise's convoluted metaphysical position, agency is equally a matter of a free will originating in the Real and a mechanical determinism that functions as the metaphysical core of the machines. The synthesis of Real and simulation compromises the integrity of both systems of metaphysics.

The Oracle's "you cannot see beyond the choices you don't understand" is superficially impressive but less than philosophically conclusive.

The most obvious intrusion of the simulated form into the Real occurs in the affectivity of the One. The Matrix is a perversion of the Real, a trancelike hallucinogenic state in which sensuality is divorced from the physical body. The spectacle offers the transformation of the banality of the Real into the hyperkinetic visuality of the simulation. Residual self-image is the *only* image-form of the One. The Matrix offers the uninhibited expression of the repressed self (or a self imprisoned within the cave of the Real, yet perceiving the possibilities of a simulated "self-image"). The capacity for transformation is infinite, subject only to the parameters of the imagination that reflects on the limited form of the Real. In peril on a rooftop, with escape possible only in a military helicopter, Neo asks of Trinity: "Can you fly that thing?" She replies, "Not yet." The ability to fly the helicopter is literally realized through a download into the imaginary, and infinitely discursive, consciousness. A number of theorists have commented on the disparity between the subtext of the franchise as anti-technological while reveling in the possibility of technology to make the self "more than real." I will not labor the point except to say that the hypermythological (which connotes also the simultaneous awareness and appreciation of contradictory mythic utterances) functions as an aestheticization of the Real, which is to say, a license for rejecting technology while reveling in technical innovation on film. Lucas did something very similar with the *Star Wars* franchise.

The transformation of Thomas Anderson into the One constitutes the initiation of the analogue self—the corporeal, tactile body of the Real—into the digital coding of the simulated Matrix. *The Matrix Revolutions* offers a death in the simulacrum as the original offered a birth. The One is resurrected *within* the Matrix—the virtual consciousness awakes to the kiss of life while the inert, inactive body remains asleep. The quasi-religious enlightenment is not to "read through" the Matrix, as Trost suggests,[108] but to *read and write* it. The evolution in the consciousness of the One (the Matrix as chrysalis) is not the extrication of the subject from the simulation but the immersion in the residual mythic recuperation of the original utterance. When the One exits the phone booth, reborn in the simulation, he ascends into a simulated heaven with simulated mythical wings (or equally, a simulated mythical cape). He wears simulated mirror shades. Immersed in the simulated spectacle, the One reads, writes, and *consumes* the code that constructs its discursivity. The critical transformation occurs at the point of resurrection in which the One no longer sees the Platonic object, but the digital code—streams of data as semblance of form—that constructs it.

The image of Neo as a re-presentation of Christ on the cross (at which point the Deux Ex Machina utters, "It is done"[109]) performs an absence rather than a presence of the Christian mythic structure. Neo is Christ*like*, but he is not Christ. He is not an avatar, descended (or arisen) into a fallen world to save humanity from its sins. It only *appears* this way from a monomythic perspective. The dominant aesthetic of spectacle cinema is *image-consumption*, in which original mythic utterances are reorganized as commodities in a simulacrum. The residually Real functions as a commodity, alterable, in flux, rereadable, rewriteable. The spectator, divorced from the sacred origin, consumes and simultaneously aestheticizes the commodity as replacement. The potentiality of the cinematic spectacle offers the discursive text as fractured reflection of the Real, aware of its constructedness, its component parts, its inherent artifice, its inauthenticity. Rather than seeking a newly arisen Christ, it seeks a new Christ *image*, subject to an eternal return, but also an eternal transformation (consider also that Neo is the sixth One, a return of the previous five but equally a transformation of the prior form). The newness of the One, the essential "Neo," is an incarnation of an original mythic form that has been recuperated into obsolescence. Neo is only Christ insofar as he coheres in a simulated Matrix "with a set of quotation marks that hover above [him] like an ironic halo."[110]

The play of myth and text in the simulacrum is not Jameson's pastiche. That kind of pastiche functions not merely as recuperation, but as a strategy of deterioration—its performance results in a *lessening* of the original utterance, or a loss of an essential meaning. In such a postmodern aesthetic, Plato is always less than Plato when re-presented. But equally, the hypermyth is not necessarily a consequence of what Hutcheon has called the irony of postmodern textual strategies.[111] Rather it is a consumption of the *modalities of the Real*; the Real is not effaced, but merely perpetually transformed. This consumption does not require the spectator/theorist's awareness of its status as reproduction. In fact, I would argue that very little so-called postmodern cinematic reception is founded on irony. I disagree that irony is a useful strategy for cultural resistance to a hegemonic social structure. Such strategies need development and mobilization, and irony, as Hutcheon acknowledges, is profoundly subjective.[112] Rather, the performance of the hypermyth presents the Real for consumption: a history that is rewritten, remythologized, and commodified as the One sees fit.

The Visibility of Style: Image Strategies in Contemporary Cinema

Digital Code . . . has radically altered the epistemology and ontology of the moving image.[113]

What remains of *Breathless* today, what speaks to a contemporary, young audience—when jump cuts figure in every second TV commercial?[114]

Deleuze locates the great transformation of modern cinema after the Second World War, at which point the action-image was exhausted of its capacity to provide a meaningful aesthetic in cinema. The image loses its credibility as an "account" of movement and time after suffering a brief crisis "defined by a number of characteristics: the form of the trip/ballad, the multiplication of clichés, the events that hardly concern those they happen to, in short, the slackening of the sensory-motor connections." These conditions "made possible, but did not constitute, the new image."[115] According to Deleuze, after the war, films increasingly demonstrate a conformity to the time-image, a condition in which cinema is a "purely optical and sound situation."[116] Filser concludes that the time-image constitutes a cinematic language in which "the real and the imaginary, which in organic narration are discrete, opposed, are occluded. Real and virtual become indistinguishable."[117] The future of the time-image, and thus the ontology of a future cinema, in Filser's estimation, would equate with an "audio-visual image in its most complex form, permanently interrogating information as to its source and its addressee. Perhaps this future cinema à la Deleuze may be defined as follows: that which forces information to think and us to think information."[118]

An interesting body of work has found a foothold in film theory over the last decade. This work is neither traditional literary/cultural theory nor contemporary film theory but a synthesis of "apparatus" theory[119] (in which the significance of the medium is emphasized as a site of meaning) and visual arts theory (specifically, contemporary design and an aesthetics of new media).[120] While there are obviously dissimilarities within the body of work (the notion of a synthesis is a generalization, but a useful one), these authors attempt to theorize an alteration in the ontology of the visual image, as Deleuze did in his books on cinema. This new ontology permits an approach to cinema vastly removed from the instrumentalist theory of culture, which I have argued is founded on a traditional realist aesthetic. It permits also an exploration of the aesthetic mode, or cinematic stylistics, that suffers in traditional film theory. Simply put, it offers a conceptual framework within which the spectator/theorist may ask: What are the implications of a visual/aural stylistics of cinema?

In this chapter, I have discussed various departures from traditional cinematic practices in terms of intertextual quotation and the recuperation of myth. The following section is an account of the stylistic innovations of contemporary cinema, focusing on "bullet-time" in *The Matrix* franchise and various image-strategies that are increasingly apparent in mainstream cinema. I contrast my own version of the spectacle of contemporary cinema with theories of new media and art and its conception of the spectator's immersion in the digital image of the contemporary avant-garde.

In the 1940s, the Hollywood studio film conveyed to the spectator a seamless reality that functioned self-evidently on relations of cause and effect in the pursuit of historical truth (the quest for a narrative truth offered a cinematic substitute). Thus, a remarkable number of studio films depict protagonists who attempt to solve a mystery using a prescribed set of clues that amount to a comprehensive back-story, the plot (what was actually depicted), and probable future developments (the causal consequences). Narrative closure was presumed (in spite of increasingly convoluted storylines) and rarely challenged. The spectator was subjected to a "realist" performance of the image conveyed in a seamless reproduction of what she took to be a reality shared by herself and other spectators. This subjection was accomplished through the invisibility of style (visual and aural components synthesized in a way that deflected the gaze from the inherent constructedness of the image) and the emphasis on narrative and plot development. The image functioned as a conduit to narrative solution and was thus merely a means to an end. In this sense, realism and genre (invisible stylistics and familiar narrative patterns) were fundamentally attached, forming a dominant cinematic aesthetic. This aesthetic has prevailed ever since, albeit it in a somewhat altered form.[121]

A second feature to which Bordwell alludes[122] and on which Ray significantly expands[123] is a hermetically sealed frame of representation. In the studio film, action depicted was required to cohere within the sacrosanct boundaries of the film narrative. Formal cinematic technique was predetermined by the story, of which narrative was merely a necessary and unobtrusive function. Cinematic narrative was an enclosed, insular plane that functioned without intrusion of an extraneous agency, whether creative or administrative. The studio film narrative presented the story according to the dictates of a "real world" that was presumed by the spectator to inform the cinematic world holistically. Indeed, directors such as Frank Capra and John Ford were esteemed in American film culture because of a fidelity to the Real. Ford's long shots of Monument Valley in *The Searchers* are an elegy for that which makes the American frontier what it is in the collective (and reflective) imagination. Paradoxically, the hermetically sealed world of the studio narrative ensured the lasting influence of realism in American mainstream cinema.

The "new" cinematic image, divested of the burden of the Real, draws attention to itself as a component of a manufactured media. But it also declares its rejection of the once glorified ontological status of the image as reproduced reality (Bazin). Codognet offers the following assessment of the status of the new image:

> An important characteristic of virtual environments is the possibility for the spectator to interactively move within such spaces and perceive the virtual world as through a subjective camera . . . But with virtual worlds we are moving away from the metaphor of the map to that of the path, from the third-person point of view ("God's eye") to the first-person point of view. . . . We are thus leaving, in the virtual *experience* and exploration of an unknown artificial world, the Cartesian paradigm of the Euclidean, homogenous and objective space in which points could be described in an allocentric manner by triple (x, y, z) co-ordinates for a new paradigm of a more constructive, egocentric, and indeed subjective space.[124]

He shares the fascination of theorists of new media and art with the possibility of the spectator to engage with the image, to wrestle it to a unique and wholly subjective form. In Deleuzian terms, the spectator is able to unburden herself of the itinerary of the action-image and explore the convolutions of spatial and temporal (and thus virtual) time-images. This is perhaps what Courchesne has in mind in his conception of a reformed cinema and the "immersion" of the spectator: "Cinema and television are good storytelling devices, but will always fall short of providing a believable interactive experience. In my opinion, cinema couldn't become immersive without a deep transformation of its content's structure and development, and if it did it would have to be called something else."[125] In this model, to embrace the possibilities of a new media that reorganizes the relationship between the screen and the spectator, cinema would need to be reconstituted entirely.

But perhaps an ontological transformation of the image on this scale is not entirely necessary. To what extent has Deleuze's time-image, or the ontology of the image in various interactive media, intruded into mainstream or art cinema? While it is clear that the mainstream film image partakes of elements of the time-image, the limitation of theories of new media lies precisely in its specificity as a medium and its relative obscurity to popular culture. While I would agree that mainstream cinema offers the spectator a site of engagement with the product (the cinematic text), immersion in interactive art forms presents something else entirely. Courchesne suggests that the immersion aesthetic of installation art has intruded on some mainstream cinematic practices that extends to the origins of cinema: "This [immersion] is exemplified . . . by Abel Gance's multiple-screen feature film, *Napoléon* in 1926, or by Waller's *Cinerama* in the 1950s and today's IMAX and OMNIMAX technologies."[126] The notion of IMAX as immersion is particularly interesting insofar as it has gradually expanded from the purely visual and documented (Discovery Channel documentaries) to the narrative (the recent *Polar Express* is a good example). But even so, the narrative structure of mainstream cinema and its emphasis on "telling stories" is a limitation on the visual image as a site of spectator immersion. IMAX is not a regular screening forum for a Hollywood blockbuster, and in any case its technology and capacity for immersion would not be commensurate with the narrative (and specifically genre) form. Mainstream cinema requires a viewing perspective from which the spectator can address the image *holistically*. The image is addressed as a single entity rather than a splicing together of separate and distinct visual components. In the immersion of the spectator in the interactive work, "immersion is cognitive before being perceptive. The 'reality' of immersive work is distinctly invented and recreated by the viewer—and not just perceived and undergone."[127] However, seated anonymously in the darkened movie theater, the spectator inheres in an imaginary *centrality* in relation to the image. Regardless of her location in the room, the spectator assumes a position shared by every other spectator. Equally, the spectator locates herself in a viewing relation to the image that is guided by the shot and spatial coordinates of the image: point of view, overhead, low angle, long, medium, close-up, zoom, etc. The spatial dimension of the shot steers the spectator's gaze in a particular direction. This is often accomplished through a shift in focus—an image that moves out of focus recedes from the spectator's gaze.

Spectator immersion or viewer interactivity in Courchesne's model connotes a fluid relation between spectator and image, a multiplicity of viewing points and "screens" upon which the image is presented, and an open-ended text that is located only in relation to the organizing subjective gaze (the traditional cinematic gaze is reconfigured as viewing *presence*). The "Real" of the spectator's presence is literally immersed (and dissolved) within the total virtuality of the representation. For the immersion to be complete, narrative must submit to the free play of visual and aural freely associated stimuli. As Courchesne suggests, "It is not appropriate to speak of narrativity in relation to the construction and experience of an interactive work. The way I see it, the only narrative, if it materializes, will originate from the visitor after she or he experiences the work and not from the work itself, which is constructed as a context for experience."[128] This establishes a functioning continuum between artwork and spectator that moves toward Filser's reading of Deleuze's time-image "which forces information to think and us to think information."[129]

The implications of such an art and media are difficult to conceptualize. I would suggest that the reorganization of the relation between spectator and artwork founded upon a destruction of the narrative form[130] is incompatible with current mainstream cinematic practices. While Courchesne mentions this incompatibility in passing, for me it is crucial and, indeed, central to the debate. Popular culture is engaged in the construction and deconstruction of its sacred narratives, which I have attempted to show through a reading of *The Matrix* franchise. But immersion in Courchesne's model is surely relegated to a fringe cultural aesthetic, practiced by the few trained in its traditions (which are in any case distinctly avant-garde and incompatible with the mainstream aesthetic). I cannot perceive this form of immersion at work in contemporary cinema. While Courchesne is optimistic about the impact of the immersion aesthetic in popular culture, I cannot fathom how such a transformation in the aesthetic sensibility of the mainstream would be achieved. Courchesne suggests that "media artists who are currently doing installation work are in the forefront of those inventing a medium, a medium whose impact in the future will be comparable to that of cinema in the not so distant past."[131] However, my conception of the spectacle aesthetic is vastly removed from the immersion of interactive art. I conceive of the spectacle as a simulation of narrative forms (hypermythology); Courchesne privileges the nonnarrative artwork and the Barthesian textual explorer that molds the text to form and is simultaneously molded by it. In this model, I can only perceive endlessly proliferating images and subjectivities in flux, which is of course precisely the philosophical trajectory of immersion art and theory.

The site of interaction between spectator and the mainstream cinematic image has not substantially changed since the rise of the studio film and the dominance of cinema as a social activity. The visit to the movie theater is a form of social ritual and a site of cultural interaction and consumption. Spectators do not visit film galleries in the way art enthusiasts visit art galleries. Spectators visit consumer spaces that house multiplexes and retail stores that form a chain in the production-consumption process. Inside these malls, the spectator finds easy access to the fast food industry via a "food court." Fast food complements the saturation screening of the latest blockbuster, particularly if the spectator purchases the tie-in drinking cup at the McDonald's counter. The cinema is a narrative site of social interaction in which the social ritual is a form of storytelling that interacts with the film. An aesthetic response to the film product is synthetically conjoined to the ritualized practices of the visit to the theater, lining up at the box office, buying popcorn and Coke, viewing the advertisements (which are as stylistically innovative as the feature film), viewing the previews, purchasing tie-in memorabilia. The immersion in the spectacle is an immersion in a series of ritualized consumptive practices. For the spectator of mainstream cinema, immersion represents an engagement with (rather than a departure from) a narrative text that extends from screen to an external reality. Mainstream cinematic practice "offers only an 'interior,' a pervasive meta-cinema (or a cinematic society in which the screen intrudes on an external reality) that has drawn the exterior 'reality' into itself at its point of inception."[132]

24: Real-Time Narrative

24 is perhaps the most stylistically innovative series to appear on mainstream network television for some time. The narrative of each series depicts the actions of a number of characters over the space of twenty-four hours. The twenty-four-part series screens in one-hour episodes. This serialization of the narrative requires each episode to end in a "cliffhanger," a moment of great drama leaving the viewer to anticipate the events of the following week's episode. The structure of the series foregrounds the passage of time. A digital display appears intermittently on screen to remind the viewer of the time that has passed and to indicate the narrative relations between the characters at any point in the story. Advertisements are inscribed into the real-time narrative. Thus, at the end of a commercial break, the digital read-out indicates that approximately four minutes have elapsed. This permits the forty-five-minute episode to comprise an hourlong segment in the viewing schedule while maintaining its real-time narrative structure.

Experiments with real-time narrative have traditionally been relegated to the art-house fringe (Sukorov's *Russian Ark*, shot in real time, is more remarkable for its single elaborate take than its simple narrative structure; Figgis's *Time Code*, while a unique cinematic experiment, fared poorly at the box office) or suffers a commercial and critical failure (Badham's *Nick of Time*). *24* offers a convoluted, multifocused genre narrative. The generic characterization and post-9/11 thematic is a major factor in the success of the series; the dexterity of its plotting is genuinely innovative. Its willingness to use split-screen shots, to reject slow-motion and other time-altering strategies, and yet to emphasize fast cuts and "forced framing" (in which the framing of a shot does not conform to a realist relation of spectator to image) foregrounds its innovative stylistics that complement a streamlined genre story. It is stylistically unorthodox and yet recognizable as a genre piece. The narrative of each episode is structured around segments of time. Season Four, Episode 1 inserted an *extranarrative* indication to the spectator that "everything is going to change in less than ten minutes." All plot elements are constructed around time constraints. For example, a bomb will detonate in thirty minutes, a virus will be released within the hour (thus forming a temporal structure to the episode). The screening of Season Four in Australia included an audience promotion: solve the *24* code within the hour to win a prize.

Real-time, functioning as a narrative frame, constitutes a striking departure from traditional realism. The long take and deep focus, according to Bazin, achieves an "image-structure" "[that] is more realistic."[133] *24* foregrounds the temporal and spatial presence of the cut, often splicing an image into multiple frames (a number of filmmakers have used this device—De Palma and Tarantino come to mind, but it is rare in commercial television). Furthermore, the cut is established as a moment in *virtual real time*. The spectator is aware of the spatial and temporal location of the cut within the narrative. A multiple-frame shot is accompanied by the digital readout that coordinates the narrative into a sequence of artificially constructed *time segments*. Rather than achieving the perfection of the realist image in Bazinian terms, paradoxically, the real-time narrative structure imposes a virtuality on the action-image. The narrative is subjected to the process of simulated time that "inscribes [the viewer] into the scene, in the first instance by perspective and in the second, into the temporality or action by the narrative."[134] The Real recedes only to bring the *real-time* generated spectacle into greater relief.

Traditional formal narrative structures such as the flashback and frame (*Double Indemnity, Sunset Boulevard*) are prohibited in the real-time

The spatial/temporal segment in 24: *constructing real-time narrative frames.*

image. In this sense, the relation between "reality" and the real-time narrative conforms to Baudrillard's conception of the relation between the Real and hyperreal. The real-time image effaces the Bazinian essentiality of the visual image, foregrounding the cut, montage, and the hyperstylized relations of the visual (cinematic) form. The real-time image finds form only in spatial and temporal *segments* rather than a fluid and uncontaminated realism. The genericity of the plotline complements the constructedness of the time sequence. Jack Bauer (Kiefer Sutherland) may just as well be Jack Ryan (Tom Clancy's intrepid patriotic hero played by Alec Baldwin in *The Hunt for Red October* and Harrison Ford in *Patriot Games* and *Clear and Present Danger*). CTU is merely the latest manifestation of the generic U.S. intelligence agency. The fact that Bauer works in the Counter-Terrorist Unit provides a post-9/11 intrigue in international terrorism and the insurgencies in Iraq and Afghanistan. Season Four focuses on a terrorist plot organized by a professional Middle Eastern terrorist cell stationed in Los Angeles.

Time segments are organized visually through a network of imaging and audio devices: satellite surveillance, infrared, subway system surveillance cameras, telescopic sights, night-vision goggles, phone taps, tracking devices, microscopic cameras. Apart from the fetish appeal, the surveillance technology employed by CTU personnel constructs a spatial and temporal simulation of the Real: environments are mediated through image reproduction. There is a tremendous vicarious thrill in the spectator's perception of the hostile character through a technologically mediated form. The spectator pursues a digital representation of the hostile rather than the Real figure. Ridley Scott was able to achieve a similar effect in *Alien* through the ingenious contrivance of the motion detector. Baudrillard's simulacrum is realized: *24* presents the thrill of the digital representation of the self (a figure on a screen) when the appeal of the Real form (the Platonic shape) has been aesthetically exhausted.

The Ontology of Bullet-Time

One obvious problem with digital cinema is that it has no novelty value, at least not for film audiences. This being the case, what will drive its future development?[135]

We're talking about cameras that are now broken from the subject matter, that are virtual. That's the next phase. That's what computers have introduced into cinematography.[136]

Each installment of *The Matrix* franchise opens on a digitized representation of the Matrix: the code of the simulation seen through the eyes of the One. The spectator assumes the One's point of view as the Matrix materializes into the form of the simulation: irreducible component into whole. The One reads the code but is simultaneously inscribed by it into the simulation. This motif is literally a deconstruction of the digitized image. The simulation is deconstructed into its component parts, digitized ones and zeros that form the simulation. The motif also functions as a framing device of the narrative that is installed into the simulation. The digital coding of the Matrix is thus a revelation of the inherent *constructedness* of the image out of its component parts. I suggest that this motif applies equally to the narrative, thematic content, and cinematography of the franchise, exemplified in the cinematographic innovation of "bullet-time."

I recall seeing the opening action sequence of *The Matrix*[137] in 1999 and being astonished at the visual incongruity of the images in terms of their relation to the sequence as a whole. As perhaps viewers of *Citizen Kane* in 1941 did, the spectator senses some transformation in the constitution of shot, sound, and movement, but cannot conceptualize the departure from the conventional mode. Joel Silver suggests that Warner Bros. agreed to the film's hundred-million-dollar budget only after seeing a previously shot version of this sequence.[138] In my opinion, it is a virtuoso performance of the virtual (spectacle) aesthetic in contemporary popular cinema.

The scene begins after a brief exchange between Cypher and Trinity over a phone line. The uniformed policemen enter the darkened room, lit only by their flashlights. The high contrasts and low-angled shots quote classical *film noir*. Repeated viewings of this sequence indicate a hyperstylized aesthetic; the Wachowski Brothers are cinematic *stylists*. What makes them more unusual in this respect than a Scorsese or De Palma is their willingness to sacrifice narrative integrity to the visual hyperstylization of a sequence. (De Palma approaches this aesthetic in *Carrie* and *Dressed to Kill* but does not achieve the full potential of the stylized sequence as cinematic quotation.)

In this sequence, shots quote prior cinematic shots, lighting and setups quote a particular tradition or generic form. Characters are textual tropes: policemen inhabit a hard-boiled world that recurs eternally within the simulation. Trinity is configured as a sadomasochist Gothic; the shot of the handcuffs over her wrists confirms this textual configuration. The hyperstylization of the scene is apparent in the visual composition. The first shot after the policemen enter is a close-up of the handcuffs fastened to the lead policeman's belt. Trinity is in the background, out of focus. What is significant here is that her shadow is held in focus. The outline looks like a sketch in a graphic novel. The shot reverses (conventional shot-reverse shot) to a close-up of Trinity with her hands held behind her head, waiting for the policeman to fasten the handcuffs over her wrists. The first noticeably incongruent image appears. The camera, positioned above Trinity's right shoulder, holds both Trinity's face and the policeman in the background of the shot, perfectly in focus. The deep focal length is held as the policeman advances. Rather than a deliberate and heavy-handed shot innovation, the Wachowski Brothers initiate the sequence by reverting to a traditional stylistic technique in which deep focus stands in opposition to orthodox focal lengths. Deep focus is often used in mainstream cinema, but its appearance in this sequence in *The Matrix* is less a strategy of representation than a distinct cinematic quotation. It is less an innovation here than a quotation of a once-innovative aesthetic impulse.

The policeman slaps the handcuffs onto Trinity's wrist. The exaggerated sound (a sharp metallic grate) functions as a coda on the first movement of the sequence. The scene then devolves into a series of fast cuts and kinetic movements. Trinity spins, twists the policeman's arm, breaks it, and slams her hand into his face. The scene cuts to an overhead shot to capture the recoil of the policeman's head from Trinity's hand, and then to a medium shot of Trinity as she leaps into the air—and freezes. The camera rotates (it appears to dolly) on a 180-degree arc from Trinity's left to right. The shot is held in freeze-frame as the camera completes this movement. Reset on the opposite side of the room, the sequence is set in motion, and Trinity completes the kick that sends the policeman crashing spectacularly into a wall. The point at which the scene freezes, allowing the camera to dolly to the opposite side of the room, is the first instance of bullet-time in *The Matrix* franchise.

Bullet-time is less a shot in the conventional sense than a time-segment divorced from the narrative. The narrative literally pauses (Trinity is held suspended in freeze-frame) to allow the camera to reposition itself, and resumes after the camera has been repositioned on the opposite side of the room. Bullet-time achieves the effect of a sequence of cuts in which the camera is repositioned without the cut occurring in the film.

Virtual cinematography: the bullet-time image.

The movement of the camera (which is in fact only a simulated movement—the movement of the camera in bullet-time is captured through photographing separate visual frames and splicing the sequence together digitally) occurs external to the operation of the narrative, and offers an intrusion of a virtual space that spontaneously comes into being within the narrative. The bullet-time segment inserts a virtual frame into the narrative reality and achieves what Baudrillard conceptualizes in his simulacra: "that the real is no longer real."[139] Equally, the intrusion of the virtual into the Real contaminates the purity of the realist image. Narrative reality is subject to the spatial and temporal dimensions of the virtual (computer-generated) simulation.

The ontology of the image in bullet-time is reconstituted within a simulated or virtual representative plane. In the realist mode, the image is subjected to a narrative itinerary. The narrative functions literally as a control on the spatial and temporal ordering of a sequence. This is precisely why Bazin valued Welles's deep focus: it resisted the montage as a guiding cinematographic "voice" and revealed the Real in its unmediated purity. The narrative sequence in traditional realism is subject to causal determinism: action on film should conform to its physical attributes and dimensions in the external reality. The dimensions of a shot, camera position, and *mise en scène* in classical cinema follow deterministic patterns.

If cinema after Bazin has exemplified a departure from the Real, bullet-time achieves an advance beyond the spatial and temporal cinematographic strategies of earlier movements. It represents an incursion of *virtual reality* into an art form dominated by a realist aesthetic. Gaeta suggests that bullet-time is merely one manifestation of the possibilities of digitally produced imagery: "We're talking about cameras that are now broken from their subject matter, that are virtual. That's the next phase. That's what computers have introduced into cinematography."[140] It is also what earlier cinematic traditions did not have access to: the ability to map the image on screen according to a computer-generated simulation.

"Today abstraction is no longer that of the map, the double, the mirror, or the concept. . . . It is the generation by models of a real without origin or reality."[141] Digital imagery is the perfect realization of the simulacrum: the reality of the image on screen functions only as a reproduction of the simulated form. If Godard's work is exemplary of the departure from Deleuze's action-image, digital cinema installs a simulated image completely severed from a self-organizing deterministic reality. It is what Patricia Pisters, working through Deleuze, suggests is a "metacinematic universe that calls for an imminent conception of audiovisuality, and in which a new camera consciousness has entered our perception."[142]

The jump cut (Godard, *Breathless*), freeze-frame (Truffaut, *The 400 Blows*), and slow-motion/fast-motion montage (Peckinpah, *The Wild Bunch*) are each subject to the narrative frame. Godard claimed that he had used the jump cut to shorten the running time of *Breathless*. Even if we were to take him at his word, the jump cut offers a profound transformation of the ontology of the image. Subject to the jump cut, the temporal and spatial dimensions in which the narrative coheres are essentially reorganized. Causal determinism is affected by the capacity to leap time segments. The jump cut is not entirely disorienting in *Breathless* (the sequence rarely skips more than a few frames), though Godard's experimentation with fractured narratives in later films (primarily through editing) revealed the capacity to shift the ontology of the image in modern cinema and a willingness on the part of the spectator to accept this new relationship between the image and an external reality.[143] Yet in each of these cinematographic strategies (the jump cut is surely the most ambitious), the narrative is maintained as a hermetically sealed frame of representation. The jump cut intrudes upon and alters the cause-effect functioning of the narrative, but cannot sever the image from its location within a narrative form.

According to Gaeta, bullet-time cinematography was "conceived specifically for *The Matrix* . . . as a stylistic way of showing that you're in a constructed reality."[144] The technology allows the image to "go forward in motion and forward in time with the event."[145]

> I can also choose to stop the camera abruptly and start moving backwards while the action continues to move forward. I can shoot the move coming away from both sides at the same time, crisscrossing over, and ending. I can shoot in waves . . . cycles of film.[146]

The Real no longer dictates the direction of the shot or the spatial and temporal dimensions of the image. The cinematographic eye is no longer constricted by the physical presence of the camera. While *The Matrix* is ostensibly a genre action film with an interest in speculative science fiction, Gaeta is correct to suggest that the technology of virtual cinematography offers a new *potentiality* of the cinematic image that is only tentatively explored in *The Matrix*. The "burly brawl"[147] in *The Matrix Reloaded* offers a bullet-time shot in which Keanu Reeves has been replaced by a virtual figure; the *action* film partakes of the computer game (virtual) aesthetic.

I have argued that the synthesis of the Real and simulation in the narrative is a thematic that informs the visual aesthetic of the film, particularly its cinematography. With virtual cinema, this synthesis is realized in the visual aspect of the film. The ontology of the image in bullet-time (and Gaeta alludes to the fact that bullet-time is merely one innovation in virtual cinematography) is fundamentally altered, divorced at last from its cherished realist origins. For Purse, bullet-time realizes the most "heightened moments of hypermediacy . . . [in which] the spectator is drawn fully into the diegetic space, disrupting the conventional spatial relationship between the spectator, the screen, and the filmic world."[148] In this formulation, Purse approaches something resembling Filser's notion of a shared information between subject and text, or immersion.[149] I would not want to discuss bullet-time as a form of "immersion art." And yet, it achieves something equally radical in its acknowledgment of the possibilities of the digital (or virtual image) to transcend the classical montage, deep focus, or any manifestation of a perceived reality on film.

Notes

1. Debord, *Society of the Spectacle*, 13.

2. Bruce Sterling, "Every Other Movie Is the Blue Pill," in *Exploring* The Matrix: *Visions of the Cyber Present*, ed. Karen Haber (New York: St. Martin's Press, 2003), 23.

3. Umberto Eco, "*Casablanca*: Cult Movies and Intertextual Collage," in *Modern Criticism and Theory*, ed. David Lodge (London and New York: Longman, 1988), 447. This quote indicates the great distance we have crossed in our ideas of popular culture since Benjamin's "The Work of Art in the Age of Mechanical Reproduction" and the prevailing aura of authenticity.

4. Benjamin, 1171.

5. Barthes, "From Work to Text," especially 159–160.

6. Roland Barthes, "From Work to Text," 147.

7. Barthes, "Death of the Author," 148.

8. Ella Shohat and Robert Stam, *Unthinking Eurocentrism* (London and New York: Routledge, 1994), 178.

9. I refer here to Harold Bloom's massive study of Shakespeare and modern thought, *Shakespeare: The Invention of the Human* (New York: Penguin and Putnam, 1998). Bloom's contention is that Shakespeare's characters inform the prevailing sense of "humanity" or the essence of being human. In Bloom's universe, and in a modern parlance, this "personality" of the modern human is "a Shakespearean invention, and is not only Shakespeare's greatest originality but also the authentic cause of his perpetual pervasiveness. Insofar as we ourselves value, and deplore, our own personalities, we are the heirs of Falstaff and of Hamlet, and of all the other persons who throng Shakespeare's theatre of what might be called the colors of the spirit" (4).

10. Ohmann, 68–69.

11. Tara Brabazon, "We'll *Always* Have Tatooine," *Australian Journal of Communication* 26, no. 2 (1999), 4. For a similar sentiment regarding Hebdige's *Subculture: The Meaning of Style*, see Jonathan Sterne, "The Burden of Culture," in *The Aesthetics of Cultural Studies*, ed. Michael Bérubé (Boston: Blackwell, 2005), 89.

12. Hebdige, 129.

13. Stuart Hall, "Notes on Deconstructing the Popular," in *People's History and Socialist Theory*, ed. Raphael Samuel (Boston: Routledge, 1981), 239.

14. Felski, 34.

15. Brabazon, 8.

16. Brabazon, 1.

17. Jeremy G. Butler, "The Star System and Hollywood," in *American Cinema and Hollywood: Critical Approaches*, ed. John Hill and Pamela Church Gibson (Oxford: Oxford University Press, 2000), 116. My emphasis.

18. See Bruce Isaacs and Theodore Louis Trost, "Story, Product, Franchise," In *Jacking in to* The Matrix *Franchise: Cultural Reception and Interpretation*, ed. Mathew Kapell and William G. Doty (New York and London: Continuum, 2004), 73.

19. See Slavoj Žižek, "The Matrix: Or, the Two Sides of Perversion," in *The Matrix and Philosophy*, ed. William Irwin (Chicago and La Salle, IL: Open Court, 2002), 240–266. The article's title works as an in-joke with Jameson's "Postmodernism: Or, the Cultural Logic of Late Capitalism"—the two together offer a veritable prison-house of theory. Žižek's conclusion is formulated on a crucial misreading of the scene in which Neo exits the telephone booth as the reborn One. "At the same time, Neo addresses people still caught in the Matrix as the Savior who will teach them how to liberate themselves from the constraints of the Matrix" (263). But Neo does not address people caught in the Matrix. Rather, he addresses the Machines: "I'm not here to tell you how this will end. I'm here to tell you how it will begin." And as Morpheus says, those imprisoned in the Matrix must ultimately "free themselves," attested by the fact that at the conclusion of *The Matrix Revolutions* the machines will free only those who *want to be freed*. The film's conclusion is thus not an inconsistency in the way that fits with Žižek's theoretical bent.

20. For an extensive and detailed analysis of the "misreadings" of film and television violence, see *Ill Effects: The Media/Violence Debate*, ed. Martin Barker and Julian Petley (Routledge: London and New York, 2001). Of particular interest is Martin Barker's chapter, "The Newson Report: A Case Study in 'Common Sense'" (27–46).

21. Barry Keith Grant, "American Psycho/sis: The Pure Products of America Go Crazy," in *Mythologies of Violence in Postmodern Media*, ed. Christopher Sharrett (Detroit, MI: Wayne State University Press, 1999). 23–24.

22. Grant, 23.

23. Grant, 33.

24. I am thinking here of the scene in which Mr. Orange (Tim Roth) is shot by a female driver while escaping the scene of the robbery. He is then forced to shoot her at close range, killing her, and this allows Mr. White (Harvey Keitel) to engineer their escape.

25. Linda Hutcheon, "Representing the Postmodern," in *A Postmodern Reader*, ed. Joseph Natoli and Linda Hutcheon (Albany: State University of New York Press, 1993), 256.

26. John Belton, "Digital Cinema: A False Revolution." *October* 100 (2002), 107–108.

27. Belton, 114. The Australian critic David Stratton has said the same thing of digital cinema, rejecting the innovations of the Dogma '95 Group; Stratton seems to cherish Bazin's "myth of total cinema." Ironically, the Dogma group championed digital technology to distance itself from the emphasis on spectacle and special effects cinema of the Hollywood mainstream (see Lessard).

28. For two mainstream reviews exemplary of the film's critical reception in the U.S., see Todd McCarthy, "The Matrix Revolutions," *Variety*, Nov. 2, 2003; and A. O. Scott, "The Game Concludes with Light and Noise," *The New York Times*, Nov. 5, 2003.

29. Eco, "*Casablanca*: Cult Movies and Intertextual Collage," 454.

30. Bruce Isaacs, "Popular Postmodernism: The Cultural Logic of *The Matrix*," *New Media Poetics* Vol. 1 (2003), 1.

31. William Gibson, "Afterword," in *The Art of the Matrix*, ed. Spenser Lamm (London: Titan Books, 2000), 451; see also Sterling, "Every Other Movie Is the Blue Pill."

32. Aude Lancelin, "Baudrillard Decodes *Matrix*," *Le Nouvel Observateur*, trans. anon, no. 2015 (Jun. 19, 2003); posted in trans. Nov. 8, 2003, http://www.teaser.fr/~lcolombet/empyree/divers/Matrix-Baudrillard_english.html. Accessed Nov. 24, 2003.

33. Žižek, "The Matrix: Or, the Two Sides of Perversion," 244–250.

34. Chris Seay, *The Gospel Reloaded: Finding Spirituality and Faith in* The Matrix (Colorado Springs, CO: Piñon Press, 2003), 158.

35. Andrew Gordon, "*The Matrix*: Paradigm of Postmodernism? Part II," in *Taking the Red Pill: Science, Philosophy and Religion in* The Matrix, ed. Glenn Yeffeth (Dallas: Benballa Books, 2003), 96. I would suggest that *Star Wars* has not had as significant a response from the academic community. There are indeed dozens of articles and the occasional college course, but the academic material brought to bear on *The Matrix* franchise is of a scholarly register that cannot be found in other popular franchises. While films such as Scott's *Blade Runner* and Kubrick's *2001: A Space Odyssey* have received significant scholarly attention, their relative impact on popular culture at large has been minimal—I can only draw on box office receipts and personal experience to make this judgment.

36. Brabazon, 8.

37. Barthes, "From Work to Text."

38. Zygmunt Bauman, "Postmodernity, Or Living with Ambivalence," in *A Postmodern Reader*, ed. Joseph Natoli and Linda Hutcheon (Albany: State University of New York Press, 1993), 21–24.

39. See, for example, Laura Bartlett and Thomas B. Byers, "Back to the Future: the Humanist Matrix," *Cultural Critique* 53 (2003), 28–46; see also Seay. For a similarly orthodox narrative reading of the *Star Wars* franchise, see Lawrence.

40. Barthes, "From Work to Text," 157. Original emphasis.

41. Stuart Hall, "Cultural Studies and Its Theoretical Legacies."

42. Bauman, 22.

43. Barthes, "From Work to Text," 156.

44. Eco, "Innovation and Repetition," 177.

45. Jameson, "Reification and Utopia," 134.

46. Eco, "Innovation and Repetition," 170.

47. Eco, "Innovation and Repetition," 170.

48. Eco, "Innovation and Repetition," 170. Eco's discussion here is detailed and fascinating. He goes on to suggest that "the topos in *Raiders* is quoted in order to contradict it (what we expect to happen, based on our experience, will not)" (170). Interestingly, Spielberg had intended to follow through precisely in accordance with Eco's topos, that is, an elaborate set piece in which Indiana Jones (Harrison Ford) battles the giant. But Ford, suffering from food poisoning in Tunisia, was unable to complete the sequence. Removing the sequence entirely, Indiana Jones, in perhaps the most iconic moment in the franchise, casually dispatches the Giant with a single bullet.

49. Eco, "Innovation and Repetition," 170.

50. Eco, "Innovation and Repetition," 170.

51. See also Eco, "*Casablanca*: Cult Movies and Intertextual Collage."

52. A number of critics have viewed *Scream* as exemplary of the postmodern incorporation of art as commodity and the centrality of pastiche to postmodern aesthetics. In such criticism, there is a sense of this mode as redundant. See, for example, David Sanjek, "Same as It Ever Was: Innovation and Exhaustion in the Horror and Science Fiction Films of the 1990s," in *Film Genre 2000*, ed. Wheeler Winston Dixon (New York: State University of New York, 2000), 113–114: "Neither Williamson (*Scream*) nor very many of his contemporaries appear to be interested in critiquing or subverting those [genre] parameters. Instead, they merely call attention to them in the most blunt and obvious fashion. As a result, and unlike the work of those aforementioned directors and scriptwriters, the ideological dimension of much if not most of the horror and science-fiction narratives of the 1990s is paltry or pacified." Sanjek makes the obligatory mention of George Romero (*Night of the Living Dead*, *Dawn of the Dead*, *Day of the Dead*). Where I object to his reading of *Scream* is in its comparison of the lack of ideological intent in *Scream* with Romero's ideologically suffused films. While on one level the distinction is obvious (Romero's *Night of the Living Dead* works as a neat metaphor for the paranoia of the 1960s and *Dawn of the Dead* is a vague critique of 1970s American capitalism), it must also be said that Romero was a B-grade horror director who started out with midnight screenings of his films. *Scream* was a studio production directed by Wes Craven. A more

apt comparison would perhaps be Romero's *Dawn of the Dead* with the independent Canadian production *Cube*, or the Japanese cult film *Ring*. This is to say that *Scream* and *Night of the Living Dead* do not operate on audiences in the same way, or for that matter, on the same audiences at all.

53. Eco, "Innovation and Repetition," 170.

54. Eco, "Innovation and Repetition," 176.

55. For a sample of the wealth of material discussing *The Matrix* franchise as gender-conservative, or more broadly ideologically conservative, see Martina Lipp, "Welcome to the Sexual Spectacle: The Female Heroes in the Franchise," in *Jacking in to The Matrix Franchise*, ed. Mathew Kapell and William G. Doty (New York and London: Continuum, 2004), 65–79; see also John Shelton Lawrence, "Fascist Redemption or Democratic Hope?" in *Jacking in to The Matrix Franchise*, 80–96.

56. Consider a similar iconic scene in *The Empire Strikes Back* in which Princess Leia finally confesses her love to Han Solo before he is frozen in carbon, perhaps never to return:

> Leia: I love you.
> Han Solo: I know.

The exchange works very much in the way Eco suggests of the Indiana Jones/Arab Giant confrontation insofar as the viewer expects Han Solo to reply, "I love you, too," "consummating" their love in a generic exchange. Solo's alteration is all the more intertextually innovative for its recuperation of, and departure from, the generic form.

57. For an oft-cited attack on the insularity of external and internal frames of text, see Paul de Man, "Semiology and Rhetoric," *Diacritics* 3, no. 3 (1973): "The development of intrinsic, formalist criticism in the twentieth century has changed this model [literary 'form' as superficial]: form is now a solipsistic category of self-reflection, and the referential meaning is said to be extrinsic. The polarities of inside and outside have been reversed, but they are still the same polarities at play: internal meaning has become outside reference and the outer form has become the intrinsic structure" (27–28). De Man wishes to negate this divide between the inside and outside of the text.

58. For an interesting analysis of audience-oriented theory, see Will Brooker and Deborah Jermyn, "Introduction," in *The Audience Studies Reader*, ed. Will Brooker and Deborah Jermyn (London: Routledge, 2003), 1–4. See also Sut Jhally and Justin Lewis, "Enlightened Racism. *The Cosby Show*, Audiences and the Myth of the American Dream," in *The Audience Studies Reader*, 279–286; and Tamar Liebes and Elihu Katz, "The Export of Meaning: Cross-cultural Readings of *Dallas*," in *The Audience Studies Reader*, 287–304. It is worth noting here the degree to which the authors rely on empirical research in the service of cultural theory.

59. Eco, "*Casablanca*: Cult Movies and Intertextual Collage," 455.

60. Plato, *Republic*, in *Dialogues of Plato*, ed. and trans. J. D. Kaplan (Pocket Books, 1950), 361–362.

61. William G. Doty, *Mythography* (Tuscaloosa: University of Alabama Press, 1986), 174.

62. Sterling, "Every Other Movie Is the Blue Pill," 23.

63. Sterling, "Every Other Movie Is the Blue Pill," 25.

64. Sterling, "Every Other Movie Is the Blue Pill," 24–25.

65. Rage Against the Machine.

66. See Aylish Wood, "The Collapse of Reality and Illusion in *The Matrix*," 120. I concur with Wood that "*The Matrix*, whilst very different to *eXistenZ*, is as full of gaps and uncertainties, and that these gaps and uncertainties lead to a mistrust of the reality status of *both* the Matrix and the Real World. In *The Matrix*, the extent of the illusion, or the depth of the rabbit-hole, is not the only thing in doubt; so too is the question of where it begins and ends." The second and third installments of the trilogy further compromise the dialectic between Real and illusion, though I will say more about this in due course.

67. Sterling, "Every Other Movie Is the Blue Pill," 28. For a provocative reading of religious pluralism and its self-defeating philosophy in *The Matrix*, see Gregory Bassham, "Religion in *The Matrix* and Problems of Pluralism," in *The Matrix and Philosophy*, ed. William Irwin (Chicago and La Salle, IL: Open Court, 2002), 111–125.

68. Harold Bloom, "Dumbing Down American Readers," *Los Angeles Times*, Sep. 24, 2003. My emphasis.

69. Campbell, 30–32.

70. Jewett and Lawrence, *The American Monomyth*, 169–197.

71. For a detailed and thorough analysis of the mythic structure of *Star Wars*, see Andrew Gordon, "*Star Wars*: A Myth for Our Time," *Literature/Film Quarterly* 6, no. 4 (1978), 314–326.

72. Cited in Richard Corliss, "Popular Metaphysics," *Time*, Apr. 19, 1999.

73. See Roger Ebert, "*The Matrix Reloaded*," *Chicago Sun-Times*, May 14, 2003. Ebert writes that "it [*The Matrix Reloaded*] plays like a collaboration involving a geek, a comic book artist and the smartest kid in Philosophy 101."

74. Hall, "Cultural Studies and Its Theoretical Legacies," 278–279.

75. For an interesting discussion of the significance of mirror shades in cyberpunk fiction, see Bruce Sterling, "Introduction," in *Mirrorshades: The Cyberpunk Anthology*, ed. Bruce Sterling (London: HarperCollins, 1994).

76. The ingenious contrivance of the narrative is that, for the spectator in the movie theater, who is assumed herself to inhabit the Matrix, external reality and its historicity is a construct, a simulation of a prior (but no longer extant and recoverable) Real. Thus, *film noir* as a cinematic tradition exists *only* in the Matrix. The Real is severed from history in the city of Zion, a postapocalyptic limbo beneath the surface of the earth.

77. Larry Wachowski and Andy Wachowski, "*The Matrix*: Shooting Script," in *The Art of* The Matrix, ed. Spenser Lamm (London: Titan Books, 2000), 280.

78. Chuck Palahniuk, *Fight Club* (New York: Norton, 1996).

79. Donna Haraway, *Simians, Cyborgs and Women: The Reinvention of Nature* (New York: Routledge, 1991), 151.

80. For two excellent analyses of Buddhism in *The Matrix*, see James L. Ford, "Buddhism, Mythology and *The Matrix*," in *Taking the Red Pill: Science, Philosophy and Religion in* The Matrix, ed. Glenn Yeffeth (Dallas: Benballa Books, 2003), 125–144;

and Michael Brannigan, "There Is No Spoon: A Buddhist Mirror," in *The Matrix and Philosophy*, ed. William Irwin (Chicago and La Salle, IL: Open Court, 2002), 101–110.

81. Doty, 16.

82. Eco, "*Casablanca*: Cult Movies and Intertextual Collage," 455.

83. For a fascinating "reading" of his novel, see Umberto Eco, *Reflections on* The Name of the Rose (London: Secker and Warburg, 1985).

84. I use "pastiche" here in the sense of being an empty reproduction. This is a definition of the term I do not share with Jameson and others. I argue essentially that pastiche is intrinsic to the spectacle aesthetic.

85. Anne Lancashire, "*The Phantom Menace*: Repetition, Variation, Integration," *Film Criticism* 24, no. 3 (2000), 24.

86. Timothy Druckrey, "Fugitive Realities, Situated Realities, 'Situational Realities,' and or Future Cinema(s) Past," in *Future Cinema: The Cinematic Imaginary After Film*, ed. Jeffrey Shaw and Peter Weibel (Cambridge, MA: MIT Press, 2003), 60. Discussing the traditions of cinematic apparatus, Druckrey suggests "three 'regimes' of 'presence,' 'representation,' and 'simulation.'" This conforms roughly to the "regimes" of signification I have discussed—denotative, connotative, discursive. Druckrey focuses on the image-apparatus of the cinema, and his argument has something in common with Deleuze's distinction between the action-image and the time-image. For Druckrey, a contemporary immersive art is predicated on an aesthetic of simulation.

87. Barbara Filser, "Gilles Deleuze and a Future Cinema: Cinema 1, Cinema 2—and Cinema 3?" in *Future Cinema: The Cinematic Imaginary After Film*, ed. Jeffrey Shaw and Peter Weibel (Cambridge, MA: MIT Press, 2003), 214. Filser draws on Deleuze here in a conceptual of the fragmentation of the "action-image": "Description stops presupposing a reality and narration stops referring to a form of the true at one and the same time" (Deleuze, *Cinema 2*, 135).

88. Collins, 255. Original emphasis.

89. Lancelin.

90. Bartlett and Byers, 30.

91. Christopher Norris, *Uncritical Theory: Postmodernism, Intellectuals and the Gulf War* (London: Lawrence and Wishart, 1992), 11.

92. Norris, 31.

93. Baudrillard, *Simulacra and Simulation*, 10.

94. Baudrillard, *Simulacra and Simulation*, 11.

95. For a now classic formulation, see Marshall McLuhan, *The Medium Is the Massage* (New York: Bantam Books, 1967): "All media work us over completely. They are so pervasive in their personal, political, economic, aesthetic, psychological, moral, ethical, and social consequences that they leave no part of us, untouched, unaffected, unaltered" (26).

96. Norris, 25.

97. Lyotard, 29.

98. Norris, 27.

99. Morpheus describes the image of the self in the Matrix as "residual self image." The simulated self is literally a residual component of the self that originates in the Real.

100. Jewett and Lawrence, 59.

101. Palahniuk, 201.

102. *The Matrix.*

103. Wachowski and Wachowski, 393.

104. Philip K. Dick, "We Can Remember It for You Wholesale," in *Preserving Machine and Other Stories* (London: Victor Gollancz, 1971), 129–149.

105. See, for example, Philip K. Dick, *Ubik* (New York: Doubleday, 1969); and Philip K. Dick, *The Three Stigmata of Palmer Eldritch* (Gainsville, FL: Triad, 1978).

106. William Gibson, *Neuromancer* (Glasgow: HarperCollins, 1993), 12.

107. Lipp, 29.

108. Theodore Trost, "My Own Personal Jesus Christ: The Curiously Christian Worldview in *The Matrix*," (paper delivered at the annual meeting of the Academy of Religion in Nashville, TN, 2000).

109. Gospel of John 19:30.

110. Collins, 256.

111. Hutcheon, "Irony, Nostalgia, and the Postmodern," 5.

112. Hutcheon: "Irony is not something *in* an object that you either 'get' or fail to 'get': irony 'happens' for you (or, better, you *make* it 'happen') when two meanings, one said and the other unsaid, come together, usually with a certain critical edge" ("Irony, Nostalgia, and the Postmodern," 5).

113. Gene Youngblood, "Cinema and the Code," in *Future Cinema: The Cinematic Imaginary After Film*, ed. Jeffrey Shaw and Peter Weibel (Cambridge, MA: MIT Press, 2003), 156.

114. Adrian Martin, "*A Bout de Souffle (Breathless)*," in *1001 Movies You Must See Before You Die*, 370.

115. Deleuze, *Cinema 2*, 3.

116. Deleuze, *Cinema 2*, 3.

117. Filser, 214.

118. Filser, 217.

119. See Teresa De Laurentis and Stephen Heath (ed.), *The Cinematic Apparatus* (London: Macmillan, 1980).

120. See, for example, Darley; Jeffrey Shaw and Peter Weibel (ed.), *Future Cinema: The Cinematic Imaginary After Film* (Cambridge, MA: MIT Press, 2003); and O. M. A., Rem Koolhaus, and Bruce Mau, *SMLX* (New York: Monacelli Press, 1995).

121. For a discussion of the transformation of genre in recent cinema, see Wheeler Winston Dixon, "Introduction," in *Film Genre 2000*, ed. Wheeler Winston Dixon (Albany: State University of New York Press, 2000), 1–12.

122. See David Bordwell, "Classical Hollywood Cinema: Narrational Principles and Procedures," in *Narrative, Apparatus, Ideology*, ed. P. Rosen (New York: Columbia University Press, 1986), 17–34.

123. Ray, 32–55.

124. Philippe Codognet, "Artificial Nature and Natural Artifice," in *Future Cinema: The Cinematic Imaginary After Film*, ed. Jeffrey Shaw and Peter Weibel (Cambridge, MA: MIT Press, 2003), 463. Original emphasis.

125. Luc Courchesne, "The Construction of Experience: Turning Spectators into Visitors," in *New Screen Media*, ed. Martin Reiser and Andrea Zapp (London: British Film Institute, 2002), 265.

126. Courchesne, 256.

127. Codognet, 464.

128. Courchesne, 266.

129. Filser, 217.

130. I have argued that the spectacle in contemporary mainstream cinema has de-emphasized the narrative in film. However, this de-emphasis does not equate with a destruction of the ontological status of the narrative form. *Wayne's World* and *True Lies*, while de-emphasizing narrative to some extent, are overtly narrative films. In fact, the spectacle in contemporary cinema could be considered a simulation of the traditional narrative founded on originality and creative genius into generic textual quotation.

131. Courchesne, 257.

132. Bruce Isaacs, "Non-Linear Narrative," in *New Punk Cinema*, ed. Nicholas Rombes (Edinburgh: Edinburgh University Press, 2004), 138.

133. Bazin, "Evolution of the Language of Cinema," 35.

134. Malcolm Le Grice, "Virtual Reality—Tautological Oxymoron," in *New Screen Media*, 232.

135. Belton, 114.

136. John Gaeta, "Bullet-Time," *The Matrix*, DVD (Warner Bros., 2001).

137. This is the scene in which Trinity is confronted by three uniformed police in the Heart of the City Hotel and then chased over the rooftops of the surrounding buildings.

138. Joel Silver, "Making *The Matrix*," *The Matrix*, DVD (Warner Bros., 2001).

139. Baudrillard, *Simulacra and Simulation*, 13.

140. See note 136.

141. Baudrillard, *Simulacra and Simulation*, 1.

142. Pisters, 16.

143. For a discussion of Godard's "revision" of cinema, see Peter Wollen, *Signs and Meaning in the Cinema* (Bloomington: Indiana University Press, 1972), 164–165.

144. Gaeta, "Bullet-Time."

145. Gaeta, "Bullet-Time."

146. Gaeta, "Bullet-Time."

147. This is the sequence in which Neo confronts an endlessly replicating Agent Smith.

148. Lisa Purse, "The New Spatial Dynamics of the Bullet-Time Effect," in *The Spectacle of the Real: From Hollywood to Reality TV and Beyond*, ed. Geoff King (Bristol: Intellect Books, 2005), 157.

149. Filser, 217.

4

The Cinematic Real: Image, Text, Culture

The Spectacle Aesthetic, Or the Cinematic Real

> In talking about cinema, I have been talking about life as well; however, I do not want to make too many claims. I am not arguing that this perspective offers in some sense a better view of the world (there is no hierarchy). I simply want to indicate that some mutations are taking place, both in the image and in the world. Developments in science, art and philosophy all indicate changes in perception and changes in our relation to the world. It may be that this involves a generational shift. . . . Ultimately, we have no choice but to change.[1]

This chapter presents an analysis of recent popular cinema, focusing on filmmakers, films, and cinematic trends that I believe represent a profound intrusion into a prior dominant realist aesthetic. I argue that within a complex filmic arena in which the blockbuster and the so-called alternative aesthetic are often produced by the same studio,[2] these cinematic trends not only reflect but increasingly *express* a new ontology of the cinematic image and text. Equally, these traditions express a transformation in the ontology of the spectator, which must instantiate a similar transformation in the ontology of the film theorist.

The chapter also functions as a conclusion to this book in its attempt to chart the phenomenon of a new film aesthetic. The spectacle aesthetic is simultaneously about what contemporary film *is* and how it is *consumed*. Consumption, as I have argued, is a profoundly aesthetic engagement with the product at the level of textuality and ideology. Mass culture cinema is market oriented. Its aesthetic system, which I have attempted to recuperate, is immersed in the market system. I am astonished at what constitutes mainstream cinema in what is a dynamic and increasingly discursive filmic arena. The 2006 Best Picture Oscar for *Crash* is a case in point. Reports immediately after the victory described *Crash* as the lowest money earner to win an Academy Award in a decade. The film seemed to come and go at the U.S. (and Australian) box office with hardly a whimper. Yet *Crash* was subsequently rereleased in the U.S. to cash in on the Oscar win, demonstrating once again that a small, relatively independent production is able to integrate into a discursive U.S. filmic environment. It matters little what *Crash is* in a traditional aesthetic sense; rather, what matters is how it *performs*, and *is performed*, for a discursive popular film culture.

An attempt to identify the performance of the spectacle aesthetic is necessarily discursive in its point of origin and summation. I have traced the formation of a classical realist aesthetic in the studio era, drawing on the films and theorists I consider to have influenced the development of filmic traditions. In this chapter, I consider a number of cinematic transformations manifested in recent cinema: a new status of the film image, a new ontology of postmodern cinematic narrative, a new notion of genre. I offer a transformation on classical, or "pure," genre theories, drawing more concretely on Collins's notion of "genericity," which I will develop as intrinsic to the performance of metacinema in contemporary film. The staple film form—genre—is reconstituted as a new system of text, a *discursive formality* manifested in the films of Sergio Leone, Quentin Tarantino, Clint Eastwood, Robert Zemekis, and, to a lesser degree, John Carpenter.

The chapter will return to a more conventional approach to text in which the analysis is grounded in a comparative overview of several films and filmmakers. This approach is to reveal a film aesthetic that is anchored in the activity of film viewing, film reflection, and film "discussion." Discussion connotes an aesthetic engagement with film in a communal forum in which meaning is derived not in some traditional unraveling of the text, but rather something approaching Barthes's "playing" of the post-structuralist text. This is fundamentally a collective and, increasingly in film aesthetics, communal experience. The spectacle aesthetic is implicated in questions of a new authenticity, a new cinematic Real, and ultimately a "performance cinema" that renders the demarcation between text and spectator obsolete.[3] I will argue also that this aesthetic is intrinsic to a cinematic subjectivity, for which everything is in a sense performed onscreen.

In concluding this book, I return to a point at which it began: engaging the aesthetic impulse. I am convinced by McCann's assessment of what needs to be done to make film theory meaningful for a contemporary culture that knows its films in ways far removed from traditional theorists:

> Film theory needs to think less of itself and more of the movies. It must spend less time seeking to ingratiate itself with academic grandees and more time trying to appeal to movie audiences. It has come to respect the film, but it has still to love the movie. If film theory is to be for something really worthwhile, it had better be for people other than theorists.[4]

I am not aligning myself with each of McCann's claims; my project is at least in part indebted to a rich legacy of film theory and analysis. Yet I share his view that film theory stops well short of "loving" the movies, and until such a transformation in the ontology of the theorist takes place, film theory resides in an opposing camp to the object of its theory, and this will always be a profound limitation.

The Metacinematic Lens

Broadly speaking, I perceive three forms of the metacinematic aesthetic that will form a foundation to the argument that follows: the performance of genre ("genericity"), various image strategies in recent cinema, and the inception of postmodern narrative devices. In the section on postmodern narrative, I trace a departure from the classical narrative frame that functioned as a staple of studio-era cinema. *Singin' in the Rain* and *Double Indemnity* are two noteworthy examples of the conventional use of the frame in which the action departs from and then returns to a point of origin. In *Reservoir Dogs*, *Pulp Fiction*, and Fincher's *Fight Club*, I will argue that the narrative frame is collapsed, and that the distinction between diegetic and nondiegetic utterance is blurred.

The aesthetic I attempt to chart is founded upon a rejection of classical realism. But whereas *Citizen Kane* and classical *noir* cinema are merely retroactively "metacinematic," the cinema of Sergio Leone and Quentin Tarantino embrace this aesthetic as the point of artistic inception. In this new aesthetic sensibility, cinema is ultimately a cinema of style and an aestheticization of prior cinematic representations. This is all to say that Leone and Tarantino (or the less well known John Carpenter and Brian De Palma) approach the aesthetics of cinema in a very different way than their much-idealized predecessors of the Hollywood studio era or the European art-cinema scene of the 1960s and 1970s. Leone and Tarantino *think differently* about film: about the way it is "created," the way in which it functions on an audience—about what it essentially is. I contend that their audiences are required to do the same.

The innovation toward metacinema—and more specifically, the departure from classical realism—occurs earlier than Tarantino and his postmodern coterie. But whereas something like Antonioni's masterpiece about the irresolution of the cinematic image—*Blow-Up*—clearly establishes a dialectic between meaning and a lack of meaning, Tarantino's cinema embraces only a unique form of *cinematic* meaning in which the traditional dialectic is rendered obsolete. Tarantino's cinema "means" *only* through cinematic *topoi* (to recall Eco's very useful term). Antonioni's great modernist defeat of meaning—one recalls the photo-grapher's (David Hemmings) eyes as they traverse the path of an imaginary tennis ball in the concluding scene in *Blow-Up*—seems a quaint intellectualism when measured alongside Tarantino's cinematic "caricatures," or the character ephemera of past cinema, television, pulp novels, tabloid magazines, and mainstream film iconomania. For Tarantino, the cinematic imaginary is indeed "even better than the real thing." As the photographer vanishes from a once-resolute and wholly integral realism of the image in Antonioni's film, so the classical modernist auteur of the 1960s, viewed retrospectively from the 1990s, becomes a thing of the past. Antonioni's meditation on the ephemeral image is tragic and yet triumphant in its expression of a dialectic of truth/reality, constructed images and the psychological imaginary. Tarantino's cinematic simulacra have little of this pathos or profundity. I should however stress that, in my argument, such a lack in Tarantino's cinema (or Leone's) is not regarded as debasement of an earlier modernist aesthetic mode.

Character Acting

In Tarantino's *Reservoir Dogs*, an undercover policeman, Mr. Orange (Tim Roth), must insinuate his way into a party of criminals who are planning to rob a bank. The film is not a conventional heist film; the heist is conspicuously missing from the final cut, apart from a momentary flashback to its aftermath. *Reservoir Dogs* might be considered an unconventional character study, although this would surely not take account of the generic aspects of the characters and storyline. The anonymity of the characters (and their designation by color) is a familiar trope of this kind of genre crime story. Paul Auster uses a similar device in *Ghosts*, a novella in *New York Trilogy*.[5] The device in Auster's novel functions as a neat realization of the ubiquity of types in generic fiction. I want to make of Tarantino's films a claim similar to that which Auster seems to make of the novel: that the representation of an object (whether cinematic or novelistic), or an "objective reality," draws that object field into its mimetic construct. This chapter is in part an attempt to conceptualize and ultimately come to terms with this kind of textual awareness as it is performed in mainstream cinema.

The challenge posed by *Reservoir Dogs* seems to be a self-aware mediation between the serious character film ("I don't believe in tipping" as social commentary, "you're fuckin Baretta" as a pop culture [and all the more serious] take on contemporary mainstream masculinity) and the generic escapism of crime capers such as *The Hot Rock* or *Topkapi*. The viewer must negotiate these separate aesthetic modes—a verisimilitude to a traditional form of realism, and equally a verisimilitude to a traditional form of *generic* realism. Before Mr. Orange (Tim Roth) can meet his crew, he must literally assume his character. He must materialize within the script in which Mr. Orange plays the lead role; in a sense, the action involving Mr. Orange in *Reservoir Dogs* is always already a script within a script. Tarantino does the same for Jules (Samuel Jackson) and Vincent (John Travolta) in *Pulp Fiction*. Arriving early to collect Marsellus Wallace's briefcase, they "hang back" to discuss the incident involving Tony Rocky Horror. Here the duo assume the mantle of New Age sensitive (hit)men who debate a broad range of issues. When Vincent suggests a foot massage is inherently more than platonic, Jules says, "It's an interesting point." The measured remark functions as a coda to one of several inventive dialogue set pieces.

The discussion is left behind as Jules says, "Let's get into character," and the two assume the mantle of *generic* hitmen, leaving behind the less-than-conventional hitmen they were out on the landing. The hitmen of the landing resemble their counterparts in *Reservoir Dogs*. The opening sequence of *Reservoir Dogs* is an elaborate introduction to the "band of outsiders" in which they discuss the subtext of Madonna's *Like a Virgin* and debate the merits of tipping at a coffee shop. In *Pulp Fiction*, Jules and Vincent, shortly before assuming their conventional hitmen personae, discuss the contemporary mores of dating. The transition from one kind of hitman/robber into the generic role is an act of "getting into character" for the personas that inhabit Tarantino's metacinematic universe. The implication of this textual strategy is that all characters are merely imitating prior textual roles—in Tarantino's case, almost exclusively cinematic. In the shooting script of *Kill Bill, Volume 1*, Tarantino designates a fast zoom as "a quick Shaw-Brothers-style Zoom into her [the Bride's] eyes."[6] The next sequence, a flashback, is designated in the script as "Flashback— Spaghetti Western Style."[7] The set piece in the church that concludes with the massacre is almost a reproduction of two sequences in Leone's *Once Upon a Time in the West*: the arrival of Jill McBain (Claudia Cardinale) in Flagstone and the confrontation between Frank (Henry Fonda) and Harmonica (Charles Bronson). The Bride is of course the generic *Woman with No Name*. For Tarantino, even the cinematic shot (setup, cropping, cut) is a composition of prior filmic references. Leone did the same thing in each of his films. While a great deal has been written about allusion-ism, pastiche, blank irony, quotation (which has been explored at some length in this book), I am not convinced that current theories of post-modern cinema appreciate this aesthetic mode for what it is.

"Bad acting is bullshit in this job."
Mr. Orange receives instruction from his partner to use a "humorous anecdote" for authenticity. From the rooftop in which Roth is instructed to play a part as undercover cop (in the same sense in which all Tarantino characters are undercover players), the scene cuts to Mr. Orange's apart-ment in which he is preparing to go downstairs to meet Nice Guy Eddie (Chris Penn). The sequence is a Tarantino-esque ritual in which a film character must "get into" a generic character.[8] Mr. Orange wanders through the apartment to a song that apparently plays on a radio. The country-western tune is less evocative of a real time and place than of a cinematic past; Tarantino no doubt recalls the road film and its plethora of diner and road stop scenes in which jukeboxes are perpetually playing the same-sounding tunes. Mr. Orange says his spiel in front of a mirror (in which he transforms into "fucking Baretta," who is "super-cool"). The medium shot is held in a deeper focus to bring into relief a poster Mr. Orange has on his bedroom wall: *Silver Surfer*. *Silver Surfer* is a comic strip character that identifies Jim McBride's remake of Godard's *Breathless*.[9] Significant here (and exemplary of Tarantino's cinema) is his acknowl-edgment on film (a cinematic self-awareness) of a lineage of films that are generic performances. Both Godard's and McBride's *Breathless* are cut in this mould; perhaps Tarantino prefers McBride's version because it is all the more explicit as a commentary on cinema, and specifically, genre cinema.

Tarantino's films make unique demands of its audiences. I have never considered *Reservoir Dogs*, *Pulp Fiction*, or even *Kill Bill, Volumes 1 and 2* as revolutionary as some critics have in their use of unconventional plotlines, characters, dialogue, dramatic situations, settings, or music. Mamet's *Glengarry Glen Ross* has wittier dialogue; Lynch's *Mulholland Drive* is more interesting narratively and thematically; Scorsese's *Goodfellas* or *Casino* (or anything by Leone) is surely more innovative (and inventive) stylistically (and more specifically, photographically) than anything in Tarantino's oeuvre. But I do contend that Tarantino's cinema inaugurated a new wave as influential and potentially transforming as the Italian Neo-Realism of the 1940s or the French New Wave of the 1960s. The initial transformation did not occur at the site of a new media culture or pop culture sensibility, but at the point of a transformation in the ontology of the cinematic story itself, which relies increasingly in the last two decades on reality's immersion in cinematic texts, and on the ascendance of film as the dominant art form. I argue that Tarantino is the first real film auteur because his cinematic texts know no boundaries other than those that are already cinematic. In this respect, I regard Godard's *Breathless* as a genuine precursor to the new aesthetic. But for Godard, cinema was always a site of contestation. It was always necessarily a political art form, if not "merely political." Tarantino's brand of auteurism is a convergence of spectator/filmmaker/theorist that expresses a new cinematic culture divorced from prior aesthetic modes. Tarantino vacillates between an auteuristic self, creating such diverse works as *Reservoir Dogs* and *From Dusk Till Dawn*, and the quintessential pop culture consumer, appearing in 2004 as a guest judge on *American Idol*. (Apparently, Tarantino is a fan of several Reality Television shows.) I cannot imagine Godard or any of the New Wave auteurs doing the equivalent in 1960s European popular culture forums.

Shortly after the release of *Pulp Fiction*, film and literature courses found space in their syllabuses for Tarantino. Film scholars wanted to write about Tarantino *now*—as if to do so in retrospect would be to lose the essence of his cinema, or to shed the vitality of this quintessentially "postmodern" cinematic moment. One of my formative experiences as a film scholar was studying postmodernism through the rubric of Tarantino and Lynch; Lynch was "serious" postmodernism, Tarantino was "playful" postmodernism. Vincent's utterance in Jack Rabbit Slim's—"That's a fuckin good milkshake. I don't know if it's five dollars, but it's pretty fuckin good"—seemed to offer something altogether new, yet analyses of Tarantino fell back on the wholly conventional. Tarantino "did good dialogue" or Tarantino responded to the fascination and repulsion toward violence in contemporary cinema.[10] Perhaps the best way to express what I consider genuinely revolutionary in Tarantino's cinema is to say that he infuses his characters and storylines with a plethora of pop terminology and iconography, past and present, a functioning "wax museum with a pulse." Yet even this observation does not take account of the impact of the imbrication of such an aesthetic sensibility. Jameson might call it pastiche, the limitations of which I discussed in Chapters Two and Three. Other critics have called it a form of blank irony, which is invariably substituted for pastiche at some point. But in what sense is this cinematic performance—genericity—*creative*, and more crucially, impacting aesthetically on a mainstream audience?

Simply put, what accounts for the almost universal designation of the 1990s as the decade of Tarantino, as perhaps the 1970s was the decade of Scorsese, Coppola, and Altman? How does one conceptualize Tarantino's legacy and a legacy of cinema that defines an aesthetic of what Jim Collins calls "genericity"? I use the term legacy pointedly here: I am arguing that what is now quaintly "Tarantino-esque" or "postmodern chic" was manifested in the cinema of this period and self-consciously in the films of Tarantino. If Scorsese, Coppola, and Altman were serious-minded filmmakers (rather than artists), Tarantino was the equivalent for the 1990s— but without the "critical distance," to use Adorno/Jameson parlance. If Scorsese, Coppola and Altman wanted to "say something," Tarantino wanted to "make movies." I recently saw an interview with Tarantino in which he lamented the end of the mission/war film hybrid that gained popularity in the 1960s; he mentioned *Where Eagles Dare* in this context. It was his contention that the serious war film of the 1970s—*Apocalypse Now*, *The Deer Hunter*—rendered the action/adventure/war film hybrid obsolete. His next project, he claimed, was an epic scale war film that was going to be *fun*.

In attempting to trace this cinematic legacy prior to Tarantino, I draw on Sergio Leone's *Dollars* trilogy[11] and *Once Upon a Time in the West*, Clint Eastwood's *Unforgiven*, and to a lesser extent, the impact of Robert Zemekis and John Carpenter on mainstream and B-grade Hollywood cinema. It is more than merely noteworthy that a character in Carpenter's *Assault on Precinct 13* says: "I have something to do with death," quoting a line of dialogue from Leone's *Once Upon a Time in the West*. It is also significant that the line is quoted as a seminal cinematic quotation, a statement that has become synonymous with Leone's films and the Spaghetti Western in general. Carpenter's quotation is exemplary of a film aesthetic that is an essential part of contemporary cinema and mainstream viewing practices. It is fascinating to observe a cinematic "conversation" between several filmmakers through a single cinematic sequence.[12] In *Kill Bill*,

Volume 1, Copperhead (Daryl Hannah) is set on finally executing the Bride (Uma Thurman). Tarantino has suggested that Hannah's character is drawn loosely from a figure in an obscure Swedish action/revenge film, but the sequence in which Hannah walks down a corridor is a stylistic quotation of several sequences in Brian De Palma's films. The use of split-screen, which seems so outmoded in contemporary cinema, fits perfectly into Tarantino's metacinematic commentary. The spectator recalls De Palma's *Carrie* or *Dressed to Kill* and the almost obsessive use of the split-screen in those films. And yet Tarantino's quotation is merely a "reply" to De Palma's quotation of Hitchcock in *Carrie*, *Sisters*, or *Obsession*. Thus, Tarantino's invocation of De Palma's split-screen quotation of Hitchcock is simultaneously an invocation of the stylistics of Hitchcock. Tarantino and De Palma are performing cinema rather than representing a non-cinematic Real. The several quotations function as a stream of *metacinematic* dialogue.

I am not arguing that contemporary popular cinema is dominated by the metacinematic text. Instead, I argue that conventional textual realism has always been and currently remains the dominant aesthetic mode. Cinema continues to be classified as the nearest approximation of an external reality; a cinema that no longer engages mimetically with this external reality is considered aberrant. However, the most significant, innovative, and potentially impactful challenge to cinematic realism lies in "metacinema," and for this reason it is crucial to any theory of a new film aesthetic.

Foregrounding Genericity: The Limitations of Classical Film Genre

[There are] two aspects that define the text as an utterance: its plan (intention) and the realization of this plan. The dynamic interrelations of these aspects, their struggle, determine the nature of the text. Their divergence can reveal a great deal.[13]

Studies of genre have been at the forefront of cinema since its inception in the late nineteenth and early twentieth centuries. Porter's *The Great Train Robbery* (1903) is an early example of the Western and a precursor to the heist film, a hybrid genre form that developed in subsequent decades (*Rififi* is noteworthy is this respect). *The Wizard of Oz* can be seen as a fantasy adventure story. *Samson and Delilah* is a biblical epic of the kind that was a Hollywood staple in the 1940s and 1950s. Even *Citizen Kane* offers a generic plotline in its conventional mystery story and investigation of the meaning of "Rosebud." In fact, later in his career, Welles conceded that the Rosebud solution was more a gimmick for audiences craving an answer to Kane's inherent mystery.[14] Rosebud was the narrative trope the film needed to transform a conventional biography into a generic entertainment. *Kane* might be the greatest film ever made, but one wonders if the accolades would have been forthcoming for a Hollywood product with a genuinely nonrealistic thematic/narrative/character conceit.

Genre is a form of classification, a retrospective molding together of qualities that define either the genre film or a film genre, a distinction Schatz upholds.[15] The distinction forms a problematic in the conceptual framework of genre theory. On the one hand, a genre film conforms to setting, character traits, and recognizable themes: Ford's *Stagecoach* and *The Searchers* reconstruct a vision of the American West as frontier territory inhabited by character types. Both films engage with the uniquely American symbolism of the frontier as a New World, a conduit between an older form of civilization and a new modernity. *The Searchers* is particularly interesting in this respect. Ethan Edwards (John Wayne) is a man returned from the Civil War, in which an older system of values has been eradicated. Ford's humanism stands in opposition to later visions of the loss of self and traditional morality. Sergio Leone, whom Baudrillard considers the first postmodern filmmaker,[16] perfects the generic typing of setting and character in his *Dollars* trilogy, in which the anti-hero is a metageneric "Man with No Name." Leone reprised the Man with No Name type in the character of Harmonica (Charles Bronson) in *Once Upon a Time in the West*.

The *genre film* is problematic insofar as it intrudes into the neatly (and retrospectively) formed *film genre*. The problem arises in the definition of genre itself, for which we can revert to Bakhtin. The film genre component of Schatz's paradigm works with Bakhtin's text as formal system, the "dynamic interrelations" of the text's intention and mode of realization. Thomson describes (negatively) a traditional formalist approach to genre as "an abstract construct that is situated at a higher level than the individual literary work. Missing from what is essentially a hierarchical and classificatory scheme is an account of how we move from specific text to generic type."[17] Bakhtin offers an advance on this rigid hierarchical model: "As an utterance (or part of an utterance) no one sentence, even if it has only one word, can ever be repeated: it is always a new utterance (even if it is a quotation)."[18] In this sense, the genre film, while conforming to type, offers a reorganization of the contours of the film genre. The necessity of Schatz's distinction—and the veracity of Bakhtin's theory—is certainly played out in the Spaghetti Western of the 1960s. Leone's films are a commentary on the genre form, yet they are simultaneously *generic*. Few spectators would argue that the *Dollars* trilogy consists of something other than Westerns, yet it very deliberately offers a departure from the classical Western of Ford (*Stagecoach, My Darling Clementine, The Searchers*) or Hawks (*Red River, Rio Bravo*). A film such as *The Good, the Bad, and the Ugly* bears the intent (Bakhtin) of the filmmaker to create a system of generic types while concurrently reorganizing and altering the generic form, semantically and syntactically.[19] Leone explicitly quotes Ford's long shots of Monument Valley (*Once Upon a Time in the West*) or the inventive camera shot beneath a running locomotive[20] that features in Ford's *Stagecoach*. Yet the storyline of *Once Upon a Time in the West*—a generic plot in which the Old West makes way for the New Frontier—is handled with a sincerity and absence of irony that recalls *The Searchers*, or the stoicism of George Stevens's *Shane*. The exchange between Harmonica and Frank (Henry Fonda) about the loss of the traditional hero is a moving account of what Leone's films embody: a passing of a kind of Western, and indeed, a kind of cinema. The passing of the Old West in Leone is equally a passing of the Old *Western*, and as such maintains a duality as genre form and generic quotation. The elaborate Civil War battle in *The Good, the Bad and the Ugly* achieves a similar effect, combining the (original) generic utterance and the generic utterance as quotation. Eastwood cares for a fatally wounded soldier in perhaps the most tender moment in Leone's work, only to don the antiheroic mantle that must lead inexorably to the metacinematic Western shootout between the Good and the Bad. (Leone also inserts the fool, Tico [Eli Wallach], who is ultimately spared.)

Underwood's *City Slickers* achieves a more recent synergy of original utterance and generic quotation. The protagonist (Billy Crystal) is cast as a man suffering a midlife crisis in the midst of a cattle-drive weekend vacation. The vacation is a literal transposition of the Western setting and character into a contemporary simulation. The frontier of the New World is reconfigured as a theme-park Wild West (Baudrillard's reading of Disneyland is interesting in this respect[21]) but maintains the value system of 1990s Middle America. The presence of Jack Palance functions as an explicit quotation of his character in *Shane*, though Palance is recast here as a sanguine reflection of the unremittingly evil villain. The protagonist learns to "be a man" by steering cattle through a storm and partaking of the Wild Western ways of the traditional (and generic) American cowboy. Billy Crystal's "everyman" is a 1990s incarnation of Tom Dunson (John Wayne) in Hawks's *Red River*. The stirring "*Yeehaaahhh!*" that initiates the cattle drive sequence in *City Slickers* is a quotation of its forebear in *Red River*. (Slim Pickens rides an atomic bomb after the same exclamation in Kubrick's *Dr. Strangelove*.)

If the genre film is an intrusion into the formalism of the film genre, in what way is genre maintained as a classificatory and ordering system, and in what way are genre films able to maintain their "genericity"? If, as Altman suggests, early genre theory follows an either/or methodological approach to the semantic and syntactic components of film genre,[22] what might a fuller account of film genres and genre films constitute? And what accounts for the resilience of genre theory in the broader discipline of film studies?

First, genre foregrounds and ultimately privileges the formal *organization* of texts, and this is particularly true of popular cinema. As Eco suggests, "A popular song, a TV commercial, a comic strip, a detective novel, a Western movie were seen as more or less successful tokens of a given model or type. As such, they were judged as pleasurable but non-artistic."[23] The "organizational aesthetic" (repetition, innovation, quotation) is thus connected to the value of art as *entertainment*.[24] The genre film is easy to follow; it has a familiar storyline and a foreseeable outcome; it provides types and forms we recognize and feel comfortable with; it assures us that conflict is necessary but resolvable, that distinctions between good and bad exist (even if they are not always distinct from each other), and that they are maintained by a value system external to the plot. The genre film is accessible to a mass culture because this culture has internalized its conventions and functionality. In this culture, genre is the dominant cinematic form. It was the staple of the Hollywood studio system of the 1930s, 1940s, and 1950s, and has remained so in the era of blockbuster cinema and the film franchise.

The visual structure of genre emphasizes what Carroll calls the "pictorial representation":

> These images [single shots—a close-up or long shot] are, for the most part, representational, but, more important, they are *pictorial* representations. They refer to their referents by way of *picturing*, by displaying or manifesting a delimited range of resemblances to their referents. By recognizing these similarities, the spectator comes to know what the picture depicts, whether a man, a horse, a house, and so on.[25]

Carroll accounts for the popularity of mainstream cinema as "pictorial representations [that] differ radically from linguistic representations. The speed with which the former is [*sic*] mastered suggests that it does not require special learning. . . . Rather, the capacity to recognize what a picture depicts emerges in tandem with the capacity to recognize the kind of object that serves as the model of the picture."[26] Carroll's contention seems to be that popular cinema functions through an inherent familiarity; the pictorial offers the accessibility of a recognizable form. While I feel this oversimplifies the appeal of popular cinema, I agree that the popularity of mainstream cinema is related (if not proportional) to its degree of accessibility. *The Silence of the Lambs* is a rich and complex genre hybrid, yet it was also one of the box office hits of 1991 and can be credited with establishing the commercial viability of the serial killer genre as divorced from the staple and tested "crime film." Generic oversimplicity perhaps accounts for recent box office flops such as *Catwoman* and *Daredevil*, or the tawdry crime films *Double Jeopardy* (the reference to *Double Indemnity* is misleading; the film achieves nothing of *Double Indemnity*'s virtuosity as *noir*) and *The Bone Collector*.

The acceptability of genre by mass culture (the crucial legitimation that is withheld from the art film) derives from its status as a popular form. Genre is truly "of the people," a popular form constructed and conventionalized for the masses, but also authorized and legitimated *by its popularity*. One of the more obvious contrasts between the genre film of classical Hollywood cinema and the art film of the 1960s and 1970s[27] produced within the Hollywood system is the linear structure of genre's narrative and its emphasis on resolution and narrative closure. There are remarkably few films that could be considered mainstream successes that depart from conventional narrative forms. Similarly, one could contrast Jim Carrey's Joel Barish (*Eternal Sunshine of the Spotless Mind*) with his embodiment of the generic everyman in Truman Burbank (*The Truman Show*). Barish exemplifies an art-film whimsy and dissociation from a conventional (generic) external reality, while Truman is the epitome of that generic role; Carrey's often hyperbolic performance even lends itself to caricature.

Jancovich, discussing the work of James Naremore and Andrew Tudor, suggests that approaches to the study of genre, while dissimilar structurally,

> illustrate the point that genre definitions are not simply of academic interest, but have far greater currency and significance.

Both also emphasize that genre definitions are produced more by the ways in which films are understood by those who produce, mediate and consume them, than they are by the internal properties of the films themselves.[28]

The currency stems from the notion that generic properties are in some sense a reflection of a cultural reality; genre is an indicator of the kinds of stories, characters, and ideas that pique the enthusiasm of mainstream audiences and mainstream cultures. This is no doubt the case. Genre cinema is connected to the structure of an external reality as formulaic, or already familiar. Perhaps there is also a sense of the generic role or story as partaking of a collective mythic store and reconfiguring that myth as textual trope. However, the shortcoming of Jancovich's approach lies in the less thorough treatment of the internal properties of genre films, a shortcoming that is all the more apparent when one considers the stylistics and thematics of the work of Leone, Tarantino, Fincher, Paul Thomas Anderson, and Christopher Nolan as *genre* properties. In this field of postmodern cinema, or New Punk cinema, or however we designate contemporary innovative film practices, the integrity of genre matters.

Genre and Contemporary Cinematic Forms

It is clear that the centrality of genre films in popular culture demands a strategy for assessing the formal characteristics of generic forms, as well as their impact on audiences and cultures. "What can be said about genre? It seems universally true that escapism rules when it comes to blockbusters."[29] I would add that escapism functions on a textual familiarity. The recent increase in the number of remakes or sequels in Hollywood reflects the essential conservatism in the studio production ethic. Genre cinema is bankable.

The pervasiveness of formal genre principles in the dominant mode of contemporary cinema (the franchise or blockbuster film) is a crucial aspect of any study of mainstream cinema. If the dominance of cinema in popular culture is contingent on an element of escapism, genre is central to the development of this trend from classical Hollywood to the present. Braudy suggests that

the typical genre situation is a contrast between form and content. With the expectations of stock characters, situations, or narrative rhythms, the director can choose areas of free aesthetic play within. In genre films the most obvious focus of interest is neither complex characterization nor intricate visual style, but pure story. Think about the novel we can't put down. That rare experience in literature is the common experience in film.[30]

"Pure story," I would argue, relies on a sense of storied patterns, familiar narratives, and stock character types and settings—in short, the elements of genre. Braudy is correct to suggest that genre offers a realm of aesthetic play, but it is a realm that is constrained by generic principles. The parameters of genre are an aesthetic point of impact. The boundaries of the genre story or characterization, to use Braudy's fields of inquiry, invigorate the familiar patterns into something immediate, vital, and authentic. Citing Ian Eng, Jancovich suggests that "it is not the *fact* of differences [of tastes in popular culture] but 'the meaning of differences that matter.'"[31] One could equally argue that the boundaries of genre respond to a set of prescribed tastes that are different in specific ways and that reflect the differences in generic plots and characters. The internal properties of genre matter as sites of cultural meaning when consumed by the spectator. Thus, even familiar plotlines or characters are in some sense invigorating. This is not to conflate invigoration as a response to a mode of creativity with a more traditional sense of "originality"; I am not arguing that genre cinema aspires to a classical aesthetic of originality.

While genre studies presents a number of shortcomings as a cinematic metatheory,[32] cinema is increasingly reliant on generic forms to be commercially viable. But of even greater significance is the pervasiveness of generic tendencies in even the most self-conscious art film. Bordwell contends that "the art film defines itself explicitly against the classical narrative mode, and especially against the cause-effect linkage of events."[33] But the nature of the distinction between art film and commercial genre product is increasingly difficult to locate. I appreciate Bordwell's detailed analysis of the distinction between genre films and art films, but a complication arises if we revert to Schatz's distinction between the genre film and film genre, which might equally (and even more pronouncedly) apply to the distinction between the art film and "film art." While Bordwell draws on a hefty body of work from the 1950s, 1960s, and 1970s in service of the art-film aesthetic (Fellini, Antonioni, Bergman, Godard, Truffaut), the kind of obvious thematic and, particularly, formal disparities between, for example, *Blow-Up* (1966) and *In the Heat of the Night* (1967) are not as common in 2005.[34] While art-house cinemas have continued to operate in spite of the assault on cinema-going practices by the multiplex, art *films* have greatly changed. Who could fill the oversized, auteur-empowered shoes of an Antonioni, Fellini, or Kurosawa, particularly as auteur theory has suffered a galvanizing attack by Schatz and other genre theorists? David Thomson's lament for an auteurist cinema of the past privileges the director with too much control of the cinematic product and conflates film with a more individualist creative art. For Thomson, "Robert Bresson, Bergman, Kurosawa, Antonioni" constitute the great auteurs. "But there is not an American filmmaker working today, or even alive, who is unmistakably of the first rank."[35] For Thomson, no living filmmaker is good enough simply because the material and aesthetic conditions for the production of the "art film" no longer exist.

The emphasis on the art film as inherently a kind of film art that is divorced from genre is increasingly obtuse when measured alongside the films produced each year by the major studios. To some extent, it may be said that Fellini, Antonioni, and Bergman draw their formal inspiration from a mode of European modernism and the avant-garde. For these filmmakers, cinema was an art form. The production aesthetic of this form of cinema was more concretely established as an auteuristic impulse or a traditional form of creativity. Film production—even production of a genre cinema in Hollywood's 1940s and 1950s—was equally art if it was *artful*. This was particularly the case of the French New Wave revisionist assessment of the Hollywood auteurs Welles, Ford, and Hitchcock. In contrast to what Thomson considers the golden age of cinematic invention in the 1970s, contemporary cinematic practices (from production to consumption) have effectively divorced the product from the realm of artistic authenticity. It is increasingly difficult to talk about any form of contemporary cinema (art film or genre film) as film art; increasingly, and belatedly, the film theorist no longer feels the obligation to do so.

Cinema is simply no longer a traditional art form that conforms to the hierarchical gradations of high art, mediocre art, and trash. Rather, the once-vital art-film aesthetic finds dilution in major production and distribution deals, but more significantly, in self-acknowledged generic or formulaic stories. Teaching a class recently on a range of what I considered "essential films," I was astonished to discover that James Cameron's *Aliens* was effortlessly dispatched by the majority of my students as mainstream trash, or generic junk. Even more interesting was the corollary notion that while a film might be "essential" to a particular spectator (or theoretical discourse), it might also be of little artistic merit and thus unworthy of the *kind* of spectating demanded by the previous week's essential films, *Apocalypse Now* and *Taxi Driver*. *Aliens* was exemplary of a time and place—a "cultural logic," to use Jameson's terminology—divorced from any meaningful criteria of artistic value. It became apparent that for the majority of this class, a sustained viewing of the film was commensurate with a lessening of the integrity of the spectator as theorist or critic. *Aliens* was thus an aberration on acceptable viewing practices.

The limitation of this form of artistic evaluation is that, on the one hand, *Aliens* is increasingly considered a benchmark in contemporary film aesthetics; it thus demands investigation. And second, Cameron's form of blockbuster cinema with a B-grade Hollywood aesthetic traverses the spectrum of traditional hierarchical value usually reserved for high-culture art forms. Jancovich suggests that a traditional notion of artistic value is increasingly difficult to apply to recent cinema; he refers to *Alien* and *Aliens* in support of this contention.[36] But even more provocative is something like Almodóvar's *Bad Education*, which is magnificent as *film noir*, or neo-*noir*, while simultaneously drawing on the generic brand of the art film. *Bad Education* conforms to the aesthetic of "genericity," which is to say, the purest and yet most corrupt form of genre cinema. Art films in contemporary cinema include *I Heart Huckabees*, *The Triplets of Belleville*, *2046*, and *Sin City*, none of which conform to the great auteurist/art cinema Thomson describes. In each of these cinematic works, the art film is less an innovative piece than a kind of *generic film art*.

The emergence of genre cinema and genre theory is connected to the emergence of popular culture as the dominant cultural entity. This is nowhere more apparent, and professionally coordinated, than in television and its corollary interests (news media, corporate advertising, Reality Television). The police procedural drama (*Law and Order*, *NYPD Blue*) offers hybrid generic configurations of the 1980s crime stories and popular mysteries. Chris Carter describes *The X-Files* as a reworking of the television late-night horror shows of the 1970s, including *Kolchak: The Night Stalker*.[37] Perhaps the best series to appear on television since Lynch's *Twin Peaks*, *The Sopranos* offers the most complex form of genericity (the series in fact foregrounds this genericity in its numerous quotations of gangster films and reality [Tony is compared to John Gotti on several occasions]). I discussed the remarkable innovation of *24* and stress here only its genre hybridity (rather than genericity, a distinction on which I will elaborate shortly). The phenomenon of Reality Television functions as generic reality for prime-time audiences. *Survivor* draws on *Robinson Crusoe*'s shipwrecked everyman and the communalization of *The Swiss Family Robinson*. (The hit series *Lost* also ties into these generic *topoi* but engages with a Stephen King brand of the popular macabre, an

intriguing metaphysical structure completely unrecognizable in mainstream television, and a *Survivor*-type challenge of the human spirit.) *Big
Brother* is perhaps the most interesting example of Reality Television in
its generic depiction (and yet hyperstylization) of the banality of "real"
life. These banal existences are only palatable (and intriguing) when
molded to generic form through a complex editing strategy. Nondescript
individuals gradually germinate into recognizable generic types.

The following analysis of new genre strategies in cinema attempts to
employ what Jim Collins and others (Rick Altman among them) have
described as "genericity." In Collins's work, I take this to mean more than
a conformity to genre or generic types in cinema. Rather, for Collins
genericity is a complex cinematic aesthetic evident in such films as *Blue
Velvet, Back to the Future, Part III*, and *Thelma and Louise*. What distinguishes genericity from the genre film is

> the recognition that the features of conventional genre films that
> are subjugated to such intensive rearticulation are not the mere
> detritus of exhausted cultures past: those icons, scenarios, visual
> conventions continue to carry with them some sort of cultural
> "charge" or resonance that must be reworked according to the exi-
> gencies of the present.[38]

While I will later address this in some detail, we can begin here by
assuming that genericity has meaning only in relation to former generic
strategies, and that it presents a qualitative transformation of those strategies. I argue that genericity represents a vital transformation of the
generic text. Schatz, Neale, Altman, Braudy, and others have examined
the semantic and syntactic features of genre. Genre theory has focused
on the Western, the Musical, the Adventure Film, and the Biblical Epic
as staple generic styles in the classical Hollywood era. Genericity offers
a new approach that reconfigures genre and genre studies, and finally
permits a means by which to approach genre cinema as aestheticized
patterns and textual structures, an invigoration of formulaic art and a
reinvention of pastiche as a profoundly creative aesthetic strategy.

The three phases of genre—the classical (or "pure") genre film, the
genre hybrid, and genericity (which is notable in the work of Leone in
the 1960s)—are not chronological, and certainly not uniform in their
appearance and development. I am not offering a historical account of
the way in which genericity developed, except to say that it appears to
have emerged as a textual strategy in the 1960s, but gained credibility

in the mainstream only in the 1990s. While it is true that *film noir* as a category of story is more obviously discernible in *The Big Sleep* or *Double Indemnity* (though the two are as interesting for their dissimilarities as for their generic commonality), departures from the "pure" generic form occurred in the classical era as well as in later films.[39] It should be stressed that genre is a theoretical tool, often servicing broad generalizations about film and culture. It is simple to classify a film as fitting a particular genre after the genre has been well established in film theory and practice. But it is also clear that genre films of the last two decades have undergone a profound transformation that was not clearly apparent or overtly manifested in the studio film of the classical era. Tarantino's version of the heist film in *Reservoir Dogs* does not mirror Dassin's version in *Rififi*. Almodóvar's "femme fatale" in *Bad Education* offers a gender reconfiguration of Barbara Stanwyck in *Double Indemnity*. And while *Back to the Future, Part III* is in some sense a Western, simply put, something else is going on that dissociates its generic*ness* from the traditions of genre cinema.

The "pure" genre is a necessary conceptual tool in formulating a theory of genericity. Film genre has never been pure, even in its formative period in the classical Hollywood system. Generic "purity" in my usage equates to a recognizable generic structure that informed the classical genre film, rather than a body of films that exemplify the generic form; this is a useful schematic for organizing film history even though it is also a generalization. Ryan conceives of classical genre cinema as existing only in relation to the elements of its generic form:

> A return to the individual film and its analysis enables us to find an appropriate role for the system-building, the taxonomic and inventory-oriented activity that characterizes genre criticism. Instead of asking the question, "To what genre does *Mildred Pierce* belong?," it is necessary to probe the consequences of positioning the film in relation to the various genres to which it has a family resemblance.[40]

In this sense, genre is also a reinvention of the generic plotline or character in which the film exists in relation to other films of its kind. Ryan situates genre studies within the very broad rubric of classical genre films, and this strategy will be useful to maintain as we proceed. Even a classic genre film such as *Double Indemnity* is not "pure" or self-contained genre fare. Classical genre cinema, particularly *film noir*, was based upon a formula, but it was rarely *formulaic* in the current pejorative sense.[41] As Bakhtin suggests, the *diversion* from the form or system offers a dynamic way in which the text makes meaning. The "pure" genre film is perhaps best thought of as a blueprint of film types that demonstrate a conformity to a single generic structure. *The Maltese Falcon* may partake of a number of film types, but it is clearly an early example of *film noir* (though *noir* was itself a development of earlier crime genres and a European aesthetic sensibility, particularly German Expressionism). *Stagecoach* is an early John Ford Western and has a very clear resemblance to his 1955 film *The Searchers*, though *The Searchers* is thematically more complex and filmed in color. Genre theory has rarely settled on a conceptual framework that describes the similarities and differences in films that form various genres. Neale suggests that "aside from *film noir* and melodrama . . . genre critics and theorists have identified around a dozen major genres."[42] For the purposes of this conceptual paradigm—pure genre, genre hybrid, genericity—I designate Neale's dozen genres "pure genre" forms.

The genre hybrid may describe a particular film or film type. Hitchcock's *To Catch a Thief* is a combination of action-adventure, mystery, and romantic comedy. *Psycho* is a mystery, suspense thriller (a genre almost synonymous with Hitchcock), and perhaps the earliest example of the horror/slasher film. *Sunset Boulevard* is a variation on *film noir* but it is also an early entry in a genre form that would develop in the sixties and seventies, "films about Hollywood."[43] One could equally discuss *Sunset Boulevard* as partaking of the aesthetic of genericity; Gloria Swanson's casting in the role of Norma Desmond (and her attempt at a "return" in a Cecil B. DeMille film) establishes a "cinematicality" to this narrative.

However, the genre hybrid can also refer to a combination of "pure'" genres. Scott's *Alien* offers a hybrid form of the horror and science fiction genres, while Cameron's sequel, *Aliens*, introduces the war film and adventure film into the original hybrid form. The hybrid is less a rigid splicing of separate generic forms than a synthesis. Occasionally a film foregrounds its generic hybridity (*From Dusk Till Dawn*—action thriller becomes vampire/slasher film), but I would argue that this is a manifestation of genericity rather than a traditional genre hybrid. Eastwood's *Unforgiven* (which I will discuss in some detail shortly) is a similar case in point in its awareness of its generic structure as well as the genre tradition of which it is a part. Neale argues that "many Hollywood films—and many Hollywood genres—are hybrid and multigeneric. This is as true of the feature film as it is of an obvious hybrid like musical comedy."[44] The hybrid, then, is less an innovation or commentary on pure genre forms than a textual structure that was concurrently employed by the major studios.[45] The genre hybrid can be regarded as a genre unto itself.

Genericity: Beyond Genre

Genericity implies a *performance* of genre and a stylization of the generic form. If the pure genre and genre hybrid were classical narrative forms that developed under the auspices of the studio system,[46] genericity is a textual strategy that developed within the postmodern aesthetic of reflexivity and textual self-awareness. The genericity film foregrounds its construction out of generic (and often genre-clichéd) components. But unlike the pure genre and hybrid, genericity is a cinematic aesthetic, a creative strategy that actively comments upon and reconstitutes earlier generic types and texts. The pure genre and hybrid merely serviced a storyline. As Braudy suggests, the classical genre form is "pure story."[47] The contemporary spectator did not address *Double Indemnity* as a generic system that manifested its constructedness. Recent film theory has addressed classical *noir* cinema as *generic*, but the classical narrative did not practice an aesthetic in which generic composition was instrumental. Rather, its generic*ness* was merely a consequence of the commercial viability of genre forms and their acceptance by a mass audience. Genre was a form of escapism into broad character types and recognizable story patterns.

The genericity film demonstrates two significant transformations on the pure genre and genre hybrid forms. Collins alludes to genericity as a textual strategy: "I use the term 'genericity' here because I want to address not just specific genre films, but genre as a category of film production and film viewing."[48] In the studio era, genre films were crucial to the success of the studio. Studios invested in a number of genre films each year to guarantee a return on their investment. The studio genre film was considered a product for the masses that guaranteed the financial prosperity of the industry. "Maintaining certain formulas that would stabilize audience expectations and, by extension, stabilize those audiences, was obviously in Hollywood's best interests."[49] The genre film compensated for the experimental projects, *Citizen Kane* and *The Lost Weekend* (though a studio could still bank on Billy Wilder to carry some weight as director). The genre film was thus associated with the cultural masses and the hegemony of the studio system, while dissociated from the art film and independently produced film (which were relatively rare). Genre cinema was commodity cinema, the art film was individual-ized, creative, and *authored*, rather than produced.[50]

In contrast to the bankable genre film that developed in a society for which cinema was a relatively new art form, genericity took place in the era of a cinematic society that Collins describes as a "media culture" mani-festing a "profound ambivalence [to traditional film genres] that reflects the lack of any sort of unitary mass consciousness."[51] Even more crucially, Collins recognizes the contemporary film spectator as attuned to a new "cinematic literacy" that recognizes the "entertainment value that the ironic manipulation of the stored information [exemplifying the generic-ity aesthetic] now provides."[52] Genericity functions as a viable cinematic aesthetic only in a postmodern culture in which audiences are familiar with a plethora of recyclable cinematic narratives. There is an element of what Collins calls "cinematic literacy"[53] in contemporary mainstream film viewing that I would argue was not a part of mainstream viewing practices in the classical era of cinema.

A second facet of genericity is the self-awareness of the genre text, a knowing and acknowledged textual artifice. While the pure genre is a hermetically sealed frame of representation that encapsulates story, character, and theme, the generic performance necessarily foregrounds its generic component structure, re-presenting what was once an original textual utterance. Collins offers a detailed reading of *Back to the Future, Part III* as an *articulation* of the Western.[54] In Zemekis's trilogy, film is itself subject to quotation; it is a spoken (or written) utterance that is "*always already* so highly mediated."[55] In *Back to the Future, Part II*, Hill Valley of 2015 is a vibrant stream of cinematic tropes. Marty is the cine-matic flaneur who traverses a pop culture arena incorporating a Café 80s (in which Michael Jackson, Ronald Reagan, and the Ayatollah Khomeini contest for cultural supremacy) and a holographic billboard of *Jaws 19* (in which "the shark still looks fake"). Crossing a street and almost run over by a car, Marty McFly Jr. calls out, "Hey, watch it! I'm walking here, I'm walking here," speaking the words of Ratso Rizzo (Dustin Hoffman) in Schlesinger's *Midnight Cowboy*. *Back to the Future* is a deliberate and explicit quotation of the Americana of the 1950s that developed on film.[56] In fact, the cinematic 1950s in *Back to the Future* intrudes into the real-ity of the 1950s as recorded history. Thus, Marty McFly (Michael J. Fox) is overheard singing "Johnny B. Good" by Marvin Berry, the cousin of Chuck Berry: "Chuck! It's Marvin . . . *Marvin Berry*. You know that sound you've been looking for? Well, listen to this." A Chuck Berry that exists in the imaginary realm of the cinematic 1950s inaugurates rock 'n roll by quoting a performance of "Johnny B. Good" by a 1980s American every-teenager (!). Zemekis manages to rewrite history on film in a similar way in *Forrest Gump*.

In each of these cases, but most explicitly in *Back to the Future, Part III*, the film demonstrates an awareness of its own immersion in "generic legacies." What makes Collins's reading of *Back to the Future, Part III* all the more compelling and provocative is the notion that this self-awareness and exhibition of generic components provides a "cultural charge" to the spectator that is indeed a new way of experiencing mass entertainment.

Performing Genericity

Contemporary film criticism has been utterly unable to come to terms with these very profound changes in the nature of entertainment because this hyperconscious eclecticism is measured against nineteenth-century notions of classical narrative and realist representation.[57]

Drawing on Todorov's work on the notion of verisimilitude in relation to "the fantastic," Steve Neale suggests that "negotiating the balance between different regimes of verisimilitude plays a key role in the relations established between spectators, genres, and individual films. In markedly nonverisimilitudinous genres these relations can be particularly complex—and particularly fragile."[58] He concludes by suggesting that the emphasis on realism as an ideology in cinema (and more generally, art) "is to refuse to acknowledge the generic status of realism itself."[59] Presumably, verisimilitude forms the basis of aesthetic and other forms of artistic engagement. Neale's claim regarding nonverisimilitudinous genres such as science fiction, musicals, and horror films is that, at some level, the generic representation must bear some relation to the object it represents. To disavow this relation is to negate the status of the representation. Perhaps one might discuss abstract art as a move toward this negation of the object, though even this has limitations: abstract impressionism bears some relation to a prior objective point of reference, namely, impressionism. Neale's study of genre is a defense of the importance of generic forms—plotlines, characters, and themes—to contemporary cinema and culture. For Neale, the verisimilitude inherent in generic representation on screen is a verisimilitude that matters.

At this point, it is instructive to set Neale's verisimilitude in opposition to Baudrillard's notion of the reproduction without an antecedent object discussed in Chapter Three. I drew on the simulacrum—the

Matrix—as a useful metaphor to traverse the gap between Baudrillard's seemingly absurd claim regarding origins and points of reference and the necessity of observing the very real challenge to traditional verisimilitude, or classical realism. The Matrix is a reproduction of the Real that bears the "residual image" of its antecedent object. Rather than an image that is a literal reflection or reflective representation of the object, the relation between the Real and the simulacral representation lies in the status of the *residual* image. The residual image, partaking of the original but transformed by the performance of the simulation, operates as a discursive (rather than denotative or connotative) system of meaning. The cinematic image is a hermetically enclosed frame of meaning, drawing on its own self-reflective origins, forming its own cinematic language. Metacinema in the current usage refers to a cinema that is about cinema. In my usage, the connotation is nearer to a cinema that is always already *of* cinema.

Tarantino's brand of metacinema imbues the cinematic image with a life that is derived from an antecedent object located in a cinematic universe. The performance of quotation, generic utterance, and, ultimately, genericity, reinscribes the original utterance (the veracity of which is now redundant) into a cinematic simulacrum. Tarantino's cinematic images bear the verisimilitude of a cinematic simulation. In *Pulp Fiction*, Butch (Bruce Willis), fleeing the scene of the fight he has "fixed," sits in the rear seat of a cab driven by Esmeralda Villalobos (Angela Jones). When Esmeralda asks the meaning of his name, Butch replies: "This is America. Our names don't mean shit." This is an American pop culture and pop cinema is which names are inscribed as cinematic tropes. Much of the extended sequence (which was trimmed in the final cut from a very lengthy [and labored] dialogue) is shot from the front of the taxi, with Esmeralda and Butch in focus. Tarantino uses a screen to shoot the exterior backdrop, which displays the winding, dimly lit road the cab is traversing. The use of the screen in this case is particularly significant. Tarantino simulates a shot that would have been used in a studio film of the 1940s or 1950s. The backdrop is noticeably contrived, deliberately artificial. The quotation of a generic car interior (the yellow cab synonymous with New York City [though almost all "New York" exteriors of the classical studio films were shot on Hollywood backlots]) and the backdrop that shifts in and out of a deliberately contrived focus recalls scenes out of Wilder's *film noir* or Hitchcock's suspense thrillers. But whereas Wilder and Hitchcock were attempting the purest form of realism that current technology made available (the most perfect verisimilitude at hand), Tarantino encapsulates the shot in a wholly anachronistic cinematic time and space. The result is a disorienting shot from the exterior of the cab of a classical studio vista in a 1990s film. Tarantino's characters inhabit a world bordered only by cinema itself; the yellow cab traverses a winding road that exists only onscreen.

I argued in Chapter Three that *The Matrix* requires a sophisticated awareness of its intertextual strategies to make sense of its storyline—specifically, to authorize Neo's resurrection at the conclusion of the film. I argue something similar in the case of Tarantino. Tarantino's films require an awareness of their intertextual (but more crucially, *metacinematic*) strategies to appreciate their aesthetic possibilities. Collins describes this aesthetic engagement as a "cultural charge." This is no doubt the case. But there is something more than culture at stake. There is also the inscription of a new aesthetic value founded on the play of the cinematic text within the language of cinema. I am suggesting that Tarantino's cinema demands a transformation in the ontology of the spectator/theorist, and this transformation (which is equally a transformation in the ontology of the artist-filmmaker) is something as profound and creative as the early challenges to classical realism posed by auteurs such as Antonioni and Godard. Tarantino's films are hermetically enclosed cinematic quotations that proliferate into a diversely articulated popular culture as quotation themselves, generating new cinematic trends and a new reality of metacinematic awareness. The attempt to create a new form of cinema out of the detritus of a past cinema is hardly original to Tarantino, but Tarantino's auteurism is new in its embrace of the corruption of the ideal, or really real, or authentic. Creativity here lies in an illegitimate authenticity that stems from a love of cinema (or better still, a love of "movies") rather than a love of "art."

At the same time that Tarantino was being accused of a vacuousness apparently endemic to the MTV Generation, or Generation X, or the "Me Culture," he was also being accused of a kind of cinema that is nonserious, superficial, and, in its worst incarnation, irresponsible. It is a cinema that represents, according to Christopher Sharrett, "an inhumane vision, a worldview that prefers the cynicism and self-absorbed death-fantasies that have always been the hallmark of capitalist civilization."[60] In short, Tarantino's films are themselves a waste depot, a detritus of junk parts synthesized into a product without meaning or value. In addition to this, as Tarantino refuses to take his screen images seriously (the argument goes), he divorces himself ethically from the consequences of his images on the culture that views his films. Tarantino is part of a contemporary culture that experiences violence, gender, and race only as cinematic representations, desensitized to real acts and real consequences. But he is more insidious than this. His films scrape away at a system of cherished and proven artistic values, reveling in the kind of chaotic referentiality that exemplifies a debased culture. How can the serious critic validate the pop culture references, particularly when Tarantino appears to offer little distinction between pop culture, pop capitalism (monologues about McDonalds, for example, or the merits of a certain kind of fast food over another), pop racism ("you're my nigger"), and pop urban violence ("We gonna go to work on my homes here with a blowtorch and pair of pliers . . . we gonna get medieval on his ass")? Tarantino offers it all in a kaleidoscope of pop iconomania, lovingly depicted in the kind of detail and authenticity that is the hallmark of a "serious-minded" artist.

This kind of criticism of Tarantino (which can be designated the "argument of nonseriousness") is inevitably ideologically motivated. What is perceived as nonseriousness in Tarantino's films is instead the apparent lack of a distinct *kind* of seriousness evident in cinema prior to the advent of Tarantino's "allusionism and bankruptcy of codes."[61] Thomson reflects on Coppola and Scorsese as America's halcyon days, or Bergman and Fellini as the equivalent in Europe.[62] For Sharrett, Tarantino's brand of cinema that savors a "pop culture detritus" is a consequence of the ubiquitous market, late capitalistic production, conspicuous consumption, and the industrialization of filmic processes.[63] Crucially for Sharrett, and exemplary of this form of criticism of the so-called postmodern aesthetic, it manifests a lack of "worth or concern outside the realm of cheap commercial representation."[64] One assumes that Tarantino's allusionism has little in common with Joyce or Eliot. Rather, this allusionism has nothing to sustain its performance or support its aesthetic ambitions. It is merely a dispersal of meanings into an overcharged, chaotic, ultimately valueless arena in which pop culture holds tenuously to its transparent meanings.

My argument is that the film theorist must come to terms with the ontology of the cinematic text as discursive. Inherent in this discursivity is the performance of cinema as cinematic trope, or a sophisticated system of pop culture allusionism. The theorist cannot search for value in the ruins of a classical aesthetics. Such an aesthetic pursuit is futile in a postmodern cinema in which a traditional classical aesthetic system is meaningless. Sharrett might question the value of a new aesthetics in which myths of urban alienation and disenfranchisement are mediated by the street philosophy of Eminem and Dr Dre; these same street philosophers chart the abjectivity of the contemporary self through the itinerary of megacorporate entities such as iPod or Limewire. I argue that such questions can only be meaningfully explored if the initial point of contact between theorist and object is a mutual *experience* rather than abstract criticism. Metacinema is a *performance* and, as such, is subject to an aesthetic appreciation.

For Neo, the Matrix provided access to a "residual self image" that synthesized and ultimately made redundant the really real self. I argue that the self that coheres in what Lisa Purse calls a "hypermediate"[65] culture is derived through a textual performance that implicates the subject in its textual itinerary. This is not the claim that audiences revel in allusion-spotting in *The Simpsons*, *Seinfeld*, or a Tarantino film. Rather, what I perceive in what Sharrett implies is a *culture* of allusionism is a sense of collective self (and ultimately community) that materializes in the textual system—the allusive fabric. For those engaged in this culture, and this *experiential process*, I suspect it is a very real collusion between artist, text, and subject.

The Metacinematic Aesthetic: Tarantino—Leone—Eastwood

In one of the iconic film sequences of the last two decades, Ringo (Tim Roth) and Honey Bunny (Amanda Plummer) hold up a coffee shop ("Why not?") in *Pulp Fiction*. Rather than a conventional hold-up—suspense, violence, the separation of criminal and victim—this set piece presents a sophisticated reworking of the generic hold-up. Amid the absurdity of the situation (the fact that Jules and Vincent end up in the same coffee shop as Ringo and Honey Bunny is an ingenious and unpredictable development), Tarantino locates the scene within a frame of reference that extends from cinema/television's origins to its present. The coffee shop is an imaginary space that partakes of a lineage of generic themes: transformation, revitalization, violence, beginnings, and endings. The characters that enter this coffee shop inhabit its cinematic space and time; they are well versed in *Green Acres*, *Happy Days*, and *Kung Fu*. This is a time and space in which popular culture is *performed*, and in which the screen and the object it seeks to represent are no longer distinct. Collins describes a similar synthesizing of the screen and object in relation to *Back to the Future, Part III*. Marty McFly must travel back to 1885 to rescue Doc Brown from the Old West. In the sequence in which Marty time travels, he speeds the Delorean up to 88 miles per hour, driving directly into a drive-in movie screen displaying a marquee-type representation of Indians. Collins suggests that

> when the characters travel back in time to the Old West, their trip is actually a voyage *into* the Old Western . . . his avenue to the past is a film screen, a metaphor literalized by his driving a time machine through a drive-in movie screen in order to reach the past. The screen, then, is a portal to a nineteenth century that can exist only in the form of images, in the form of cinematic reconstructions, and their very materiality is overtly foregrounded by the text, a point made especially explicit by the fact that the drive-in happens to be located within Monument Valley.[66]

After entering Hill Valley of 1885, Marty assumes the role of the Man with No Name (though in an inventive twist, he gives his name as Clint Eastwood); the banter of Doc Brown and Marty recall Butch Cassidy and the Sundance Kid; Mad Dog Tannen is a caricature of the Western villain (perhaps Liberty Valance [Lee Marvin] in Ford's *The Man Who Shot Liberty Valance*: both characters, Liberty Valance and Mad Dog Tannen, conspicuously refer to their nemesis as "dude"); and Hill Valley itself represents the building of a new town in Western cinematic mythology, recalling Leone's *Once Upon a Time in the West*. In *Back to the Future, Part III*, there is also an unfinished railroad that will materialize in the future, at which point the old railroad as new frontier (traversed by steam engines) is usurped by electric trains and Deloreans! The culmination of Western cinematic mythology in *Once Upon a Time in the West* (and perhaps the realization of all that Leone had wanted to say on the topic) materializes at the point at which Jill McBain (Claudio Cardinale) provides water to the men who build the station house in Sweetwater. A train whistle is heard, the steam engine moves in and out of shot, and Harmonica (Charles Bronson) rides off into the distance, a Western hero erased by the coming of the New West and the New Western.

Remarkable in Tarantino's cinema is the imbrication of this meta-cinematic aesthetic without a textual indicator. Zemekis provides the screen that functions as a metaphor of the transition between cinema and an external reality. *Back to the Future, Part III* presents a *cinematic* Western, a Western that not only finds the Old West on film but inscribes itself as part of cinematic legacy. Tarantino's cinematic universe seems to materialize with the first sounds and images of the film. *Reservoir Dogs* opens with the muted discussion of "Like a Virgin" that incorporates several other pop culture references. *Pulp Fiction* begins in the diner and moves into the "Royale with cheese" discussion. Tarantino does not explicitly indicate the parameters of this cinematic universe (as Zemekis does through *Back to the Future, Part III*). Jack Rabbit Slims, a *"wax museum with a pulse,"* is a microcosm of the wax museum that encapsulates each frame of Tarantino's cinema.

Kill Bill, Volumes 1 and 2 achieve perhaps the most perfect realization of metacinema. The cinematic space is explicitly constructed from the opening shot, including Tarantino's novelistic chapter structure. Characters inhabit the screen ephemera of their cinematic precursors. The Bride (Uma Thurman) is a gender transition on Eastwood's Man with No Name of Leone's *Dollars Trilogy*. The opening shot on the Bride's bloodied face functions on several levels as metacinematic performance. Bill's (David Carradine) disembodied voice reincarnates the figure of Kane (David Carradine) in the cult TV show *Kung Fu;* in *Pulp Fiction*, Jules (Samuel Jackson) says to Vincent (John Travolta): "I'll just walk the Earth—like Kane in *Kung Fu.*" In *Kill Bill, Volume 1*, Kane rematerializes in an old church in some anonymous town in the Old West. The opening in the church (which is replayed from several perspectives in the film) functions as a performance of two earlier film sequences. The initial performance appears in Leone's *Once Upon a Time in the West* in the sequence in which Jill McBain (Claudia Cardinale) arrives in Flagstone. Frayling describes a single tracking shot in this sequence as the most complex shot Leone had attempted up to that point in his career.[67] The camera begins on Cardinale as she moves from the locomotive toward the station-house (this is the same station-house seen in the first sequence of the film, which is a majestic set piece that seamlessly quotes Zinneman's *High Noon*). The tracking shot holds Cardinale as she moves onto the station-house platform and enters through the door, shifting out of shot. Now the camera tracks upward (on a crane) and above the station-house roof to survey the magnificent vista of the generic Western town, Flagstone, which moves with the frenzied activity of a town with a newly established railroad. The camera pause at the top of the pan is accompanied by Ennio Morricone's powerful theme.

This sequence is reproduced with remarkable acuity in Zemekis's *Back to the Future, Part III*. Instead of the widow entering a new town, Marty McFly enters Hill Valley of 1885. The town is a motif for Zemekis's Americana trilogy as it is for Leone, or John Ford, to whom Leone is obviously indebted for several sequences in *Once Upon a Time in the West*. Zemekis's camera replicates the complex camera track, surveying a newly built Hill Valley with its functioning railroad. Alan Silvestri's

A "Cinematic" Conversation – Leone – Zemekis – Tarantino.

Leone's complex tracking shot: Flagstone, the generic Western Town.

Zemekis—the simulacrum of the generic Western Town.

A Tarantino/Leone "collaboration."

score replicates the movement (if not the melody) of Morricone's. In this sequence, Zemekis is offering an explicit, self-aware quotation of Leone's sequence. As Marty McFly passes through the makeshift entrance to the new Western township of Hill Valley, the camera rises on a crane (reproducing Leone's camera move) and survey's the majesty of Hill Valley for the first time from above the town entrance (if not a station-house). Zemekis's shot is in fact a repetition of several similar shots of Hill Valley of 1985 (*Back to the Future*), 1955 (*Back to the Future*), 2015 (*Back to the Future, Part II*), and 1885 (*Back to the Future, Part III*).

Tarantino offers a stylistic quotation of the same sequence, relocating the town entrance at the entrance of the church, where the Bride is shot. Instead of the track from below to above the station-house in Leone and Zemekis, Tarantino uses an equally complex pan and tracking maneuver to shift from the interior to the exterior of the church, again rising from the ground to a position above the church. It is significant that this cinematic space (setting) in *Kill Bill, Volumes 1* and *2* is visited several times and from several different perspectives.

From the opening sequence in the church, the film moves to the Bride, who lies comatose in a hospital bed. The interior will comprise the space of Tarantino's "De Palma" set piece. Her passage from the hospital to the final showdown with Bill is a reenactment of Bruce Lee's passage in *Game of Death* to confront his final opponent. In the miraculous set piece in the House of Blue Leaves, the Bride is clad in a tracksuit identical to Lee's in *Game of Death*. Prior to the confrontation, the Bride rides a motorcycle through the streets of a cinematic Tokyo in which airplane passengers carry samurai swords on their person. The confrontation between the Bride and O-Ren Ishii (Lucy Liu) recalls a discursive performance of prior cinematic encounters, in which the sole figure must find her passage to her nemesis.

Prior to Tarantino's *Pulp Fiction*, the notion of metacinema (or metafiction, for that matter) referred to a cinema *about* cinema.[68] As I have indicated, my usage of metacinema refers to a cinematic spectacle that is always already *of cinema*. In this performance of a new cinematic aesthetic, Sharrett's grievances concerning a detritus of allusive fragments seem obtuse. The new aesthetic is not merely intrinsic to a very significant part of recent cinema, but it is also necessary for an aesthetic engagement with a kind of cinematic text. I would argue that the new cinematic subjectivity is increasingly receptive to this mode of experiencing its art forms.

Eastwood's *Unforgiven* is perhaps the most elegant metacinematic representation of the Western since Leone's *Once Upon a Time in the West*. Frayling's authoritative commentary on *Once Upon a Time in the West* (available on the DVD) illuminates the degree to which Leone's film is a simulation of prior iconic Western moments. Locations, props, even the choice of actor in many cases is merely a cinematic trope installing into the film a prior frame of reference. *Unforgiven*, however, attains a degree of self-awareness by installing Eastwood as character, actor, filmmaker, and mythic figure into the universe of the film. In fact, Eastwood as actor forms the basis of a major strand of Western cinematic mythology since the early 1960s. Had Leone and Eastwood not parted after *The Good, the Bad and the Ugly*, one could well imagine Eastwood reprising his persona in *Once Upon a Time in the West* (though what would that film be without Charles Bronson!).

The Man with No Name is often described as an anti-hero despite embodying certain overtly heroic tendencies. At the end of *A Fistful of Dollars*, the Man with No Name rescues a boy and his mother from Escobar (Gian Maria Volonté), the villain of the piece. The child, named

Jesus, establishes the Man with No Name as "the good," a moral/ethical status he will reprise in *The Good, the Bad and the Ugly*. While Leone's Man with No Name is far removed from the basic incorruptibility of Gary Cooper in *High Noon* or Alan Ladd in *Shane*, he manages to reflect the unremitting evil of Lee Van Cleef's turns as the bad in *For a Few Dollars More* and *The Good, the Bad and the Ugly*, or the organized villainy of Escobar in *A Fistful of Dollars*. Zemekis's reflection of the Man with No Name in the every-teenager Marty McFly is particularly inventive. Marty is a rogue with a heart of gold, but he is not beyond a little opportunism (which comprises the storyline of *Back to the Future, Part II*, in which Marty purchases a sports almanac in 2015 to take with him to 1985). Zemekis prefigures the coding of the Man with No Name in Marty's character in *Back to the Future, Part II*. Marty confronts Biff with his knowledge of the almanac as Biff watches the ending to *A Fistful of Dollars*. In the showdown in *Back to the Future, Part III*, Marty places a metal plate beneath his poncho (which inscribes him as the Man with No Name, Eastwood) before facing Mad Dog Tannen. The fact that Marty pulls out of the showdown merely functions as a knowing transformation of an earlier Western *topos*.

Unforgiven finds the Man with No Name in his later life, widowed with two young children, working a small farm. The casting of Eastwood in the role (and the fact that Eastwood as director establishes a lineage to his *The Outlaw Josey Wales* [1976] and Leone's Westerns of the 1960s) inscribes *Unforgiven* as a metacinematic presentation of a Western cinematic mythology. The opening credits situate this story in a tradition of Westerns; cinematic tropes in this form of metacinema establish familiarity rather than originality of story, character, and theme. William Munny's (Eastwood) "character arc" knowingly engages with the *topoi* of the Man with No Name and, more specifically, the incarnation of the Man with No Name in the physical presence of Eastwood. The *topoi* of the classical Western format find a new expression in *Unforgiven* that reflects on an original presentation. Munny must rediscover the essence of his cinematic self—literally a self inscribed on film. Rather than a debunking of the Western myth, *Unforgiven* is also a celebration of a cinematic mythology that has been re-presented for a cinematic audience aware of its origins. Munny recalls Bronson's Harmonica, who rides off into the sunset, indelibly inscribed with a sense of passing. In Cheyenne's (Jason Robards) words, "Men like that have something inside. Something to do with death." Eastwood's Munny brings new life to a cinematic myth, and a mythical being, but it is less a myth projected on an American West than on an American Western. *Unforgiven* is in this sense a functioning simulacrum of a cinematic form, divorced from origins, reflecting only on its prior cinematic performances. It is for Eastwood what *Once Upon a Time in the West* was for Leone: an expression of the form through the language of the Western genre. Mainstream criticism approached *Unforgiven* as a critique of the mythology of the American and Spaghetti Western.[69] I do not wish to reject such interpretations out of hand. However, Munny's final stand, configured as a quotation of the generic Western confrontation[70] is equally a transformation of the original Western myth (a revision of a familiar *topos*), in which Munny descends into a violent past, and a romanticizing of that generic past, in which the Man with No Name remains incarnate in Munny's presence. Eastwood could have killed off the Man with No Name at the end of *Unforgiven*, but he chooses not to.

Metacinema and Postmodern Narrative: The New Auteurism

Kill Bill, Volumes 1 and *2* permit the discussion of Tarantino's oeuvre in terms of genre, and more specifically for this discussion, the strategy of genericity that, I have argued, forms the basis of a metacinematic aesthetic. The fact that Baudrillard has written similarly about Sergio Leone, an obvious precursor to Tarantino, suggests that such a discussion is not merely a welcome addition to studies of Tarantino, but a critical trajectory necessary for coming to terms with his legacy as a filmmaker. While narrative has received little attention from critics of Tarantino's work,[71] in the following section I attempt to discuss narrative in *Pulp Fiction* in formal terms, reflecting on the characteristics of "postmodern narrative" described by Lyotard in *The Postmodern Condition*. Lyotard's contention is that the basic aesthetic of postmodern narrative is founded upon instability, or the process of fragmentation, which he attributes to the ubiquity of "language games":

> It is useful to make the following three observations about language games. The first is that their rules do not carry within themselves their own legitimation, but are the object of a contract, explicit or not, between players. . . . The second is that if there are no rules, there is no game. . . . The third remark is suggested by what has been said: every utterance should be thought of as a "move" in a game.[72]

Lyotard's contention is that the presence of language games within narrative renders the narrative form subject to extraneous "moves," and ultimately an inherent instability. Furthermore, the notion that an utterance constitutes a move in the game implicates external and internal players in the performance of the narrative. I wish to illustrate this principle by discussing two narrative frames in recent films. To recall the degree of Tarantino's innovation on classical narrative, I want to focus on a narrative device in *Pulp Fiction* that, at least to my knowledge, has gone unnoticed.

The film opens on Ringo (Tim Roth) and Honey Bunny (Amanda Plummer) in the quintessential American diner scene with a twist. Deciding that restaurants are safer to hold up than gas stations, Amanda Plummer (on crowd control) leaps onto a table and says: "Any of you fucking pricks move and I'll execute every motherfucking last one of you." The camera freezes and we move to credits. In the film's final set piece, we discover (from a different point of view) that Ringo and Honey Bunny's hold-up forms a frame to this unwieldy narrative. Linear narrative has been dispensed with: Vincent (John Travolta) sits on a toilet though he was shot by Butch (Bruce Willis) in an earlier scene. Vincent's brief confrontation with Butch in a dimly lit bar takes place shortly after the "Bonnie Situation." In the final sequence of the film, returned once again to the diner, we shift from Vincent and Jules for the moment it takes Ringo and Honey Bunny to announce the hold-up. We watch again as Plummer leaps to the table for her (now) anticipated line: "Any of you fucking pricks move and I'll execute every one of you motherfuckers!"

On a first viewing, or perhaps even on several cursory viewings, the line functions as a neat installation of a traditional narrative frame. However, rather than maintaining the linear sequence in which cause must eventuate in effect, Tarantino fractures the frame—the one coherent and wholly conventional narrative device. The narrative frame recalls an entire cinematic tradition, encompassing Billy Wilder's *Double Indemnity* (1944) and *Sunset Boulevard* (1950), seminal American *noir* films made within the studio system and emblematic of its great achievement. The narrative frame extends to the realist novel of the nineteenth century, particularly Mary Shelly's *Frankenstein*, and is predicated on a conventional causality. Cause and effect *must* operate to return the beginning of the narrative to its natural end.

In this sequence, the frame is fractured by Honey Bunny when she "revises" her earlier exclamation. "Any of you fucking pricks move and I'll execute every motherfucking last one of you" becomes "Any of you

fucking pricks move and I'll execute every one of you motherfuckers."
Though not overtly a narrative self-awareness, it is a narrative *reflexivity*
that reflects the growing acceptance of nonrealist narrative devices and,
more specifically, the intrusion of ulterior narrative frames into a master narrative. Plummer's revised line makes literal what was only met-
aphorical in classical Hollywood and, notably, *Citizen Kane*: that story
is ultimately and resoundingly the contrivance of its narrative framing,
subject to revision, reversion, or, in the case of David Lynch's best work,
dissolution. Tarantino's cinema is ultimately a language game in which a
conventional narrative structure and a realist aesthetic metamorphoses
into the metacinematic "frame."

David Fincher's *Fight Club* offers a similar intrusion of the nondiegetic
space into the diegetic, which I would argue is a profound transformation
of realist cinematic practices. The film charts a presentation of a postmodern odyssey into destruction, oblivion, and, ultimately, the recuperation
of the self; in this it diverts from Palahniuk's novel which, in its conclusion, is unremittingly bleak: the protagonist ends up in a mental institution when his explosive charge malfunctions, and history is relegated to a
perpetual present.[73] The film's narrative appears to function conventionally, again with the use of the traditional framing device. In the opening
scene, the nameless narrator (Edward Norton) and Tyler Durden (Brad
Pitt) share a conversation, which digresses into a depiction of the events
that culminate in that conversation. When the viewer returns to the
scene, Tyler is unveiled as a destructive (and, paradoxically, regenerative)
split personality, a degree of sensationalism that weighs upon the film's
magnificently rendered (and very fashionable) antisensationalism.

One of the film's motifs involves depicting a scene in reversion. The
title sequence inverts the conventional cinematic gaze: we begin inside
the narrator's mind and exit through a point between his eyes to view
the barrel of a gun held by Tyler. The film's preponderance of experimental cinematic devices—jump cuts, fades, a reduced color ratio—convey
the constructedness of the narrative. Tyler's splicing of porn images into
family entertainment parallels Fincher's control of the film narrative,
deframed by Norton's fractured self. The Tyler persona intrudes initially
in Norton's narration in fleeting still shots, mirroring Tyler's splicing of
frames of film into a master narrative; it is worth watching the first twenty
minutes of the film very closely to observe this bold and yet remarkably subtle intrusion into the linear, cause-effect narrative. The nearer
we come to Tyler's entrance into the film, the more frequent the spliced
frames of Tyler's figure.

Unlike Tarantino's frame, which collapses without the impetus of a character, Fincher places the narrative in the control of the characters framed within it. The narrative is written and rewritten at the whim of the characters, who are traditionally its components. An example of the reflexive narrative frame (Plummer's line in *Pulp Fiction*) expanding to the self-aware, ironic placement of characters as creative agents occurs when we return to the frame in the final scene of *Fight Club*. The shot materializes on Norton sitting on a stool with a gun in his mouth. The opening credit sequence—a shot reverting from a central point (Norton's psychosis) to the exterior reality—recurs with Norton's voiceover: "I think this is about where we came in." The two alternate versions of the conversation (the narrative frame) are reproduced below.

The Opening
Tyler: Three minutes. This is it. Ground Zero.
Would you like to say a few words to mark the occasion?
Narrator: I can't think of anything.

The Closing
Tyler: Three minutes. This is it. The beginning. Ground Zero.
[The narrator's voiceover: *This is about where we came in.*]
Would you like to say a few words to mark the occasion?
Narrator: I still can't think of anything.
Tyler: Hmm . . . flashback humor.

A Tarantino-like alteration occurs with Tyler's insert "The beginning," which does not appear in the original conversation. However, Tyler's acknowledgment of the narrator's "flashback humor" reflects a radical narrative self-awareness. And beneath that is Fincher's ironic appreciation of the essential constructedness and contrivance of the traditional narrative form. On one level, the "flashback humor" is presented as functioning within the narrator's psychosis—that is, it makes sense because it is only to be expected of an irrational mind fumbling over an otherwise accepted sequential narrative. On another level, a narrative origin (cause) is unrecoverable because it is reflected upon by an internal presence. The narrator is also a narrative trickster insofar as he is able to alter a narrative sequence (conversation 1) required to perform its repetition (conversation 2). Tyler and the narrator's simultaneous awareness of the narrative revision fractures what began as whole and must thereafter regress to a point of entropy. This is not to say that the narrative fractures into nonsense, but merely a radically indeterminate *kind* of sense.

Linearity and causality, Fincher seems to declare, are merely select ways of telling a story subject to the intrusion of an indeterminate narrative voice that is aware of its presence within a hermetic structure. It is a textual conceit that ultimately has very little to do with an external reality. Various narrative realities converge, each an indeterminate construct of the other, each compromised in its integrity by the existence and performance of the other.

Narrative self-awareness is merely one element of a broader ironic relationship that exists between the mainstream cinematic text and a contemporary audience. The implications of this shift in aesthetic sensibilities are difficult to evaluate and, indeed, conceptualize. If cinematic narrative reflects an increasing uncertainty in narrative truth, ideological right, and existential purpose, these contemporary auteurs, rather than shying away from the disturbing implications, seem to have embraced the aesthetic possibilities. Aesthetic innovation, insofar as it is able to establish a "wave," requires a sensibility and mindset willing to receive it. Contemporary mainstream audiences are aware of cinematic traditions less as incarnations of an inherent and external Real than as a cinematic mythology. The hermetically sealed frame of representation, in contemporary cinema, has been inverted: accessing this cinema requires a profound and complex knowledge of cinematic traditions, to varying degrees of esotericism. To what extent does an aesthetic appreciation of Tarantino's *Kill Bill* rely on a prior knowledge of Leone's *Once Upon a Time in the West*? To what extent is contemporary cinema merely a cinematic performance of prior texts and past traditions?

One characteristic of the films of the so-called postmodern generation is the hyper-revisionism of their content, aesthetically and thematically. The cinematic image is a commentary on film, and by extension, a running commentary on itself. The film-savvy culture of the milieu permits and embraces a radical new kind of mainstream cinematic appreciation that seems to explore (if not embrace) an alternative aesthetics—narrative experimentation, self-awareness, and the artistic frame as simulation or metacinema—marketed by major studio subsidiaries for mass audiences. The implication of this hyperrevisionism is the loss of an essential and literal realism that was once so pervasive in the Hollywood studio film. Tarantino and Fincher reflect obsessively on a cinematic past, a cinematic mythology that informs the narrative frame of their films. Their protagonists are not only able to stand outside of the mimetic construct, they are able to locate themselves within a prior cinematic tradition.

The new auteurism of Tarantino and Fincher (which is a profound transformation on the auteurism of the French New Wave or the Hollywood auteurs of the 1970s) lays bare the inherent cinematicality of the image. Narrative takes its place alongside other textual tropes in a performance space. Bazin's "reality myth," in this context, has been reconfigured for a cinematic culture practicing a new film aesthetics. Perhaps we might adopt a position similar to the residual self-image of the simulacral Matrix, in which a screened reality offers itself merely as a vestige of the Real.

Conclusion

I am first and foremost a film fanatic. I've always wanted to make movies, to be part of that world. My most important experiences as a viewer are amazingly varied: they go from Nicholas Ray to Brian De Palma, from Terry Gilliam to Sergio Leone, from Mario Brava to Jean-Luc Godard and Jean-Pierre Melville, and even include Eric Rohmer.[74]

Auteurism in an age in which the classical auteur has been well and truly killed off (if Barthes, Foucault, and other post-structuralists were not entirely successful in the realm of film, writers like Schatz very effectively described a cinematic text that had little use for a single genius[75]) finds a new form in the era of metacinema. I agree with Thomson that Godard, Antonioni, and Fellini are no longer reproducible. The cinematic culture has lost the material conditions required to produce "film art." Auteur filmmakers are no longer aesthetes but pop culture flaneurs traversing the boundaries of a new cinema inscribed by a very real cultural agency. And perhaps even more crucially, the new auteur's expression of authenticity resides in an awareness of film, film references, and the cultural detritus of so many scenes, set pieces, and throwaway lines of dialogue. This is the cultural screen on which film *means*. To ask what "allusionism" means is to impose an aesthetic sensibility wholly incompatible with the process of cinematic meaning in the contemporary mainstream scene. Rather, the spectator (and the theorist) should ask how it is *performed*.

This is a kind of cinema that has drawn the Real into itself, making it cinematic, offering a series of tropes and *topoi* (which Eco discusses in relation to *Casablanca* or *Raiders of the Lost Ark*) that bounce off of the spectator immersed in the cinematic spectacle. This kind of cinema is necessarily hyperstylistic. It is fundamentally *experiential*. It is exhibited in all of Tarantino's films, but perhaps most elegantly in *Pulp Fiction*, in which a yellow taxicab, superimposed on an artificial background, maintains its position in movie stasis while the backdrop recedes into the distance of a cinematic simulacrum.

Butch (Bruce Willis) and Esmeralda Villalobos (Angela Jones):
a classical cinematic frame that recedes in the distance.

Notes

1. Pisters, 223.

2. For an analysis of the convergence of major studio productions and smaller "art-film" enterprises, see Timothy Corrigan, "Auteurs and the New Hollywood," in *The New American Cinema*, ed. Jon Lewis (Durham, NC, and London: Duke University Press, 1998), 43–52. Michael Moore's recent *Fahrenheit 911* is an example of the convergence of the studio film distribution chain and the art-film aesthetic (radical political documentary). In this case, distribution was undertaken by Miramax, a subsidiary of Disney.

3. See Purse, who offers a similar conclusion in her analysis of bullet-time in *The Matrix*: a convergence of the spatial frame occupied by cinematic text and spectator (157). See also Collins. However, I would argue that such formulations, now passé in contemporary theories of film, are indebted to the classical wave of post-structuralist theory. In my own experience of this movement, Barthes is a voice to which I invariably return.

4. McCann, 33.

5. Paul Auster, *New York Trilogy: City of Glass, Ghosts, The Locked Room* (London: Faber and Faber, 1987), 133–196.

6. Quentin Tarantino, "Chapter 2," shooting script, *Kill Bill, Volumes 1 and 2*, Internet Moviescript Database, http://www.imsdb.com/scripts/Kill-Bill-Volume-1-&2.html (accessed Oct. 10, 2005).

7. Tarantino.

8. For an excellent reading of this sequence, see Peter Travis, "The Critics Commentary," *Reservoir Dogs*, collector's edition DVD (Lion's Gate, 2006).

9. Travis, "The Critics Commentary."

10. See, for example, Grant; for an analysis of sequences in *Pulp Fiction* as "orchestrated violence" (and Tarantino's use thereof to explore conventions of cinematic violence), see Marsha Kinder, "Violence American Style: The Narrative Orchestrations of Violent Attractions," in *Violence and American Cinema*, ed. J. David Slocum (New York and London: Routledge, 2001), 81–84.

11. *Per Un Pugno di Dollari (A Fistful of Dollars)*; *Per Qualche Dollaro in Più (For a Few Dollars More)*; *Il Buono, Il Brutto, Il Cattivo (The Good, the Bad and the Ugly)*.

12. See Gerald Peary (ed.), *Quentin Tarantino Interviews* (Jackson: University of Mississippi Press, 1998): "When I was 18 or 19, I was going to write a book on genre filmmakers—John Flynn, Joe Dante, John Milius, Richard Franklin—and engage them in a conversation about movies " (28). Implicit in Tarantino's comment is the notion that films are connected in a way that filmmakers and films recognize.

13. M. M. Bakhtin, "The Problem of the Text in Linguistics, Philology and the Human Sciences: An Experiment in Philosophical Analysis," in *M. M. Bakhtin: Speech Genres and Other Late Essays*, ed. Caryl Emerson and Michael Holquist, trans. Vern W. McGee (Austin: University of Texas Press, 1986), 104.

14. Welles and Bogdanovich, 53.

15. Thomas Schatz, *Hollywood Genres: Formulas, Filmmaking, and the Studio System* (Austin: McGraw-Hill, 1981), 16.

16. Cited in Christopher Frayling, "Commentary," *Once Upon a Time in the West*, two-disc special ed. DVD (Warner Home Video, 2003).

17. Clive Thomson, "Bakhtin's 'Theory' of Genre," *Studies in Twentieth Century Literature* 9, no. 1 (1984), 30.

18. Bakhtin, 108.

19. See Rick Altman, "A Semantic/Syntactic Approach to Film Genre," *Cinema Journal* 23, no. 3 (1984): "The semantic approach stresses the genre's building blocks, while the syntactic view privileges the structures into which they are arranged" (10). Altman argues that the explanatory power of genre criticism has been weakened by its privileging of the semantic or syntactic approach to genre cinema.

20. Frayling describes this shot as a reproduction of a similar shot in *Stagecoach*. While Leone has not commented on this relationship, the two shots are remarkably similar. See Frayling.

21. Jean Baudrillard, *America*, trans. Chris Turner (London and New York: Verso, 1988), 1: "Vanishing Point."

22. As a response, Altman proposes that a study of "these two categories is complimentary, that they can be combined, and in fact that some of the most important questions of genre study can be asked only when they *are* combined" (11).

23. Eco, "Innovation and Repetition," 162.

24. See *Hollywood Blockbusters: The Top Grossing Films of All Time* (Rochester, NY: Grange Books, 2004), introduction: "Movies are about fun, entertainment, sharing, and above all, sheer escapism" (6). Of course, the ideological theory of the *Cahiers du cinéma* group, particularly the seminal essay by Jean-Luc Comolli and Jean Narboni, "Cinema/

Ideology/Criticism," views the escapist/entertainment aesthetic as diversion and repression strategies by an industrialised Hollywood machine.

25. Carroll, "The Power of Movies," 82.

26. Carroll, "The Power of Movies," 83.

27. Consider Bogdanovich's *The Last Picture Show* (1971), Malick's *Badlands* (1973), Scorsese's *Mean Streets* (1973), or even Polanski's *Chinatown* (1974), which is clearly not classical *noir* in the spirit of *The Maltese Falcon* (1941) or *The Big Sleep* (1946).

28. Mark Jancovich, "Genre and the Audience: Genre Classifications and Cultural Distinctions in the Mediation of *The Silence of the Lambs*," in *Horror: The Film Reader*, ed. Mark Jancovich (London: Routledge, 2002), 152.

29. For an analysis of the highest grossing films, see *Hollywood Blockbusters: The Top Grossing Films of All Time*, 8–9.

30. Leo Braudy, "Genre: The Conventions of Connection," in *Film Theory and Criticism*, ed. Leo Braudy and Marshall Cohen (Oxford: Oxford University Press, 2004), 668.

31. Jancovich, "Genre and the Audience," 152.

32. See David Bordwell, "The Art Cinema as a Mode of Film Practice," *Film Criticism* 4, no. 1 (1979), 56–60. Bordwell suggests that there are clear distinctions between the classical narrative and what he calls the "art film." In this case, a theory privileging the study of genre in cinema must neglect Antonioni's *L'Avventura*, Fellini's *La Dolce Vita*, and Coppola's *The Conversation*. However, I am persuaded by Eco that genre is more pervasive than contemporary literary theory acknowledges—see Eco, "Innovation and Repetition," 174.

33. Bordwell, "The Art Cinema as a Mode of Film Practice," 57.

34. Worth noting is De Palma's fascinating remake of *Blow-Up*, *Blow-Out* (1981). De Palma, as he has done on several occasions, reworks the art-film aesthetic as genre piece. Consider also the quotation of the Odessa Steps sequence in Eisenstein's *Battleship Potemkin*, reconfigured in De Palma's *The Untouchables* as an operatic shoot-out in Chicago's own version of Grand Central Station.

35. David Thomson, "Who Killed the Movies," 62.

36. Jancovich, "Genre and Audience," 152.

37. See Axel Kruse, "*The X-Files*: Entries on Meaning," *Sydney Studies in English* 23 (1997–8), 110–111.

38. Collins, 256.

39. Consider the femme fatale of Clouzot's *Les Diaboliques* (1954) as a variation of Stanwyck in *Double Indemnity*, though the femme fatale is maintained as generic *topos*.

40. See Tom Ryall, "Genre and Hollywood," in *American Cinema and Hollywood: Critical Approaches*, ed. John Hill and Pamela Church Gibson (Oxford: Oxford University Press, 2000), 110.

41. For an analysis of the criticism of popular art as formula, see Carroll, *A Philosophy of Mass Art*, 49–67.

42. Neale, 51.

43. For an overview of the development of this genre, see Christopher Ames, *Movies About the Movies* (Kentucky: University of Kentucky Press, 1997), 3. Notable entries in

the genre include Lumet's *Network* and Altman's *The Player* (apart from Wilder's landmark *Sunset Boulevard*).

44. Neale, 51.

45. Neale, 5.

46. For a seminal analysis, see Bordwell, "Classical Hollywood: Narrational Principles and Procedures," 17–34.

47. Braudy, 668.

48. Collins, 243.

49. Collins, 243.

50. Schatz, "The Whole Equation of Pictures," 92–93.

51. Collins, 262.

52. Collins, 249.

53. Collins, 249.

54. Collins, 242–243 and 248–249.

55. Collins, 247. My emphasis.

56. For an assessment of this form of 1980s Americana as "Reaganite Cinema," see Andrew Britton. "Blissing Out: The Politics of Reaganite Entertainment," *Movie* 31/32 (1986), 13–15. Britton considers this form of hegemonic cinema as exemplary of the Frankfurt School's culture industry. See also Robin Wood, "Papering the Cracks: Fantasy and Ideology in the Reagan Era," in *Movies and Mass Culture*, ed. John Belton (New Brunswick, NJ: Rutgers University Press, 1996), 203–228.

57. Collins, 250.

58. Neale, 35.

59. Neale, 35.

60. Christopher Sharrett, "End of Story: The Collapse of Myth in Postmodern Narrative Film," in *The End of Cinema*, ed. Jon Lewis (New York and London: New York University Press, 2001), 330.

61. Sharrett, 328.

62. Thomson, "Who Killed the Movies," 62.

63. Sharrett, 328–330.

64. Sharrett, 328.

65. Purse, 157.

66. Collins, 248. My emphasis. Monument Valley is significant because it is the location of several John Ford Western sequences, notably, *The Searchers*; for Zemekis, Monument Valley is also the site of Leone's *homage* to Ford and his own cinematic quotation that Zemekis is reproducing here.

67. Frayling, "Commentary," *Once Upon a Time in the West*—two-disc special ed., DVD (Paramount, 2001).

68. See Ames for this common usage. My notion of a cinema *of* cinema shares something with Pisters's reading of Deleuze in which she formulates the "Universe as Metacinema" (chapter one). Pisters traces this notion through Hitchcock and Deleuze.

69. See Richard Corliss, "The Last Roundup," *Time*, Aug. 10, 1992; see also Michael Sragow, *The New Yorker*, Aug. 10, 1992, 70.

70. See Isaacs and Trost, "Story, Product, Franchise," 74.

71. Most writing on Tarantino focuses on a new aesthetic of cinema, emphazising the pop culture references or a blasé approach to violence. Yet I would argue that a close examination of the narrative structure of his films is rarely undertaken. Tarantino is thus easily reduced to a celluloid figure himself rather than someone who shares in the "anonymity" of Hollywood's great auteurs—Scorsese, Lynch, or, more recently, somebody like Paul Thomas Anderson.

72. Lyotard, 10.

73. Palahniuk, 206–207.

74. Peary, 7.

75. See Schatz, "The Whole Equation of Pictures," 93–94.

Bibliography

Adorno, Theodor. "Cultural Criticism and Society." In *Prisms*, trans. Samuel and Sherry Weber, 17–34. London: Neville Spearman, 1967.

Adorno, Theodor. *Aesthetic Theory*, trans. C Lenhardt, ed. Gretel Adorno and Rolf Tiedemann. London: Routledge & Kegan Paul, 1984.

Adorno, Theodor. "Culture Industry Reconsidered." In *The Culture Industry: Selected Essays on Mass Culture*, ed. J. M. Bernstein, 85–92. London: Routledge, 1991.

Althusser, Louis. *Lenin and Philosophy and Other Essays*, trans. Ben Brewster. New York and London: Monthly Review Press, 1971.

Altman, Rick. "A Semantic/Syntactic Approach to Film Genre." *Cinema Journal* 23, no. 3 (1984): 6–18.

Ames, Christopher. *Movies About the Movies*. Kentucky: University of Kentucky Press, 1997.

Andrew, Dudley. *Concepts in Film Theory*. Oxford: Oxford University Press, 1984.

Arroyo, José. "Introduction." In *Action/Spectacle Cinema: A Sight and Sound Reader*, ed. José Arroyo, vii–xiv. London: British Film Institute, 2000.

Auster, Paul. *New York Trilogy: City of Glass, Ghosts, The Locked Room*. London: Faber and Faber, 1987.

Bakhtin, M. M. "The Problem of the Text in Linguistics, Philology and the Human Sciences: An Experiment in Philosophical Analysis." In *M. M. Bakhtin: Speech Genres and Other Late Essays*, ed. Caryl Emerson and Michael Holquist, trans. Vern W. McGee, 103–131. Austin: University of Texas Press, 1986.

Barker, Martin. "The Newson Report: A Case Study in 'Common Sense.'" In *Ill Effects: The Media/Violence Debate*, ed. Martin Barker and Julian Petley, 27–46. London and New York: Routledge, 2001.

Barker, Martin and Julian Petley. *Ill Effects: The Media/Violence Debate*. Routledge: London and New York, 2001.

Barthes, Roland. "The Photographic Message." In *Image Music Text*, trans. Stephen Heath, 15–31. London: Fontana, 1977.

Barthes, Roland. "Death of the Author." In *Image Music Text*, trans. Stephen Heath, 142–148. London: Fontana, 1977.

Barthes, Roland, "From Work to Text." In *Image Music Text*, trans. Stephen Heath, 155–164. London: Fontana, 1977.

Bartlett, Laura and Thomas B. Byers. "Back to the Future: The Humanist Matrix." *Cultural Critique* 53 (2003): 28–46.

Bassham, Gregory. "Religion in *The Matrix* and Problems of Pluralism." In *The Matrix and Philosophy*, ed. William Irwin, 111–125. Chicago and La Salle: Open Court, 2002.

Baudrillard, Jean. *The Evil Demon of Images*, trans. Paul Patton, Paul Floss. Sydney: The Power Institute of Fine Arts, 1987.

Baudrillard, Jean. *Simulacra and Simulation*, trans. Sheila Faria Glaser. Michigan: University of Michigan Press, 1994.

Baudrillard, Jean. *The Gulf War Did Not Take Place*, trans. Paul Patton. Sydney: The Power Institute of Fine Arts, 1995.

Baudrillard, Jean. *America*. Trans. Chris Turner. London and New York: Verso, 1988.

Bauman, Zygmunt. "Postmodernity, Or Living with Ambivalence." In *A Postmodern Reader*, ed. Joseph Natoli and Linda Hutcheon, 9–24. Albany: State University of New York Press, 1993.

Bazin, André. "The Ontology of the Photographic Image." In *What Is Cinema, Volume 1*, trans. Hugh Gray, 9–16. Berkeley and Los Angeles: University of California Press, 1967.

Bazin, André. "The Myth of Total Cinema." In *What Is Cinema, Volume 1*, trans. Hugh Gray, 17–22. Berkeley and Los Angeles: University of California Press, 1967.

Bazin, André. "The Evolution of the Language of Cinema." In *What Is Cinema, Volume 1*, trans. Hugh Gray, 23–40. Berkeley and Los Angeles: University of California Press, 1967.

Bazin, André. "The Virtues and Limitations of Montage." In *What Is Cinema, Volume 1*, trans. Hugh Gray, 41–52. Berkeley and Los Angeles: University of California Press, 1967.

Bazin, André. "An Aesthetic of Reality: Cinematic Realism and the Italian School of Liberation." In *What Is Cinema, Volume II*, trans. Hugh Gray, 16–40. Berkeley and Los Angeles: University of California Press, 1967.

Belton, John. "Digital Cinema: A False Revolution." *October* 100 (2002): 98–114.

Benjamin, Walter. "The Work of Art in the Age of Mechanical Reproduction." In *The Norton Anthology of Theory and Criticism*, ed. Peter Simon, 1166–1186. New York: W. W. Norton, 2001.

Black, Joel. *The Reality Effect: Film Culture and the Graphic Imperative.* New York and London: Routledge, 2002.

Bloom, Harold. *Shakespeare: The Invention of the Human.* New York: Penguin and Putnam, 1998.

Bloom, Harold. "Dumbing Down American Readers." *Los Angeles Times*, Sep. 24, 2003.

Bordwell, David. *On the History of Film Style.* Cambridge, Mass: Harvard University Press, 1977.

Bordwell, David. "The Art Cinema as a Mode of Film Practice." *Film Criticism* 4, no. 1 (1979): 56–64.

Bordwell, David. "Classical Hollywood Cinema: Narrational Principles and Procedures." In *Narrative, Apparatus, Ideology*, ed. P. Rosen, 17–34. New York: Columbia University Press, 1986.

Bordwell, David and Kristin Thompson. *Film Art: An Introduction.* Reading: Addison-Wesley Publishing, 1980.

Brabazon, Tara. "We'll *Always* Have Tatooine." *Australian Journal of Communication* 26, no. 2 (1999): 1–10.

Brannigan, Michael. "There Is No Spoon: A Buddhist Mirror." In *The Matrix and Philosophy*, ed. William Irwin, 101–110. Chicago and La Salle: Open Court, 2002.

Braudy, Leo. "Genre: The Conventions of Connection." In *Film Theory and Criticism*, ed. Leo Braudy and Marshall Cohen, 663–679. Oxford: Oxford University Press, 2004.

Britton, Andrew. "Blissing Out: The Politics of Reaganite Entertainment." *Movie* 31/32 (1986): 1–42.

Brooker, Will. "Internet Fandom and the Continuing Narratives of *Star Wars, Blade Runner* and *Alien*." In *Alien Zone II: The Spaces of Science Fiction Cinema*, ed. Annette Kuhn, 50–72. London: Verso, 1999.

Brooker, Will and Deborah Jermyn. "Introduction." In *The Audience Studies Reader*, ed. Will Brooker and Deborah Jermyn, 1–4. London: Routledge, 2003.

Buckland, Warren. "Film Semiotics." In *A Companion to Film Theory*, ed. Toby Miller and Robert Stam, 84–104. Oxford: Blackwell, 1999.

"Bullet-Time." *The Matrix*. DVD: Special Features. Warner Bros., 2001.

Butler, Jeremy G. "The Star System and Hollywood." In *American Cinema and Hollywood: Critical Approaches*, ed. John Hill and Pamela Church Gibson, 116–127. Oxford: Oxford University Press, 2000.

Calvino, Italo. *If on a Winter's Night, A Traveller*. London: Vintage, 1998.

Campbell, Joseph. *The Hero with a Thousand Faces*. New York: World, 1956.

Caputi, Jane. "Small Ceremonies." In *Mythologies of Violence in Postmodern Media*, ed. Christopher Sharrett, 147–174. Detroit, MI: Wayne State University Press, 1999.

Carroll, Noël. "The Power of Movies." *Daedalus* 114, no. 4 (1985): 79–103.

Carroll, Noël. *The Philosophy of Mass Art*. Oxford: Clarendon Press, 1998.

Carroll, Noël. "Introducing Film Evaluation." In *Reinventing Film Studies*, ed. Christine Gledhill and Linda Williams, 265–278. Oxford: Arnold, 2000.

Codognet, Philippe. "Artificial Nature and Natural Artifice." In *Future Cinema: The Cinematic Imaginary After Film*, ed. Jeffrey Shaw and Peter Weibel, 462–465. Cambridge, MA: MIT Press, 2003.

Comolli, Jean-Luc and Jean Narboni. "Cinema/Ideology/Criticism." In *Film Theory and Criticism*, ed. Leo Braudy and Marshall Cohen, 812–819. Oxford: Oxford University Press, 2004.

Collins, Jim. "Genericity in the Nineties: Eclectic Irony and the New Sincerity." In *Film Theory Goes to the Movies*, eds. Jim Collins, Hillary Radner, and Ava Preacher Collins, 242–263. New York: Routledge, 1993.

Copeland, Roger. "When Films 'Quote' Films, They Create a New Mythology." *New York Times*, Sep. 25, 1977.

Corliss, Richard. "The Last Roundup." *Time*, Aug. 10, 1992.

Corliss, Richard. "Popular Metaphysics." *Time*, Apr. 19, 1999.

Corrigan, Timothy. "Auteurs and the New Hollywood." In *The New American Cinema*, ed. Jon Lewis, 38–63. Durham, NC, and London: Duke University Press, 1998.

Courchesne, Luc. "The Construction of Experience: Turning Spectators into Visitors." In *New Screen Media*, ed. Martin Reiser and Andrea Zapp, 256–267. London: British Film Institute, 2002.

Coveney, Michael. *The World According to Mike Leigh*. London: HarperCollins, 1996.

Darley, Andrew. *Visual Digital Culture: Surface Play and Spectacle in New Media Genres*. London: Routledge, 2000.

Debord, Guy. *The Society of the Spectacle*, trans. Donald Nicholson-Smith. New York: Zone Books, 1994.

De Laurentis, Teresa and Stephen Heath, ed. *The Cinematic Apparatus*. London: Macmillan, 1980.

Deleuze, Gilles. *Cinema 1: The Movement-Image*, trans. Hugh Tomlinson and Barbara Habberjam. London: Athlone Press, 1986.

Deleuze, Gilles. *Cinema 2: The Time-Image*, trans. Hugh Tomlinson and Barbara Habberjam. London: Athlone Press, 1989.

DeLillo, Don. *Libra*. New York. Penguin Books, 1991.

DeLillo, Don. *Underworld*. London: Picador, 1998.

de Man, Paul. "Semiology and Rhetoric." *Diacritics* 3, no. 3 (1973): 27–33.

Denzin, Norman. *The Cinematic Society: The Voyeur's Gaze*. London: Sage, 1995.

Diawara, Manthia. "Black American Cinema: The New Realism." In *Film and Theory: An Anthology*, ed. Robert Stam and Toby Miller, 236–256. Oxford: Blackwell, 2000.

Dick, Philip K. *Ubik*. New York: Doubleday, 1969.

Dick, Philip K. "We Can Remember It for You Wholesale." In *Preserving Machine and Other Stories*, 129–149. London: Victor Gollancz, 1971.

Dick, Philip K. *The Three Stigmata of Palmer Eldritch*. Gainesville, FL: Triad, 1978.

Dixon, Wheeler Winston. "Introduction." In *Film Genre 2000*, ed. Wheeler Winston Dixon, 1–12. Albany: State University of New York Press, 2000.

Docherty, Thomas. "Introduction." In *Postmodernism: A Reader*, ed. Thomas Docherty, 1–31. New York: Columbia University Press, 1993.

Doty, William G. *Mythography*. Tuscaloosa: University of Alabama Press, 1986.

Druckrey, Timothy. "Fugitive Realities, Situated Realities, 'Situational Realities,' and or Future Cinema(s) Past." In *Future Cinema: The Cinematic Imaginary After Film*, ed. Jeffrey Shaw and Peter Weibel, 60–65. Cambridge, MA: MIT Press, 2003.

Durgnat, Raymond. *A Long Hard Look at 'Psycho'*. London: British Film Institute, 2002.

Duvall, John H. "Troping History." In *Productive Postmodernism: Consuming Histories and Cultural Studies*, ed. John H. Duvall, 1–22. Albany: State University of New York Press, 2002.

Eagleton, Terry. *After Theory*. New York: Basic Books, 2003.

Ebert, Roger. "Commentary." *Citizen Kane*. DVD: Two-Disc Special Edition. Warner Bros., 2003.

Ebert, Roger. "Mulholland Drive." *Chicago Sun-Times*, Oct. 12, 2001.

Ebert, Roger. "The Matrix." *Chicago Sun-Times*, May 14, 2003.

Eco, Umberto. "Innovation and Repetition." *Daedalus* 114, no. 4 (1985): 161–184.

Eco, Umberto. *Reflections on* The Name of the Rose. London: Secker and Warburg, 1985.

Eco, Umberto. "Casablanca: Cult Movies and Intertextual Collage." In *Modern Criticism and Theory*, ed. David Lodge, 446–455. London and New York: Longman, 1988.

Eisenstein, Sergei. "Beyond the Shot [The Cinematographic Principle and the Ideogram]." In *Film Theory and Criticism*, ed. Leo Braudy and Marshall Cohen, 13–23. Oxford: Oxford University Press, 2004.

Felski, Rita. "The Role of Aesthetics in Cultural Studies." In *The Aesthetics of Cultural Studies*, ed. Michael Bérubé, 28–43. Boston: Blackwell, 2005.

Fiedler, Leslie. *Love and Death in the American Novel*. New York: Stein and Day, 1967.

Filser, Barbara. "Gilles Deleuze and a Future Cinema: Cinema 1, Cinema 2—and Cinema 3?" In *Future Cinema: The Cinematic Imaginary After Film*, ed. Jeffrey Shaw and Peter Weibel, 214–217. Cambridge, MA: MIT Press, 2003.

Fiske, John. *Understanding Popular Culture*. Winchester, MA: Unwin Hyman, 1989.

Fiske, John. *Reading the Popular*. Winchester, MA: Unwin Hyman, 1989.

Ford, James L. "Buddhism, Mythology and *The Matrix*." In *Taking the Red Pill: Science, Philosophy and Religion in* The Matrix, ed. Glenn Yeffeth, 125–144. Dallas: Benballa Books, 2003.

Frank, Thomas and Scott Weiland, *Commodify Your Dissent: Salvos from the Baffler*. New York: Norton, 1997.

Frayling, Christopher. "Commentary." *Once Upon a Time in the West* DVD. Two-Disc Special Edition. Warner Bros., 2003.

Friedberg, Anne. "The End of Cinema: Multimedia and Technological Change." In *Reinventing Film Studies*, ed. Christine Gledhill and Linda Williams, 438–450. London: Arnold, 2000.

Gabriel, Teshoma. "Toward a Critical Theory of Third World Cinema." In *Film and Theory: An Anthology*, ed. Robert Stam and Toby Miller, 298–316. Oxford: Blackwell, 2000.

Gaeta, John. "Bullet-Time." *The Matrix* DVD. Special Features—"Bullet Time." Warner Bros., 2001.

Gaeta, John. "Commentary." *The Matrix* DVD. Warner Bros., 2001.

Gibson, William. *Neuromancer*. Glasgow: HarperCollins, 1993.

Gibson, William. "Afterword." In *The Art of the Matrix*, ed. Spenser Lamm, 451. London: Titan Books, 2000.

Gordon, Andrew. "*Star Wars*: A Myth for Our Time." *Literature/Film Quarterly* 6, no. 4 (1978): 314–326.

Gordon, Andrew. "*The Matrix*: Paradigm of Postmodernism? Part II." In *Taking the Red Pill: Science, Philosophy and Religion in* The Matrix, ed. Glenn Yeffeth, 85–102. Dallas: Benballa Books, 2003.

Grant, Barry Keith. "American Psycho/sis: The Pure Products of America Go Crazy." In *Mythologies of Violence in Postmodern Media*, ed. Christopher Sharrett, 23–40. Detroit, MI: Wayne State University Press, 1999.

Hall, Stuart. "Notes on Deconstructing the Popular." In *People's History and Socialist Theory*, ed. Raphael Samuel, 227–240. Boston: Routledge, 1981.

Hall, Stuart. "Cultural Studies and Its Theoretical Legacies." In *Cultural Studies*, ed. Lawrence Grosberg, Cary Nelson, and Paula Treichler, 277–294. New York and London: Routledge, 1992.

Haraway, Donna. *Simians, Cyborgs and Women: The Reinvention of Nature*. New York: Routledge, 1991.

Hebdige, Dick. *Subculture: The Meaning of Style*. London and New York: Routledge, 1997.

Hillier, Jim. "Introduction." In *American Independent Cinema: A Sight and Sound Reader*, ed. Jim Hillier. London: British Film Institute, 2001: ix–xvii.

Hollows, Joanne. "Mass Culture Theory and Political Economy." In *Approaches to Popular Film*, eds. Joanne Hollows and Mark Jancovich, 15–36. Manchester, UK: Manchester University Press, 1995.

Hollywood Blockbusters: The Top Grossing Films of All Time. Kent, UK: Grange Books, 2004.

Hutcheon, Linda. *A Poetics of Postmodernism: History, Theory, Fiction*. New York and London: Routledge, 1988.

Hutcheon, Linda. "Representing the Postmodern." In *A Postmodern Reader*, ed. Joseph Natoli and Linda Hutcheon, 243–272. Albany: State University of New York Press, 1993.

Hutcheon, Linda. "Irony, Nostalgia, and the Postmodern." http://www.library.utoronto.ca/utel/criticism/hutchinp.html.

Huyssen, Andreas. "The Search for Tradition: Avant Garde and Postmodernism in the 1970s." *New German Critique* 22 (1981): 23–40.

Isaacs, Bruce. "Popular Postmodernism: The Cultural Logic of *The Matrix*." *New Media Poetics* (2003).

Isaacs, Bruce and Theodore Louis Trost. "Story, Product, Franchise." In *Jacking in to The Matrix Franchise: Cultural Reception and Interpretation*, ed. Mathew Kapell and William G. Doty, 65–79. New York and London: Continuum, 2004.

Isaacs, Bruce. "Non-Linear Narrative." In *New Punk Cinema*, ed. Nicholas Rombes, 126–138. Edinburgh: Edinburgh University Press, 2004.

Jameson, Frederic. "Reification and Utopia in Mass Culture." *Social Text* no. 1 (Winter 1979): 130–148.

Jameson, Frederic. "Afterword—Marxism and Postmodernism." In *Postmodernism/Jameson/Critique*, ed. Douglas Kellner, 369–387. Washington, D.C.: Maisonneuve Press, 1989.

Jameson, Frederic. *Postmodernism, or the Cultural Logic of Late Capitalism*. Durham, NC: Duke University Press, 1992.

Jameson, Frederic. "Postmodernism and Consumer Society." In *The Cultural Turn: Selected Writings on the Postmodern 1983–1998*, 1–21. London: Verso, 1998.

Jancovich, Mark. "Genre and the Audience: Genre Classifications and Cultural Distinctions in the Mediation of *The Silence of the Lambs*." In *Horror: The Film Reader*, ed. Mark Jancovich, 151–162. London: Routledge, 2002.

Jancovich, Mark. "A Real Shocker." In *The Film Cultures Reader*, ed. Graeme Turner, 469–480. London: Routledge, 2002.

Jewett, Robert and John Shelton Lawrence. *The American Monomyth.* New York: Anchor Press/Double Day, 1977.

Jhally, Sut and Justin Lewis. "Enlightened Racism. *The Cosby Show*, Audiences and the Myth of the American Dream." In *The Audience Studies Reader*, ed. Will Brooker and Deborah Jermyn, 279–286. London: Routledge, 2003.

Kaplan, E. Ann. "Classical Hollywood Film and Melodrama." In *American Cinema and Hollywood: Critical Approaches*, ed. John Hill and Pamela Church Gibson, 46–56. Oxford: Oxford University Press, 2000.

Kellner, Douglas. "Theodor W. Adorno and the Dialectics of Mass Culture." In *Adorno: A Critical Reader*, ed. Nigel Gibson and Andrew Rubin, 86–109. Oxford: Blackwell, 2002.

Kellner, Douglas. "Media Culture and the Triumph of the Spectacle." In *The Spectacle of the Real*, ed. Geoff King, 23–36. Bristol, UK: Intellect Books, 2005.

Kennedy, Barbara. *Deleuze and Cinema: The Aesthetics of Sensation.* Edinburgh: Edinburgh University Press, 2000.

Kinder, Marsha. "Violence American Style: the Narrative Orchestrations of Violent Attractions." In *Violence and American Cinema*, ed. J. David Slocum, 63–100. New York and London: Routledge, 2001.

King, C. Richard and David J. Leonard. "Is Neo White? Reading Race, Watching the Trilogy." In *Jacking in to The Matrix Franchise: Cultural Reception and Interpretation*, ed. Matthew Kapell and William G. Doty, 32–47. New York: Continuum, 2004.

Koven, Mikel J. "Citizen Kane." In *1001 Movies to See Before You Die*, ed. Steven J. Schneider, 172. London: Quintet, 2003.

Kracauer, Siegfried. *Theory of Film: The Redemption of Physical Reality.* London and New York: Oxford University Press, 1960.

Kramer, Peter. "Star Wars." *History Today* 49, no. 3 (1999): 41–47.

Kruse, Axel. "*The X-Files*: Entries on Meaning." *Sydney Studies in English* 23 (1997–8).

Kuiper, Koenraad. "Star Wars: An Imperial Myth." *Journal of Popular Culture* 21, no. 4 (1988): 77–86.

Lamm, Spenser (ed.). *The Art of* The Matrix. London: Titan Books, 2000.

Lancashire, Anne. "*The Phantom Menace*: Repetition, Variation, Integration." *Film Criticism* 24, no. 3 (2000).

Lancelin, Aude. "Baudrillard Decodes *The Matrix*." *Le Nouvel Observateur*, trans. anon. No. 2015 (19 Jun. 2003). Posted in trans. Nov. 8, 2003. http://www.teaser.fr/~lcolombet/empyree/divers/MatrixBaudrillard_english.html.

Lawrence, John Shelton. "Fascist Redemption or Democratic Hope?" In *Jacking in to The Matrix Franchise*, ed. Mathew Kapell and William G. Doty, 80–96. New York and London: Continuum, 2004.

Lawrence, John Shelton and Robert Jewett, *The Myth of the American Superhero*. Grand Rapids, MI: W. B. Erdmans, 2002.

Le Grice, Malcolm. "Virtual Reality: Tautological Oxymoron." In *New Screen Media*, ed. Martin Reiser and Andrea Zapp, 227–236. London: British Film Institute, 2002.

Lessard, Bruno. "Digital Technologies and the Politics of Performance." In *New Punk Cinema*, ed. Nicholas Rombes, 102–112. Edinburgh: Edinburgh University Press, 2004.

Liebes, Tamar and Elihu Katz. "The Export of Meaning: Cross-cultural Readings of *Dallas*." In *The Audience Studies Reader*, ed. Will Brooker and Deborah Jermyn, 287–304. London: Routledge, 2003.

Lipp, Martina. "Welcome to the Sexual Spectacle: The Female Heroes in the Franchise." In *Jacking in to The Matrix Franchise*, ed. Mathew Kapell and William G. Doty, 65–79. New York and London: Continuum, 2004.

Lyotard, Jean-François. *The Postmodern Condition*, trans. Geoff Bennington and Brian Massumi. Minneapolis: Minnesota University Press, 1984.

McCann, Graham. "The Movie Killers." *Modern Review* 1, no. 9 (1993): 33.

McCarthy, Todd. "The Matrix Revolutions." *Variety*, Nov. 2, 2003.

McLuhan, Marshall. *The Medium Is the Massage*. New York: Bantam Books, 1967.

McRoy, Jay. "Italian Neo-Realist Influences." In *New Punk Cinema*, ed. Nicholas Rombes, 39–55. Edinburgh: University of Edinburgh Press, 2005.

"Making *The Matrix*." *The Matrix*. DVD: Special Features. Warner Bros., 2001.

Manovich, Lev. "Post-media Aesthetics." In *(dis)locations* (DVD ROM). Karlsruhe: ZKM Centre for Art and Media, 2001.

Manovich, Lev. *The Language of New Media*. Cambridge, MA: MIT Press, 2001.

Martin, Adrian. "*A Bout de Souffle [Breathless]*." In *1001 Movies You Must See Before You Die*, ed. Steven Jay Schneider, 370. London: Quintet, 2003.

Metz, Christian. *Language and Cinema*, trans. Donna Jean Umiker-Sebeok. The Hague: Mouton, 1974.

Metz, Christian. "Some Points in the Semiotics of the Cinema." In *Film Theory and Criticism*, ed. Leo Braudy and Marshall Cohen, 65–72. Oxford: Oxford University Press, 2004.

Modleski, Tania. *The Women Who Knew Too Much*. New York: Methuen, 1988.

Mulvey, Laura. "Visual Pleasure and Narrative Cinema." In *The Sexual Subject: A Screen Reader in Sexuality*, ed. Screen, 22–34. London: Routledge, 1992.

Mulvey, Laura. *Citizen Kane*. London: The British Film Institute, 1992.

Natoli, Joseph. *Memory's Orbit: Film and Culture 1999-2000*. Albany: State University of New York Press, 2003.

Neale, Steve. *Genre and Hollywood*. London: Routledge, 2000.

Newitz, Annalee. "Serial Killers, True Crime, and Economic Performance Anxiety." In *Mythologies of Violence in Postmodern Media*, ed. Christopher Sharrett, 65–83. Detroit, MI: Wayne State University Press, 1999.

Newman, Kim. "The Wizard of Oz." *1001 Movies You Must See Before You Die*, ed. Steven Jay Schneider, 154. London: Quintet, 2003.

Norris, Christopher. *Uncritical Theory: Postmodernism, Intellectuals and the Gulf War*. London: Lawrence and Wishart, 1992.

O' Connor, Brian. "Introduction." In *The Adorno Reader*, ed. Brian O' Connor, 1–20. Oxford: Blackwell, 2000.

O'Hagan, Sean. "'I'm allowed to do what I want—that amazes me!'" Interview. *The Observer*, Dec. 5, 2004.

Ohmann, Richard. *Politics of Letters*. Middletown, CT: Wesleyan University Press, 1987.

O.M.A., Rem Koolhaus and Bruce Mau. *SMLX*. New York: Monacelli Press, 1995.

O' Reagan, Tom. "A National Cinema." In *The Film Cultures Reader*, ed. Graeme Turner, 139–164. London: Routledge, 2002.

Peary, Gerald (ed.). *Quentin Tarantino Interviews*. Jackson: University of Mississippi Press, 1998.

Pisters, Patricia. *The Matrix of Visual Culture*. Stanford, CA: Stanford University Press, 2001.

Plato, *Republic*. In *Dialogues of Plato*, ed. and trans. J. D. Kaplan, 238–386. New York: Pocket Books, 1950.

Purse, Lisa. "The New Spatial Dynamics of the Bullet-Time Effect." In *The Spectacle of the Real: From Hollywood to Reality TV and Beyond*, ed. Geoff King, 151–160. Bristol, UK: Intellect Books, 2005.

Ray, Robert. *A Certain Tendency of the Hollywood Cinema, 1930–1980*. Princeton, NJ: Princeton University Press, 1985.

Rebello, Stephen. "The Inception." In *Alfred Hitchcock's Psycho: A Casebook*, ed. Robert Kolker, 29–56. Oxford: Oxford University Press, 2004.

Richardson, John H. "Dumb and Dumber." *The New Republic*, Apr. 10, 1995: 20–29.

Rivette, Jacques. "The Genius of Howard Hawks." In *Cahiers du cinéma: The 1950s*, ed. Jim Hillier, 126–131. Cambridge, MA: Harvard University Press, 1985.

Rombes, Nicholas. "A New Film Genre?" *Digital Poetics*. Blog. Apr. 15, 2005. http://professordvd.typepad.com/my_weblog/2005/04/index.html.

"Rope Unleashed." DVD Documentary. *Rope* (*The Hitchcock Collection*). Universal, 2001.

Rubey, Dan. "Not So Long Ago, Not So Far Away." *Jump Cut* 41 (1997).

Rubio, Steven. "Inventing Culture." In *The Aesthetic of Cultural Studies*, ed. Michael Bérubé, 175–184. Boston: Blackwell, 2005.

Ryall, Tom. "Genre and Hollywood." In *American Cinema and Hollywood: Critical Approaches*, ed. John Hill and Pamela Church Gibson, 101–112. Oxford: Oxford University Press, 2000.

Sanjek, David. "Same as It Ever Was: Innovation and Exhaustion in the Horror and Science Fiction Films of the 1990s." In *Film Genre 2000*, ed. Wheeler Winston Dixon, 111–124. Albany, NY: State University of New York, 2000.

Sarris, Andrew. "The Auteur Theory Revisited." In *Film and Authorship*, ed. Virginia Wright Wexman, 21–29. New Brunswick: Rutgers University Press, 2003.

Schatz, Thomas. *Hollywood Genres: Formulas, Filmmaking, and the Studio System*. Austin: McGraw-Hill, 1981.

Schatz, Thomas. "The Whole Equation of Pictures." In *Film and Authorship*, ed. Virginia Wright Wexman, 89–95. New Brunswick, NJ: Rutgers University Press, 2003.

Schwarzbaum, Lisa. "The Incredibles." *Entertainment Weekly*, 15 Sept. 2005.

Schrader, Paul. "Notes on Film Noir." In *Film Noir Reader*, ed. Alain Silver and James Ursini, 53–64. New York: Limelight Editions, 1998.

Scott, A. O. "The Game Concludes with Light and Noise." *The New York Times*, Nov. 5, 2003.

Seay, Chris. *The Gospel Reloaded: Finding Spirituality and Faith in* The Matrix. Colorado Springs, CO: Piñon Press, 2003.

Sharrett, Christopher. "End of Story: The Collapse of Myth in Postmodern Narrative Film." In *The End of Cinema*, ed. Jon Lewis, 319–331. New York and London: New York University Press, 2001.

Shaw, Jeffrey and Peter Weibel (ed.). *Future Cinema: The Cinematic Imaginary After Film*. Cambridge, MA: MIT Press, 2003.

Shohat, Ella and Robert Stam. *Unthinking Eurocentrism*. London and New York: Routledge, 1994.

"Sight and Sound Top Ten Poll." British Film Institute. http://bfi.org.uk/sightandsound/topten/.

Silver, Joel. "Making the Matrix." *The Matrix* DVD: special features. Warner Bros., 2001.

Sopranos, The. Season one, episode four: "Meadowlands."

Sragow, Michael. *The New Yorker*, Aug. 10, 1992.

Sterling, Bruce. "Introduction." In *Mirrorshades: The Cyberpunk Anthology*, ed. Bruce Sterling. London: HarperCollins, 1994.

Sterling, Bruce. "Every Other Movie Is the Blue Pill." In *Exploring The Matrix: Visions of the Cyber Present*, ed. Karen Haber, 17–29. New York: St. Martin's Press, 2003.

Sterne, Jonathan. "The Burden of Culture." In *The Aesthetics of Cultural Studies*, ed. Michael Bérubé, 80–102. Boston: Blackwell, 2005.

Sterritt, David. *The Films of Alfred Hitchcock*. Cambridge: Cambridge University Press, 1993.

Tarantino, Quentin. "Chapter 2." In *Kill Bill, Volumes 1 and 2*—Shooting Script. Internet Moviescript Database. http://www.imsdb.com/scripts/Kill-Bill-Volume-1-&2.html.

Taubin, Amy. "The Critics Commentaries." *Reservoir Dogs* DVD. Collector's Edition Two-Disc Set. Lion's Gate, 2006.

Thomson, Clive. "Bakhtin's 'Theory' of Genre." *Studies in Twentieth Century Literature* 9, no. 1 (1984): 29–40.

Thomson, David. "Who Killed the Movies." *Esquire* 126, no. 6 (1996): 56–63.

Thomson, David. *The Whole Equation*. New York: Alfred A. Knopf, 2005.

Thompson, David and Ian Christie (eds), *Scorsese on Scorsese*. London: Faber and Faber, 1989.

Travis, Peter. "The Critics Commentary." *Reservoir Dogs* DVD. Collector's Edition Two-Disc Set. Lion's Gate, 2006.

Trost. Theodore Louis. "My Own Personal Jesus Christ: The Curiously Christian Worldview in *The Matrix*." Paper delivered at the Annual Meeting of the Academy of Religion in Nashville, Tennessee, 2000.

Truffaut, François. *Hitchcock*. London: Granada, 1969.

Turner, Graeme. *Film as Social Practice*. London and New York: Routledge, 1993.

Turner, Graeme. "Introduction." In *The Film Cultures Reader*, ed. Graeme Turner, 1–10. London: Routledge, 2002.

Wachowski, Larry and Andy Wachowski. "*The Matrix* (Shooting Script)." In *The Art of* The Matrix, ed. Spenser Lamm, 271–394. London: Titan Books, 2000.

Walsh, Michael. "Jameson and 'Global Aesthetics." In *Post-Theory: Reconstructing Film Studies*, ed. David Bordwell and Noël Carroll, 481–500. Madison, WI: University of Wisconsin Press, 1996.

Welles, Orson and Peter Bogdanovich. *This Is Orson Welles*. New York: Da Capo Press, 1992.

Williams, Raymond. *Marxism and Literature*. Oxford: Oxford University Press, 1977.

Wollen, Peter. "Godard and Counter-Cinema: *Vent D'Est*." *Afterimage* (Fall, 1972).

Wollen, Peter. *Signs and Meaning in the Cinema*. Bloomington: Indiana University Press, 1972.

Wood, Aylish. "The Collapse of Reality and Illusion in *The Matrix*." In *Action and Adventure Cinema*, ed. Yvonne Tasker, 119–129. New York: Routledge, 2004.

Wood, Robin. "Papering the Cracks: Fantasy and Ideology in the Reagan Era." In *Movies and Mass Culture*, ed. John Belton, 203–228. New Brunswick: Rutgers University Press, 1996.

Wood, Robin. "The Trouble with Marnie" (Contributor). *Marnie* DVD (*The Hitchcock Collection*). Universal, 2001.

Wood, Robin. *Hitchcock's Films Revisited*. New York: Columbia University Press, 2002.

Youngblood, Gene. "Cinema and the Code." In *Future Cinema: The Cinematic Imaginary After Film*, ed. Jeffrey Shaw and Peter Weibel, 156–161. Cambridge, MA: MIT Press, 2003.

Žižek, Slavoj. *The Art of the Ridiculous Sublime*. Seattle: Walter Chapin Simpson Center for the Humanities, 2000.

Žižek, Slavoj. "The Matrix: Or, the Two Sides of Perversion." In *The Matrix and Philosophy*, ed. William Irwin, 240–266. Chicago and La Salle, IL: Open Court, 2002.

Žižek, Slavoj. "*Vertigo*: The Drama of a Deceived Platonist." *Hitchcock Annual* (2003–2004): 67–82.

Filmography

A Bout De Souffle, [*Breathless*]. Dir. Jean Luc Godard. 1959.
Adaptation. Dir. Spike Jonze. 2002.
Adventure, The. Dir. Michelangelo Antonioni. 1960.
Akira. Dir. Katsuhiro Ôtomo. 1988.
Alien. Dir. Ridley Scott. 1979.
Alien Resurrection. Dir. Jean-Pierre Jeunet. 1997.
Aliens. Dir. James Cameron. 1986.
All About My Mother. Dir. Pedro Almodóvar. 1999.
American Graffiti. Dir. George Lucas. 1973.
Année Dernière à Marienbad, L' [*Last Year at Marienbad*]. Dir. Alain Resnais. 1961.
Apocalypse Now. Dir. Francis Ford Coppola. 1979.
Armageddon. Dir. Michael Bay. 1998.
Assault on Precinct 13. Dir. John Carpenter. 1976.
Aviator, The. Dir. Martin Scorsese. 2005.
Avventura, L' [*The Adventure*]. Dir. Michelangelo Antonioni. 1960.
Back to the Future. Dir. Robert Zemekis. 1985.
Back to the Future, Part II. Dir. Robert Zemekis. 1989.
Back to the Future, Part III. Dir. Robert Zemekis. 1990.
Bad Boys. Dir. Michael Bay. 1995.
Bad Education. Dir. Pedro Almodóvar. 2004.
Batman. Dir. Tim Burton. 1989.
Batman Returns. Dir. Tim Burton. 1992.
Batman Begins. Dir. Christopher Nolan. 2005.

Battleship Potemkin. Dir. Grigori Aleksandrov, Sergei Eisenstein. 1925.

Big Sleep, The. Dir. Howard Hawks. 1946.

Birth of a Nation. Dir. D.W. Griffith. 1915.

Black Hawk Down. Dir. Ridley Scott. 2001.

Blade Runner. Dir. Ridley Scott. 1982. Director's Cut: 1991.

Blow-Up. Dir. Michelangelo Antonioni. 1966.

Blue Velvet. Dir. David Lynch. 1986.

Body Heat. Dir. Lawrence Kasdan. 1981.

Bone Collector, The. Dir. Phillip Noyce. 1999.

Boogie Nights. Dir. Paul Thomas Anderson. 1997.

Breathless. Dir. Jean Luc Godard. 1959.

Breathless. Jim McBride. 1983.

Bronenosets Potyomkin [*Battleship Potemkin*]. Dir. Grigori Aleksandrov, Sergei Eisenstein. 1925.

Bullet in the Head. Dir. John Woo. 1990

Bulworth. Dir. Warren Beatty. 1998.

Buono, Il Brutto, Il Cattivo, Il [*The Good, the Bad and the Ugly*]. Dir. Sergio Leone. 1967.

Bicycle Thief, The. Dir. Vittorio de Sica. 1948.

Carrie. Dir. Brian De Palma. 1976.

Casablanca. Dir. Michael Curtiz. 1942.

Casino. Dir. Martin Scorsese. 1995.

Catwoman. Dir. Pitoff. 2004.

C'era Una Volta Il West [*Once Upon a Time in the West*]. Dir. Sergio Leone. 1968.

Chinatown. Dir. Roman Polanski. 1974.

Chong Qing Sen Lin [*Chungking Express*]. Dir. Wong Kar Wai. 1994.

Chungking Express. Dir. Wong Kar Wai. 1994.

Citizen Kane. Dir. Orson Welles. 1941.

City Slickers. Dir. Ron Underwood. 1991.

Clear and Present Danger. Dir. Phillip Noyce. 1994.

Clerks. Dir. Kevin Smith. 1994.

Clockwork Orange, A. Dir. Stanley Kubrick. 1971.

Close Encounters of the Third Kind. Dir. Steven Spielberg. 1977.

Color Purple, The. Dir. Steven Spielberg. 1985.

Conformist, The. Dir. Bernardo Bertolucci. 1969.

Conformista, Il [*Conformist, The*]. Dir. Bernardo Bertolucci. 1969.

Crash. Dir. Paul Haggis. 2004.

Cube. Dir. Vincenzo Natali. 1997.

Daredevil. Dir. Mark Steven Johnson. 2003.

Dawn of the Dead. Dir. George A. Romero. 1979.

Day After Tomorrow, The. Roland Emmerich. 2004.

Day of the Dead. George A. Romero. 1985.

Deer Hunter, The. Dir. Michael Cimino. 1978.

Defiant Ones, The. Dir. Stanley Kramer. 1958.

Departed, The. Dir. Martin Scorsese. 2006.

Diaboliques, Les. Dir. Henri-Georges Clouzot. 1954.

Die Xue Jie Tou [Bullet in the Head]. Dir. John Woo. 1990.

Don't Look Now. Dir. Nicholas Roeg. 1973.

Do the Right Thing. Dir. Spike Lee. 1989.

Dr. Strangelove, Or: How I Learned to Stop Worrying and Love the Bomb.
    Dir. Stanley Kubrick. 1964.

Double Indemnity. Dir. Billy Wilder. 1944.

Double Jeopardy. Dir. Bruce Beresford. 1999.

Dressed to Kill. Dir. Brian De Palma. 1980.

Duel. Dir. Steven Spielberg. 1971.

Eraserhead. Dir. David Lynch. 1977.

Eternal Sunshine of the Spotless Mind. Dir. Michel Gondry. 2004.

Fahrenheit 911. Dir. Mike Moore. 2004.

Fight Club. Dir. David Fincher. 1999.

Fistful of Dollars, A. Dir. Sergio Leone. 1964.

For a Few Dollars More. Dir. Sergio Leone. 1965.

Forrest Gump. Dir. Robert Zemekis. 1994.

400 Blows, The. Dir. François Truffaut. 1959.

From Dusk Till Dawn. Dir. Robert Rodriguez. 1996.

Game of Death. Dir. Robert Clouse. 1979.

Gangs of New York. Dir. Martin Scorsese. 2002.

Glengarry Glen Ross. Dir. James Foley. 1992.

Godfather, The. Dir. Francis Ford Coppola. 1972.

Godfather, Part II, The. Dir. Francis Ford Coppola. 1974.

Goldfinger. Dir. Guy Hamilton. 1964.

Gone with the Wind. Dir. Victor Fleming. 1939.

Good, the Bad and the Ugly, The. Dir. Sergio Leone. 1967.

Goodfellas. Dir. Martin Scorsese. 1990.

Grapes of Wrath, The. Dir. John Ford. 1940.

Great Train Robbery, The. Dir. Edwin S. Porter. 1903.

Greed. Dir. Erich Von Stroheim. 1924.

Halloween. Dir. John Carpenter. 1978.

Heat. Dir. Michael Mann. 1995.

Hearts of Darkness: A Filmmaker's Apocalypse.
     Dir. Fax Bahr and George Hickenlooper. 1992.

High Noon. Dir. Fred Zinnermann. 1952.

Hiroshima Mon Amour. Dir. Alain Resnais. 1959.

Hot Rock, The. Dir. Peter Yates. 1972.

Howling, The. Dir. Joe Dante. 1981.

Hunt for Red October, The. Dir. John McTiernan. 1990.

I Heart Huckabees. Dir. David O. Russell. 2004.

Incredibles, The. Dir. Brad Bird. 2004.

Independence Day. Dir. Roland Emmerich. 1996.

Indiana Jones and the Temple of Doom. Dir. Steven Spielberg. 1984.

Indiana Jones and the Last Crusade. Dir. Steven Spielberg. 1989.

In the Heat of the Night. Dir. Norman Jewison. 1967.

Intolerance. Dir. D.W. Griffith. 1916.

Jaws. Dir. Steven Spielberg. 1975

Kill Bill, Volume I. Dir. Quentin Tarantino. 2003.

Kill Bill, Volume II. Dir. Quentin Tarantino. 2003.

King of Comedy, The. Dir. Martin Scorsese. 1983.

La Mala Educación [Bad Education]. Dir. Pedro Almodóvar. 2004.

Ladri Di Biciclette [The Bicycle Thief]. Dir. Vittorio de Sica. 1948.

Lady From Shanghai, The. Dir. Orson Welles. 1948.

Last Year at Marienbad, The. Dir. Alain Resnais. 1961.

Lola Rennt [Run Lola Run]. Dir. Tom Tykwer. 1998.

Lone Star. Dir. John Sayles. 1996.

Lord of the Rings, The: The Fellowship of the Ring. Dir. Peter Jackson.
     2001.

Lord of the Rings, The: The Two Towers. Dir. Peter Jackson. 2002.

Lord of the Rings, The: The Return of the King. Dir. Peter Jackson. 2003.

Lost Highway. Dir. David Lynch. 1996.

Lost Weekend, The. Dir. Billy Wilder. 1945.

Magnificent Ambersons, The. Dir. Orson Welles. 1942.

Maltese Falcon, The. Dir. John Huston. 1941.

Man Who Shot Liberty Valance, The. Dir. John Ford. 1962.

Manhunter. Dir. Michael Mann. 1986.

Marnie. Dir. Alfred Hitchcock. 1964.

Matewan. Dir. John Sayles. 1987.

Matrix, The. Dir. The Wachowski Bothers. 1999.

Matrix Reloaded, The. Dir. The Wachowski Bothers. 2003.

Matrix Revolutions, The. Dir. The Wachowski Bothers. 2003.

Mean Streets. Dir. Martin Scorsese. 1973.

Memento. Dir. Christopher Nolan. 2000.

Metropolis. Dir. Fritz Lang. 1927.

Midnight Cowboy. Dir. John Schlesinger. 1969.

Million Dollar Baby. Dir. Clint Eastwood. 2005.

Mulholland Drive. Dir. David Lynch. 2001.

Munich. Dir. Steven Spielberg. 2005.

My Darling Clementine. Dir. John Ford. 1946.

Nanook of the North. Dir. Robert Flaherty. 1922.

Napoléon. Dir. Abel Gance. 1927.

Network. Dir. Sidney Lumet. 1976.

Nick of Time. Dir. John Badham. 1995.

North by Northwest. Dir. Alfred Hitchcock. 1959.

Nosferatu, Eine Symphonie des Grauens [*Nosferatu, a Symphony of Terror*]. Dir. F. W. Murnau. 1922.

Natural Born Killers. Dir. Oliver Stone. 1994.

Night of the Living Dead. Dir. George A. Romero. 1968.

Obsession. Dir. Brian De Palma. 1976.

Once Upon a Time in the West. Dir. Sergio Leone. 1968.

Outlaw Josey Wales, The. Dir. Clint Eastwood. 1976.

Paisà [*Paisan*]. Dir. Roberto Rossellini. 1946.

Paisan. Dir. Roberto Rossellini. 1946.

Paris, Texas. Dir. Wim Wenders. 1984.

Patriot Games. Dir. Phillip Noyce. 1992.

Peeping Tom. Dir. Michael Powell. 1960.

Per Qualche Dollaro in Più [*For a Few Dollars More*]. Dir. Sergio Leone. 1965.

Per un Pugno di Dollari [*A Fistful of Dollars*]. Dir. Sergio Leone. 1964.

Philadelphia Story, The. Dir. George Cukor. 1940.

Player, The. Dir. Robert Altman. 1992.

Polar Express. Dir. Robert Zemekis. 2004.

Psycho. Dir. Alfred Hitchcock. 1960.

Pulp Fiction. Dir. Quentin Tarantino. 1994.

Quatre Cents Coups, Les [*The 400 Blows*]. Dir. François Truffaut. 1959.

Raging Bull. Dir. Martin Scorsese. 1980.

Raiders of the Lost Ark. Dir. Steven Spielberg. 1981.

Rear Window. Dir. Alfred Hitchcock. 1954.

Rebecca. Dir. Alfred Hitchcock. 1940.

Red River. Dir. Howard Hawks. 1948.

Reservoir Dogs. Dir. Quentin Tarantino. 1992.

Rififi. Dir. Jules Dassin. 1955.

Ring. Dir. Hideo Nakata. 1998.

Rio Bravo. Dir. Howard Hawks. 1959.

Roma, Città Aperta [*Open City*]. Dir. Roberto Rossellini. 1945.

Rope. Dir. Alfred Hitchcock. 1948.

Run Lola Run. Dir. Tom Tykwer. 1998.

Russian Ark. Dir. Aleksandr Sokurov. 2002.

Russkij Kovcheg [*Russian Ark*]. Dir. Aleksandr Sokurov. 2002.

Samson and Delilah. Dir. Cecil B. DeMille. 1949.

Saving Private Ryan. Dir. Steven Spielberg. 1998.

Scarface. Dir. Brian De Palma. 1983.

Scarface: *The Shame of a Nation*. Dir. Howard Hawks. 1932.

Schindler's List. Dir. Steven Spielberg. 1993.

Scream. Dir. Wes Craven. 1996.

Searchers, The. Dir. John Ford. 1956.

Secrets and Lies. Dir. Mike Leigh. 1996.

Se7en. Dir. David Fincher. 1995.

Sex, Lies, and Videotape. Dir. Steven Soderberg. 1989.

Shane. Dir. George Stevens. 1953.

Shoot the Piano Player. Dir. François Truffaut. 1962.

Sideways. Dir. Alexander Payne. 2004.

Silence of the Lambs, The. Dir. Jonathan Demme. 1991.

Sin City. Dir. Robert Rodriguez. 2005.

Singin' in the Rain. Dir. Stanley Donen. 1952.

Some Like It Hot. Dir. Billy Wilder. 1959.

Stagecoach. Dir. John Ford. 1939.

Stand by Me. Dir. Rob Reiner. 1986.

Star Wars, Episode IV: A New Hope. Dir. George Lucas. 1977.

Star Wars, Episode V: The Empire Strikes Back. Dir. George Lucas. 1980.

Star Wars, Episode VI: Return of the Jedi. Dir. George Lucas. 1983.

Star Wars, Episode I: The Phantom Menace. Dir. George Lucas. 1999.

Star Wars, Episode II: Attack of the Clones. Dir. George Lucas. 2002.

Star Wars, Episode III: Revenge of the Sith. Dir. George Lucas. 2005.

Strange Days. Dir. Kathryn Bigelow. 1995.

Stranger, The. Dir. Orson Welles. 1946.

Sunrise. Dir. F.W. Murnau. 1927.

Sunset Boulevard. Dir. Billy Wilder. 1950.

Superman II. Dir. Richard Lester. 1980.

Taxi Driver. Dir. Martin Scorsese. 1976.

Terminator, The. Dir. James Cameron. 1984.

Terminator 2: Judgement Day. Dir. James Cameron. 1991.

Texas Chainsaw Massacre, The. Dir. Tobe Hooper. 1974.

Thelma and Louise. Dir. Ridley Scott. 1991.

Thin Red Line, The. Dir. Terrence Malick. 1998.

Third Man, The. Dir. Carol Reed. 1949.

Time Code. Dir. Mike Figgis. 2000.

Tirez sur le Pianiste [*Shoot the Piano Player*]. Dir. François Truffaut. 1962.

Titanic. Dir. James Cameron. 1997.

To Catch a Thief. Dir. Alfred Hitchcock. 1955.

Todo Sobre Mi Madre [*All About My Mother*]. Dir. Pedro Almodóvar. 1999.

Topkapi. Dir. Jules Dassin. 1964.

Total Recall. Dir. Paul Verhoeven. 1990.

Touch of Evil. Dir. Orson Welles. 1955.

Triplets of Belleville, The. Dir. Sylvain Chomet. 2003.

Triplettes de Belleville, Les [*The Triplets of Belleville*]. Dir. Sylvain Chomet. 2003.

Triumph des Willens [*Triumph of the Will*]. Dir. Leni Riefenstahl. 1934.

Triumph of the Will. Dir. Leni Riefenstahl. 1934.

True Lies. Dir. James Cameron. 1994.

Truman Show, The. Dir. Peter Weir. 1998.

2046. Dir. Wong Kar Wai. 2004.

2001: A Space Odyssey. Dir. Stanley Kubrick. 1968.

Unforgiven. Dir. Clint Eastwood. 1992.
Untouchables, The. Dir. Brian De Palma. 1987.
Usual Suspects, The. Dir. Brian Singer. 1995.
Vera Drake. Dir. Mike Leigh. 2004.
Vertigo. Dir. Alfred Hitchcock. 1958.
Wayne's World. Dir. Penelope Spheeris. 1992.
When Harry Met Sally. Dir. Rob Reiner. 1989.
Where Eagles Dare. Dir. Brian G. Hutton. 1969.
White Chicks. Dir. Keenan Ivory Wayans. 2004.
Wild Bunch, The. Dir. Sam Peckinpah. 1969.
Wizard of Oz, The. Dir. Victor Fleming. 1939.

Television/Serials

American Idol: The Search For a Superstar. Created by Simon Fuller.
    2002–.
Big Brother. Created by Simon Hepworth and Helen Downing. 1999–.
Dragonball Z. Created by Daisuke Nishio. 1989–2003.
Flash Gordon. Universal. 1936–1940.
Green Acres. Created by Jay Somers. 1965–1971.
Happy Days. Created by Garry Marshall. 1974–1984.
Kolchak: The Night Stalker. Created by Jeffrey Grant Rice. 1974–1975.
Kung Fu. Created by Alex Beaton and Robert Butler. 1972–1975.
Law and Order. Created by Dick Wolf. 1990–.
Lost. Created by J. J. Abrams. 2004–.
NYPD Blue. Created by Steven Bochco and David Milch. 1993–2005.
Seinfeld. Created by Larry David and Jerry Seinfeld. 1990–1998.
Simpsons, The. Created by Matt Groening. 1989–.
Sopranos, The. Created by David Chase. 1999–2007.
Survivor. Created by Mark Burnett.
24. Created by Joel Surnow and Robert Cochran. 2001–.
Twin Peaks. Created by David Lynch and Mark Frost. 1990–1991.
X-Files, The. Created by Chris Carter. 1993–2002.

Music

Mamas and the Papas, The. "California Dreaming." Dunhill Records. 1965.

Madonna. "Like a Virgin." *Like a Virgin* (Album). Sire/Warner Bros., 1984.

Rage Against the Machine. "Wake Up!" *Rage Against the Machine* (Album).

Epic Records, 1992.

U2. "Even Better Than the Real Thing." *Achtung Baby* (Album). Island Records, 1991.

Index